Donated in the memory of
Peter Thurston - who worked
to the end - on behalf of our
Regional Environment's integrity.
Bless Activists Everywhere . xⱭx

GREEN RAGE

GREEN RAGE

RADICAL ENVIRONMENTALISM
AND THE
UNMAKING OF CIVILIZATION

Christopher Manes

LITTLE, BROWN AND COMPANY
BOSTON   TORONTO   LONDON

First Edition

Library of Congress Cataloging-in-Publication Data

Manes, Christopher, 1957–
    Green rage : radical environmentalism and the unmaking of
civilization / Christopher Manes. — 1st ed.
        p.   cm.
    Includes bibliographical references.
    ISBN 0-316-54513-9
    1. Environmental policy—Citizen participation. 2. Green
movement. 3. Environmental protection. 4. Radicalism. 5. Human
ecology. I. Title.
HC79.E5M353   1990
363.7'057—dc20   90-5697
                                                              CIP

10 9 8 7 6 5 4 3 2 1

MV-PA

Published simultaneously in Canada
by Little, Brown & Company (Canada) Limited

Printed in the United States of America

To Mom and Dad for their infinite patience.

To Marcy, who taught me to love the Earth.

To Gwen, who taught me to love humanity again.

And to Owl, Ferret, Spruce, River, Stone,
without whose ministrations this book
would not have been possible.

"the spear shine in the sun"

that warrior spirit
is too valuable to waste
on wars —
let it be placed
in a better context,
for instance
acting to save
our Mother Earth.
then the fire-
fangled feathers
really dangle,
the bow burn gold,
the spear shine
in the sun.

— Dennis Fritzinger

CONTENTS

Preface   xi

PART 1
GREEN RAGE
1   The Ecology of Confrontation   3
2   The Culture of Extinction   23
3   The Rise and Fall of
       Reform Environmentalism:
       An Unexpurgated History   45
4   Earth First!   66
5   Escalations   84
6   The Green World   107

PART 2
GREEN THOUGHTS
7   Deep Ecology   139
8   The Critics   151
9   Civil Disobedience   165
10   Ecotage   175

PART 3
REACTION
11   The Trials of
       Radical Environmentalism   193
12   The Natural Resources State   209

PART 4
THE UNMAKING OF CIVILIZATION
Civilization and Other Errata   225
Beyond the Green Wall   235
Epilogue   243
Notes   249
Selected Bibliography   271
Index   279

PREFACE

—————

DURING AN INTERVIEW with Edward Abbey (I believe it was one of the last he gave before he died), I asked him what gave radical environmentalists the right to use ecotage, ecologically motivated sabotage, against bulldozers and the other tools of industry that are pushing back the wild. The novelist who virtually invented the radical environmental movement out of his inkhorn paused for a moment and then said, "When someone invades your home, you don't respond objectively and reasonably. You strike back with emotion, with rage. Well, government and corporations are invading the wilderness, our native natural home. There's no time to be dispassionate about that."

Because Abbey was right and there is no time, this book does not pretend to be objective or dispassionate about the radical environmental movement and its controversial efforts to stop the culture of technology from unraveling the fragile, resplendent web of life on this planet. It is in full agreement with these efforts. It does purport to give the facts about this new cultural force and to offer an interpretation of their significance. For those who require a ritual condemnation of environmentalists whose passionate love of the Earth sometimes places them on the wrong side of the law and invariably places them on the wrong side of our technological culture, they must look elsewhere. I can only point out that there are plenty of cool, rational minds in the environmental debate who are capable of delivering that condemnation—they are, not coincidentally, the same cool, rational minds who have helped bring the ecological crisis roaring down upon us.

PART 1

GREEN RAGE

CHAPTER 1

THE ECOLOGY OF CANYON CONFRONTATION

If we can draw the line against the industrial machine in America, and make it hold, then perhaps in the decades to come we can gradually force industrialism underground, where it belongs. . . . Why settle for less? And why give up our wilderness? What good is a Bill of Rights that does not include the right to play, to wander, to explore, the right to stillness and solitude, to discovery and physical freedom?

— *Edward Abbey*

ON THE CHILL SPRING morning of March 21, 1981, seventy-five people drove into the visitors' center parking lot of Arizona's Glen Canyon Dam. They were not part of the usual crowd of tourists and boat owners come to marvel at the huge waterworks, ponder statistics on metric tons of concrete, or admire the vast power plant reservoir, inaccurately, if not disingenuously, named "Lake" Powell by the U.S. Bureau of Reclamation. On the contrary, they were more interested in what had been here before the dam, what the dam had in fact taken from them. Under five hundred feet of reservoir water lay what had once been one of the most beautiful stretches of the Colorado Gorge, the golden heart of the canyonlands, with its tamarisk and willow thickets, waterfalls and plunge pools, hanging gardens of orchids and maidenhair ferns that had found refuge in the pink sandstone recesses while mastodons still walked the continent during the Ice Age. There had been egrets and ibises that waded in the shallows, and beaver, deer, and coyotes in the cottonwood glades. There had been that abundance of life possible only, or perhaps fully appreciated only, along a desert river. It was for the sake of this submerged, half-forgotten natural world under the bone-white monument to progress that these people came to demonstrate their displeasure.

Among the crowd were Dave Foreman, Mike Roselle, Howie Wolke, Bart Koehler, and Ron Kezar. Less than a year before, during a hiking trip to the remote Pinacate Desert, in the Mexican state of Sonóra, these five environmental activists had decided to form Earth First!, a self-proclaimed radical environmental group with an obligatory exclamation point and a motto: No compromise in defense of Mother Earth. In fact, directly after this meeting Roselle and Wolke had stopped by Glen Canyon Dam on their way home to wonder if this might not be the place to put their motto into practice for the first time.

Their choice was inspired in no small part by another member of the crowd: Edward Abbey. Writer, raconteur, amiable misanthrope, and éminence grise of the environmental movement in the Southwest, Abbey had written a novel in 1975, *The Monkey Wrench Gang*, which told the story of a group of raucous, environmentally minded saboteurs who rollicked through the Desert Southwest burning bulldozers, tearing down billboards, and above all else dreaming of blowing up Glen Canyon Dam. The fictional aspirations of Abbey's characters were about to come to fruition — of a sort.

The dam occupied a special place not only along the Colorado River, but also in the history of the American environmental movement. Anxious not to appear unreasonable, the large national environmental organizations, and the Sierra Club in particular, reached a compromise with the Bureau of Reclamation in the early 1960s, in essence winning the cancellation of plans for a dam in Dinosaur National Monument, in Utah and Colorado, in exchange for allowing one to be built on Glen Canyon.[1] To acquiesce in the destruction of the world's most magnificent system of red-rock canyons without a fight stuck in the craw of many grass-roots environmentalists and began an estrangement that culminated in the rise of more militant groups like Earth First!. As if to rub salt in the environmental movement's wounds, the Bureau of Reclamation celebrated its victory at Glen Canyon with a media campaign that included the publication of a book breathlessly describing the reservoir as the "Jewel of the Colorado."[2] The book was filled with snipes at environmentalists and poetic paeans to the mastering of nature by man, including this sub-Tennysonian stanza by the reclamation commissioner himself, Floyd Dominy:

> To have a deep blue lake
> Where no lake was before
> Seems to bring man
> A little closer to God.[3]

"In this case, . . ." wrote Abbey in mock response a few years later, "about five hundred feet closer. Eh, Floyd?"[4]

Thus, to many grass-roots environmentalists Glen Canyon Dam was more than just an ugly mass of concrete and steel profaning the stark majesty of the canyonlands. It represented what was fundamentally wrong with the country's conservation policies: arrogant government officials motivated by a quasireligious zeal to industrialize the natural world, and a diffident bureaucratic leadership in the mainstream environmental organizations that more or less willingly collaborated in this process.

With howls and banners but without permits or permission, the people in the parking lot began a demonstration calling for the dismantling of Glen Canyon Dam. The Park Service officials overseeing the recreational facility were visibly nervous; they had never heard of any environmental group supporting the *removal* of a dam, and nothing in their agency's philosophy had prepared them for such a demand. From their perspective it was madness, pure and simple, to undo a technological "improvement" of the landscape. The police had somehow gotten word that there might be trouble from a new environmental group, and they therefore were present at the scene in force. Most of the security, however, was prudently concentrated in the belly of the dam, where the turbines and other vulnerable machinery were housed.

Without being noticed by the police, six of the protesters made off to the top of the dam, carrying a heavy black bundle on their shoulders. Foreman, Wolke, Spurs Jackson, and three other Earth First!ers hurried onto the concrete rampart of the dam. When they reached the midpoint of the dam's arch, they stopped, flushed with adrenaline and the fear that the police might arrest them at any moment. Seven hundred feet below lay the Colorado Gorge, the river squeezed into white plumes of water from the spillways. They lashed the corners of the bundle onto a small parapet as best they could and with the cry "Earth First!" pitched it over the side.

A three-hundred-foot black polyethylene banner slowly unfurled along the unblemished face of the dam, looking from afar like an enormous crack opening in the superstructure.[5] It was a simple and graphic gesture of protest against the destruction of nature by the artifacts of industrial society: a symbolic "cracking" of Glen Canyon Dam.[6]

Foreman went to the visitors' center and asked a ranger on duty if she had seen the dam lately. Smirking at the sight, she informed the police. The six activists hurried down and rejoined the demonstration. The police made no real attempt to find out who was responsible for the embarrassing plastic crack. They were more eager to meet Abbey, who from the back of an old pickup truck was giving a speech that included this echo from Winston Churchill: "Surely no man-made structure in modern American history has been hated so much, by so many, for so long, with such good reason."[7] Of course, they had no way of knowing that Abbey had himself contributed two hundred dollars to purchase the crack. All that the police could do was cut down the plastic, which fluttered to a grassy area below called Dominy's Football Field. Ever diligent, the FBI took possession of the crack and hauled it off as evidence. They dusted it for fingerprints, apparently with no results. The FBI would later label Earth First! a "soft-core terrorist" group. And just about five years after the cracking of the dam, it would set in motion an elaborate and expensive scheme — initiated by the scandal-shrouded attorney general under President Ronald Reagan, Edwin Meese — to use infiltrators and electronic surveillance to arrest Foreman for allegedly conspiring to cut power lines around nuclear power plants in three western states. All this, however, lay in the future. For now no charges were brought, and officialdom considered the matter closed.

As would soon become customary in its dealings with radical

environmentalism, officialdom could not have been more wrong. The metaphorical cracking of Glen Canyon Dam was the first Earth First! action to catch the attention of the public.[8] Many more would follow. Not content with merely cracking the dam, Earth First! immediately began a petition campaign to raze it, hoping to "march up to the Capitol with 20 million signatures."[9] (The radicals almost got their wish from a higher source than Congress when floods in 1983 seriously damaged the structure.) Although the cracking of the dam was merely symbolic, it seemed to let loose the very real floodwaters of a new kind of environmental activism: iconoclastic, uncompromising, discontented with traditional conservation policy, at times illegal, always motivated by a vision of the world that rejected the premise held by government, industry, and mainstream environmental groups alike that mankind should control and manage the natural world. Just as Glen Canyon Dam held back the Colorado, this grass-roots commitment to a more militant and uncompromising environmental movement had been pent up and frustrated throughout the 1970s by the cautious bureaucratic machinery of the mainstream environmental organizations. Now Earth First! was inventing a style of ecological confrontation that would give direction to this discontent.

The protagonists of the Earth First! movement realized the significance of their action even at this early stage. "We knew we were making history," said Mike Roselle years later. "The cracking of the dam was not just a media stunt, it was the real birth of the radical environmental movement — a movement all of us felt *had* to be born if the natural world was going to survive."[10]

For years after the event, Earth First! was known as the group that cracked Glen Canyon Dam. It has moved on to be known as the group that spikes trees or burns bulldozers or, for the more overwrought, like Sue Joerger, former executive vice president of the Southern Oregon Timber Industries Association, the group that "is a real threat to the American way of life."[11] Nevertheless, the Glen Canyon protest remains an important event in the iconography of the radical environmental movement, dramatizing what a growing number of activists believed: that our technological culture with its intrusions on the natural world had to be curtailed, perhaps even undone, to keep the ecology of this planet and our role in it viable. It marked a shift from a rearguard strategy to protect wilderness to an affirmative attempt to roll back the artifacts of civilization, to *restore* the world to the point where natural processes such as the flow of rivers could continue. It was the opening shot in a battle between radical environmentalists and the foundations — concrete and spiritual — of industrial society.

If at the time it was a shot not exactly heard round the world, it was at least very much part of an expanding zeitgeist of ecological militancy rising up to resist the destruction of the natural world. Radical environmentalists now exert a growing influence on public lands decisions and environmental policy — to the dismay of timber companies, government agencies, and, not infrequently, the mainstream environmental movement, which many perceive as out of touch with people's deep concern about environmental degradation. Increasingly, grass-roots activist groups like Earth First! are setting the environmental agenda and bringing national and international attention to such critical issues as the deforestation of tropical rain forests and of the temperate rain forests in the Pacific Northwest. The means they use are often both dramatic and drastic.

Over the past few years major timber companies such as Weyerhaeuser and Louisiana-Pacific have suffered an estimated $10 million in damages to road-building and timber equipment at the hands of "vandals" — the resource industry's pejorative term for radical environmentalists who have taken direct action to keep mining, logging, grazing, and any other kind of development out of America's wildlands. The radicals call their actions ecotage or, in homage to Abbey's novel, monkeywrenching. Some of the timber companies' bulldozers, graders, and trucks had their hydraulic hoses slashed or their electrical wiring cut, or they were simply set afire. Most of the damage was caused when abrasives were poured into the crankcases of road-building vehicles, destroying the engines within a few days and allowing the monkeywrenchers to be far away when the problem was finally discovered — a technique called siltation. As one Earth First!er writes, siltation is a way "to turn any internal combustion engine into an expensive boat anchor."[12] Ecotage against heavy equipment in national forests has become so prevalent that timber and mining companies now have to hire guards or use some other security measures to protect their machinery. The days when timber companies could punch roads into wild areas unopposed, except perhaps in court, are long gone.

No precise statistics on the total cost of ecotage have been compiled, not even by the law enforcement division of the U.S. Forest Service, which until recently has also lumped ecological sabotage together with acts of vandalism. In 1987 the Forest Service commissioned Ben Hull, a special agent in Region 6 (Oregon and Washington), to carry out a nationwide survey of Forest Service personnel to get some idea of the amount of ecotage being carried out. The results were kept confidential, despite several attempts by radical environmentalists to obtain the information under the Freedom of Information Act. Hull freely admits that he would prefer that the statistics never be released, because he would not want ecoteurs to know "just how much havoc they're causing."[13] The Mountain States Legal Foundation, an ultraconservative group associated with the Coors family (and formerly headed by the notorious James Watt), is also presently collecting data on ecotage, apparently with the ulterior purpose of bringing a class action suit against Earth First!.[14]

Good estimates already exist, however, and they are high, ranging from $20 million to $25 million a year. In just one incident in Hawaii in 1984, a wood chipper worth $250,000 was firebombed by environmentalists to prevent a rare tropical rain forest, dominated by hundred-foot-tall ohia trees, from being ground into fuel for local sugar mills. The company that owned the chipper was operating without a permit and subsequently went out of business. Jim McCauley, forest policy analyst for the Association of Oregon Loggers, says that the average ecotage incident in Oregon causes about $60,000 in damages, with many single incidents going as high as $100,000.[15] There have been literally dozens of such incidents reported in the Pacific Northwest in 1989 alone and, according to Dave Foreman, at least one authenticated act in every state west of the Mississippi, with others beginning to occur in East Coast states. Many more are never reported, since resource firms are anxious not to give their insurance companies another reason to raise rates in an industry already beset by safety problems. Of course, the ultimate cost of monkeywrenching goes up considerably when the responses of groups like the Mountain States Legal Foundation are tallied. According to Ecomedia Toronto, an organization that monitors government and corporate reaction to the environmental movement, at least six Pinkerton-like private agencies are investigating, and in some cases attempting to infiltrate, radical environmental groups. Just keeping track of ecotage may involve millions of dollars annually, making ecotage a very cost-effective proposition for the radical environmentalists, whose costs per incident are typically no more than a hundred dollars or so and the loss of a night's sleep.

The precipitous rise in monkeywrenching incidents began in the early 1980s. Soon after the cracking of Glen Canyon Dam, radical environmentalists destroyed seismographic equipment and pulled survey stakes on a road under construction in a successful attempt to prevent Getty Oil from drilling in the Gros Ventre roadless area of Wyoming, south of Yellowstone National Park. In the Pacific Northwest, roads under construction to timber sales (those wooded areas scheduled for cutting) and mines were so routinely "desurveyed" — that is, the survey stakes were pulled up — that the Forest Service, the agency in charge of our national forests, began to use a fluorescent powder on the stakes in the forlorn hope of catching ecoteurs among the millions of square acres of wildlands that constitute our national forest system. Not surprisingly, the ecoteurs have taken to wearing gloves. The only monkeywrencher to be convicted of desurveying a road was incriminated not by fluorescent powders, but by a hatchet-wielding Chevron employee who made a citizen's arrest in Wyoming's Bridger-Teton National Forest in 1985. The environmentalist accorded this dubious honor was Howie Wolke, one of the six who cracked Glen Canyon Dam. He later told reporters, "I did it and I'm damn proud."[16]

In 1984 the most effective and provocative technique in the radical environmentalists' repertoire appeared: tree spiking, the practice of driving large nails into trees to hinder logging operations. Tree spiking had apparently been occurring quietly on a small scale for a number of years,[17] but in October 1984 the Eugene, Oregon, *Register-Guard* received a letter, immediately brought to the Forest Service's attention, saying that sixty-three pounds of spikes — about a thousand 20-penny nails — had been driven into trees that were part of a proposed sale in Oregon's Hardesty Mountain roadless area. The letter also claimed that Smokey the Bear had been taken hostage. To its dismay, the Forest Service found the claim was true (regarding the trees, not Smokey) and had to spend thousands of dollars removing the spikes. There have been scores of tree spiking incidents since then, at least a dozen in Northern California in 1989 alone, according to Forest Service special agent William Derr.[18] Harmless to trees, the spikes can damage chain saws and expensive band saws in the mill. The idea could have come straight from the Chicago Business School, with an environmental twist: if the cost of removing the spikes is high enough, the cut will not be made, or at the very least a decreased profit margin will discourage logging in areas controversial enough to inspire this type of ecological resistance.

Public attention was focused on tree spiking and the radical environmental movement on May 13, 1987, when a spike shattered a band saw and seriously injured a worker in Louisiana-Pacific's mill in Cloverdale, California. Seemingly primed for the event, the *San Francisco Chronicle* printed a front-page headline saying "TREE SABOTAGE CLAIMS ITS FIRST VICTIM."[19] Another paper's front page read "EARTH FIRST! BLAMED FOR WORKER'S INJURIES."[20] At a highly publicized press conference a Louisiana-Pacific spokesman faulted radical environmental groups "like Earth First!."[21]

Earth First! representatives replied to the charge by denying responsibility for the spiking, noting that environmentalist tree spikers always inform timber companies about their spiking activities, the point being not to harm workers but to prevent logging. There had been no notification in the Cloverdale incident, and, moreover, the spiked tree was a second-growth redwood, not virgin timber of the type Earth First! seeks to protect. Ironically, there was some speculation in the press that the perpetrator was a radical Republican whose libertarianism was outraged by the logging going on near his property line.[22] Many radical environmentalists even suggested that Louisiana-

Pacific itself put the spike in the tree to gain public sympathy. If so, the tactic was at least a partial success, since there is rarely any public discussion of radical environmentalism without some reference to this now-infamous sixty-penny nail.[23] Nevertheless, from his hospital bed, the injured mill worker, George Alexander, unexpectedly expressed his agreement with Earth First!'s demand that Louisiana-Pacific stop clear-cutting redwood forests.[24]

The resource industry has mounted a strident political and legal campaign against tree spiking. In 1988 the congressional delegations from several Northwest timber states under the habitual leadership of Idaho senator James McClure and Oregon senator Mark Hatfield — "the Senators from Timber," according to their environmental detractors — successfully attached a rider to an antidrug bill, making tree spiking a felony.[25] "Tree spiking is a radical environmentalist's version of razor blades in Halloween candy," commented Oregon's Republican representative Robert Smith, who not surprisingly supported the bill.[26] Still unsatisfied, McClure continues to clamor for stricter laws and has even suggested, in a moment of rancor unbecoming an elected official, that for every acre of trees spiked by radical environmentalists, a hundred acres of wilderness should be clear-cut to teach them a lesson. In recent years, the states of California, Washington, Oregon, Idaho, and Montana have also passed felony laws against tree spiking. The FBI has repeatedly been asked by officials in these states to investigate tree spiking incidents, and the Forest Service, along with industry groups like Prevent Ecological Sabotage Today, has posted substantial rewards.

To no avail. No tree spiker has ever been caught, and the practice continues to spread. Since 1984 it has increased tenfold, with incidents reported from the Plumas National Forest, in California, to the George Washington National Forest, in Virginia.[27] And as if to add insult to injury, in November 1988 a delegation of Oregon's congressional aides touring a mill in southern Oregon to study the problem was treated to the sight of a two-thousand-dollar band saw shattering in a shower of metal and sparks after hitting a spike.[28]

Ecoteurs have also developed a more surreptitious variation on tree spiking called tree pinning, in which nonmetallic rock cores or hardened ceramic pins are inserted in trees. Tree pinning is virtually undetectable. Although a great deal has been written about tree pinning, only one such incident has been reported, in the Mount Hood area in Oregon. Nevertheless, timber companies understand the threat and are apprehensive that their metal-detection systems may soon become obsolete.[29]

The Forest Service is loath to talk about it, but sources in the agency and activists in the field say that at least two timber sales — in Washington State and Virginia — have been withdrawn due to tree spiking.[30] There probably have been many more. The Forest Service's reticence on this matter is understandable, since such withdrawals suggest that radical environmentalists, through ecotage, can sometimes have more influence on public lands policy than mainstream environmentalists or even the Forest Service itself.

To some extent this is exactly the case. For example, it was the media-oriented agitation by radical environmentalists using tree spiking, road blockades, and demonstrations that made a national issue of the northern spotted owl's slide toward extinction due to the logging of its ancient conifer forest habitat in the Pacific Northwest. This embarrassed national environmental organizations — which had been dragging their feet on the issue for fear of incurring the wrath of Senator Hatfield — into pressuring a recalcitrant U.S. Fish and Wildlife Service to hold hearings on listing the owl as an endangered species.[31] In September 1989 Congress passed a compromise bill purporting to give limited protection to the owl and its habitat. The compromise is wholly inadequate to save the owl and was rejected by radical environmentalists, but no action whatsoever would have been taken had it not been for radical environmental protests' beginning to appear in the news, lending passion to the otherwise arcane subject of forest management.

The spotted owl controversy is an example of how radical environmentalists have used not only ecotage, but also ecological civil disobedience to challenge government and resource industry plans to develop public lands. This often involves physically blockading timber roads. In 1983 four radical environmentalists placed their bodies in front of a bulldozer that was punching a timber road in the Kalmiopsis roadless area in the Siskiyou National Forest of southern Oregon. They were arrested, but others soon took their place. Altogether forty-five protesters were thrown into jail over several tense months in which the construction crew threatened and on several occasions even attempted to run them down. Nonetheless, the blockade halted operations long enough for Earth First! and the Oregon Natural Resources Council to get a court injunction declaring the road illegal.[32]

Since then there have been literally dozens of road blockades against the oil, mining, and timber interests that have purchased access to our public lands: on the south rim of the Grand Canyon, where a uranium mine is being operated by Energy Fuels Nuclear; in Northern California, where the giant Maxxam Corporation is cutting the last of the unprotected redwood forests to pay off the debt from a hostile takeover of the local timber company that owned the trees; in the Middle Santiam region of Oregon, where a number of timber companies are logging lucrative old-growth stands (ancient, virgin forests that contain unique species, such as the spotted owl and Pacific salamander).

In 1985 radical environmentalists set their sights higher by developing a new form of civil disobedience that has been a thorn in the side of the timber industry ever since: tree sitting. Using rock-climbing gear, six protesters ascended eighty feet into the canopy of old-growth trees in Oregon's Willamette National Forest scheduled for clear-cutting by Willamette Industries. By attaching grappling hooks to nearby trees, the tree sitters were able to prevent loggers from cutting the stand for more than a month. When the last protester was brought to the ground by police in a construction crane, his tree was finally cut down — at a cost of several hundred thousand dollars in lost harvesting time and increased law enforcement. As the tree sitter later said after engaging in several other similar incidents: "I figure I've done about a million dollars' worth of damage in the last two years. They can sue me — I don't care, I don't have any money!"[33]

This scenario has been repeated over and over again, so frequently that the Forest Service now routinely closes areas to the public where protests against old-growth logging are expected. Forest Service officials claim the closures are made for reasons of public safety, but environmental activists charge that the actions constitute a blatant attempt to stifle dissent, a kind of wilderness martial law. They are considering the possibility of a lawsuit against Forest Service closures. The situation has been made more volatile by Forest Service use of so-called pot commandos to enforce the closures and bring the protesters down from the trees. The pot commandos are a paramilitary force of five hundred law enforcement officers created by the 1986 National Forest Drug Enforcement Act, charged with preventing marijuana cultivation on public lands. Rather than being employed for this statutory purpose, however, fully half of the pot commandos may have been illegally diverted to help the Forest Service contend with environmental protests. This apparent misappropriation of funds may also soon be the subject of litigation brought by radical environmentalists against the Forest Service.

The conflict between law enforcement and environmentalists turned particularly ugly in July 1988 when pot commandos trained high-powered rifles on tree sitters in the Kalmiopsis roadless area of southern Oregon. The sheriff at the scene, Bill Arnado, was quoted as saying that if the protesters had made any hostile moves against the arresting officers, the pot commandos "would have shot their asses out of the trees."[34] Although that part of his anatomy was spared, a tree sitter in the Four Notch area of East Texas did suffer serious leg injuries when Forest Service officer Billy Ball allowed loggers to cut down the tree he was occupying in protest.[35] "I tell you, someone's going to die," said Greg Miller, executive vice president of the Southern Oregon Timber Industries Association. "That's what I fear most."[36]

In fact, timber company personnel have fired guns at radical protesters at least twice, apparently more to intimidate than to injure.[37] Local law enforcement agencies now describe the conflict between radical environmentalists on one side and the timber companies and the government agencies in charge of managing our public lands — the Forest Service, Bureau of Land Management, National Park Service, and Fish and Wildlife Service — on the other as "a range war."[38]

Physical resistance to wilderness destruction in this country is a fact that can no longer be disregarded by government, the

resource industry, or the mainstream environmental movement. And, as has already been suggested, it is a very costly
fact, running into the tens of millions. This kind of damage is
often precisely what radical environmentalists desire. To quote
Earth First!er Dave Foreman: "If enough damage is done to the
industrial tools of the incursion into wild places, then insur-
ance rates are going to go up. The Forest Service won't be able
to both build new roads and keep their old network intact if
it's being torn up. Monkeywrenching is basically a means of
self-defense."[39]

It is a defense not limited to the American wilderness. Radical environmentalism is an international phenomenon. In
1979 the Sea Shepherd Conservation Society, a radical offshoot
of Greenpeace operating out of Canada, took to the high seas
in defense of marine mammals. On July 16 the society's 206-
foot-long ship, *Sea Shepherd*, under the command of its flamboyant captain, Paul Watson, rammed and disabled a pirate
whaling ship off the Portuguese coast. Portuguese authorities
confiscated Watson's vessel, but before they could turn it over
to the owners of the crippled whaling ship, Watson reluctantly
scuttled it himself. He got the last laugh a few months later
when the pirate whaling ship was mysteriously bombed and
sunk.[40] Several years afterward, funded mainly by English
schoolchildren who raised $25,000 in a save-the-whale walka-
thon, the Sea Shepherds took on whalers from the Faeroe
Islands, a small Danish protectorate north of Great Britain,
interfering with their hunt. The incident culminated in a sea
battle between the Sea Shepherds' vessel — ringed with
barbed wire to prevent boarding — and shotgun-toting
Faeroese police in inflatable dinghies and a gunboat.[41] The Sea
Shepherd Society struck again in November 1986, this time
against Iceland, for violating the International Whaling Commission moratorium on whaling. Two members of the society
scuttled two whaling vessels in Reykjavík harbor and ran-
sacked a nearby whaling station with a fury appropriate to that
Nordic country's Viking past.[42]

On May 31, 1982, five members of a group called Direct
Action made Earth First!'s Glen Canyon Dam efforts look pale
by comparison when they blew up the $4.5 million British Co-
lumbia Hydro Substation on Vancouver Island. Over the last

few years Australian ecoteurs have caused more than $1 million in damage to dozens of bulldozers and other heavy equipment, forcing some timber contractors to close down their operations. Saboteurs in Thailand, for environmental reasons, in 1986 burned down a chemical plant producing the high-tech metal tantalum; damages totaled $45 million.[43]

Ecoteurs are particularly active in Europe. Scandinavian environmentalists have destroyed drilling equipment at one potential radioactive disposal site. A bridge leading to the Alta Dam in northern Norway was blown up by Lapps whose lands were inundated by the project. Not to be outdone by outsiders like the Sea Shepherd Society, Icelanders upset over the building of a dam used explosives to end the project. Activists associated with the West German Green movement have repeatedly vented their rage against nuclear power plants, toppling 165 electrical towers leading to plants in 1986 alone. The practice is so widespread that West Germany's Parliament recently expanded antiterrorist legislation specifically to include the destruction of electrical towers. It even appears that ecotage has made its way to the Soviet Union, where a version of Earth First! is said to be carrying out monkeywrenching Soviet style.[44]

This catalogue of ship sinkings and dam breakings is not intended to suggest that the groups involved in ecotage share a common ideology or even a common goal. On the contrary, there are distinct ideological differences between Germany's Greens, animal rights activists, Earth First!, and the Sea Shepherd Society. But the extent of radical environmental resistance proves that the battle for the world's ecology is being joined on a broad front, with ecotage as the common center of the conflict. "As the Earth's condition gets worse," says Darryl Cherney, an Earth First! activist, "radical environmentalists will become more aggressive in defense of the planet."[45]

Needless to say, mainstream environmental organizations reject these tactics. Jay Hair, president of the National Wildlife Federation, has denounced Earth First! as a terrorist organization, saying that he sees "no fundamental difference between destroying a river and destroying a bulldozer."[46] Representatives from many of the other major environmental organizations have made similar moral pronouncements. Even

Greenpeace, an organization that is no stranger to controversial direct action, suggested that members of the Sea Shepherd Society were acting like terrorists when they sank the Icelandic whaling ships.[47]

Most radical environmentalists remain unfazed by this criticism. "It doesn't even bother me whether people call us terrorists," says Barbara Dugleby, a Texas activist who has been arrested numerous times for ecological civil disobedience. "Our work is to get the message across, and those people who think we are terrorists are not damaging us. We are still getting our message across to those who are sympathizers, and the more sympathizers we reach, the stronger we become, and in the end I think people will realize that the terrorists are really the people we have been fighting, the destroyers of the Earth."[48]

Behind the unmannerly rhetoric, however, the national environmental leadership is in some instances perversely happy that Earth First! exists. "Frankly, it makes us look moderate," says Robert Hattoy, Southern California representative of the Sierra Club. "When Earth First! is out there demanding a hundred million acres of wilderness and we know we can only get ten million, I can turn to a congressman and say, Look, we're the voice of reason."[49]

The founders of Earth First! apparently had something like this role in mind for their new, aggressive brand of environmental activism — at least at the beginning. "When I helped found Earth First!," writes Howie Wolke, "I thought that it would be the 'sacrificial lamb' of the environmental movement; we would make the Sierra Club look moderate by taking positions that most people would consider ridiculous."[50]

But the self-imposed burden of being the moderate voice of reason in a time of unparalleled environmental deterioration has made the mainstream organizations less attractive to many grass-roots activists, who have come to see Earth First!'s combative stance as neither ridiculous nor extremist under the circumstances. One former member of a mainstream California environmental group puts it this way: "I've been an environmental activist for eight or ten years. And I was doing everything. I was writing letters, I was talking to my congressman, I was reading environmental impact statements, I was leading hikes to introduce people to the woods. And I was losing. Being reasonable just didn't seem to be getting anywhere. The trees were still being cut, the rivers were still being dammed, the air was dirty. And then I met Earth First!."[51]

Defections like this, according to some radical environmentalists, have prompted the mainstream groups to take stronger stands at the very same time that their moderate image is being bolstered by more militant activists. They cite Senator Alan Cranston's California Desert Protection Act, noting that the Sierra Club was at first content with 5 million acres of protected land but later demanded 8 million after Earth First! made a more sweeping proposal of almost 17 million acres.

Up to now, radical and moderate environmentalists have lived in this kind of surly symbiosis. Through ecotage and civil disobedience, groups like Earth First! have focused public attention on environmental issues, often at the same time lambasting traditional environmentalists for being wimps. The large environmental organizations, while denouncing the radicals' confrontational activities, have then been able to use their ample finances to take the campaign to Congress or the courts with the impetus of public support the radicals generated. The recent controversy over old-growth logging and the spotted owl is being played out along these lines.

Many radical environmentalists accept this as an effective arrangement. Foreman himself has often stated that there is "a need for other groups less radical than Earth First! and other methods."[52] Most radical environmentalists would agree. At unguarded moments the moderates have even returned the compliment. But there are also activists who consider the entire moderate environmental movement pernicious. Moreover, these "anarcho-environmentalists," to give them a tendentious name, seem to be growing in numbers and influence.[53]

Whatever the attitude between the moderate and radical environmentalists, in some ways the mainstream is becoming less relevant to the agenda of radical environmentalists as their various successes have won them increasing notoriety and funding. Earth First!'s Biodiversity Task Force, for instance, under the forceful leadership of Jasper Carlton, has been able to bring its own successful lawsuits on endangered species issues independent of the traditional and more cautious sources

of environmental litigation, such as the Sierra Club Legal
Defense Fund.

Despite its growing influence, size, and independence, there
have been very few principled attempts to understand the radical environmental movement. Those who have written on the
subject have been uninformed at best and malicious at worst.
In *Playing God in Yellowstone,* retired academician Alston Chase
exemplifies the former failing. Chase spends an entire chapter
discussing radical ecologists, calling them "the California cos-
mologists," though most are neither from California nor particularly interested in cosmology. According to Chase's fanciful
history, radical environmental thought came out of a "swirl of
chaotic, primeval theorizing" about Buddhism, Heidegger, and
psychotherapy.[54] The central problem, concludes Chase, is that
radical environmentalists desire to return to the Garden of
Eden, where humanity lived in bliss — a yearning that must
come as a shock to the likes of Foreman, a former marine; Mike
Roselle, a former oil field roughneck; and Wolke, a former
bouncer and wilderness guide in some of the wildest country
in the lower forty-eight states. Chase has gone on to make an
industry of interpreting radical environmentalism along these
prelapsarian lines, recently writing that radical environmentalists are "another species of missionary," out to "portray ecological decline as a conspiracy by a bunch of bad guys."[55]

Being a professionally trained philosopher from the right,
Chase can probably be excused for misunderstanding the facts
about a new social phenomenon. The left, however, should
know better. But where the politically conservative Chase sees
nothing but chaos, the left discerns a conspiracy lurking behind
the radical environmental agenda. At the July 1987 Green Conference in Amherst, Massachusetts, philosopher and social
critic Murray Bookchin laid down the first brushstrokes of this
representation, painting radical environmentalists as "eco-
brutalists" and "nature worshippers" with ties to fascism
through a "crude biologism."[56] For Bookchin, radical environmentalism is not truly revolutionary, since it does not follow
the typical leftist interpretation of the environmental crisis as
the result of capitalism. Bookchin was soon joined by a chorus
of East Coast leftists displeased with the perceived antihuman-

ism of Edward Abbey and Foreman, variously labeled as sexist, racist, and fascist.

Both Chase and Bookchin, whose positions are representative of the critical literature on radical environmentalism, are simply incorrect in their descriptions of radical environmentalism, mostly because their ideas come from reading a few articles in the popular press rather than actual knowledge of the environmental movement and the radicals' role in it. Neither of them even attempts an interpretation of ecotage, the activity that more than anything else defines radical environmentalism. More important, both men see radical environmentalism as a monolithic doctrine, a system of beliefs structured like their own, and hence a failure by that standard. It would be more accurate, however, to describe radical environmentalism as a *sensibility*, that allusive word the English language all but lost during this century. The radical environmental sensibility is not attempting to create a new philosophy to displace the dominant ideas of modern society. If anything, most radical environmentalists look at systematic philosophy as the problem, as an attempt to reduce the buzzing, howling, blossoming heterogeneity of the natural world to some abstract idea. If radical environmentalism has a watchword, it is probably its oft-repeated imperative "Let your actions set the finer points of your philosophy."[57] An ecological sensibility, according to most radical environmentalists, abides in one's actions to defend nature, not in ideological exactitude.

In other words, radical environmentalism is responding to a particular social context, a culture dominated by technology, and its relationship to that society, not a series of propositions, defines it. Certainly there are specific ideas and themes that have arisen from radical environmentalism's confrontation with technological culture — the persuasion that humankind is not the center of value on this planet, the conviction that the other species on Earth have just as much right to exist as humans do, the belief that wilderness and not civilization is the real world.[58] But the soundness of these ideas cannot be ascertained by philosophical analysis so much as by the role they are playing in a culture facing a period of ecological upheaval. As one Earth First! activist puts it, "It is the character of movements to *move."* This kinetic aspect of radical environmentalism has been lost on many commentators, who understand this new cultural force as a body of ideas rather than a body in motion.[59]

The significance of radical environmentalism does not lie in some jaundiced history of environmental philosophy, nor in the dark urge for political power. Rather, it is based on one simple but frightening realization: that our culture is lethal to the ecology that it depends on and has been so for a long time, perhaps from the beginning. The validity of the radical environmentalism movement rises or falls depending on the accuracy of this perception. To understand this new social force, therefore, requires doing something we are trained to avoid — taking a serious look at whether our culture is compatible with the natural world and its limits. If it is, then radical environmentalism is nothing more than a cultural quirk, a moribund after bloom of the sixties, hardly worth the creative misrepresentations its critics have devised.

But if, as many scientists are now saying, our global industrial society is unsustainable, then the words and deeds of radical environmentalists today may be a window to the future state of the world. And to the chagrin of those who now control the Earth's ecology, whether that window shows a living green world or a wasteland may very likely depend on the success or failure of radical environmentalism.

The understanding of radical environmentalism thus begins at the end, the end of the world as we know it, the meltdown of biological diversity that our industrial culture has recklessly set in motion.

CHAPTER 2

THE CULTURE OF EXTINCTION

To man the earth seems altogether
No more a mother but a step dame rather.

— *du Bartas,*
Divine Weekes and Workes

It's the end of the world as we know it
(and I feel fine).

— *R.E.M.*
song lyric

ENDINGS CHANGE PEOPLE. In the early 1900s a minor
Forest Service official named Aldo Leopold, intent on ridding
the Southwest of predators, shot a wolf and, watching the terrible beauty of its death, saw his own complaisant attitude
toward the natural world transformed before his eyes:

> We reached the old wolf in time to watch a fierce fire dying
> in her eyes. I realized then, and have known ever since, that
> there was something new to me in those eyes — something
> known only to her and to the mountain. I was young then,
> and full of trigger-itch; I thought that because fewer wolves
> meant more deer, that no wolves would mean hunters' par-
> adise. But after seeing the green fire die, I sensed that neither
> the wolf nor the mountain agreed with such a view.[1]

The remorseful Leopold became a passionate advocate of the
protection of wolves, cofounder of the Wilderness Society, and
principal force in establishing our national forest wilderness

system. His vision of expansive wilderness areas supporting healthy populations of predators and prey in ecological equilibrium inspired and helped define the modern environmental movement. All this, in response to the senseless slaughter of one wolf.

For Leopold, confronting humanity's destruction of the wild required a new ethic, a land ethic, which he gave this succinct and graceful formulation: "A thing is right when it tends to preserve the integrity, stability and beauty of the biotic community. It is wrong when it tends otherwise."[2] Leopold's intellectual journey presented twentieth-century industrial society with a choice: either to practice environmental humility and cultivate a richer, more egalitarian relationship with the natural world, or to pursue short-term affluence at the cost of impoverishing nature and raising the specter of ecological collapse.

Predictably, our culture chose the latter.

To understand the rise of radical environmentalism, we need to look at the consequences of this choice, because they constitute the cataclysmic backdrop against which a militant ecological sensibility took shape. "I pretty much feel," says Rick Bailey, an Earth First! activist from Oregon, "that the biological and ecological foundation of this planet is under siege right now, and something has to be done to at least slow the technological beast down to the point where we can stop and examine what we're doing."[3] This is a feeling most radical environmentalists share, and whether it is based on apocalyptic angst or firsthand observations in the wilderness, it is now being corroborated by the findings of some of the world's most distinguished biologists.

Within the last few decades, not only has the green fire of the wolf all but flickered out on this continent, but species after species has been driven into extinction by human disruptions of natural processes, disruptions summed up in the phrase of geophysicist James Lovelock as "the three deadly Cs": combustion, cattle, and chain saws. We are in fact in the midst of the greatest planetary extinction since the dinosaurs disappeared at the end of the Cretaceous period, sixty-five million years ago. According to Harvard biologist E. O. Wilson, if present measurements of habitat destruction are accurate, the world may be losing some 18,000 species a year, many of them unclassified and unexamined by scientists.[4] Others put the figure as high as 40,000 per year.[5] But whatever the exact number, species fallout is expected to rise dramatically as plant and animal populations are forced onto dwindling islands of habitat in a sea of human industrial and agricultural development.

Indeed, the use of the word "island" in this context is no mere metaphor. As logging, farming, road-building, and water projects have fragmented the world's ecology into isolated patches of wilderness, biologists have turned to the model of island ecology to understand the increasing pace of extinction.[6] On islands, whole biotic communities are vulnerable to destruction from disease or natural disaster, inbreeding, or the introduction of nonindigenous species. With the present average size of wilderness preserves worldwide being somewhere around 2 percent of each nation's landmass,[7] the same fate now awaits many other animal and plant populations.

For much of North America's wildlife the wait is over. Except in the largest parks and wildlands, the crazy quilt of small, isolated, politically determined areas that make up our national forest, wilderness, and park system has already suffered substantial species loss. Even relatively large parks like Yosemite and Rocky Mountain have lost between a quarter and a third of their native mammals.[8] If the purpose of our wildlands system is to preserve biological diversity (and, alas, it is not explicitly so by law), it must be judged a dismal failure.

In a teach-in for the environment associated with Earth Day celebrations in 1970, biologist Barry Commoner admonished students at Northwestern University that "we are in a period of grace, we have the time — perhaps a generation — in which to save the environment from the final effects of the violence we have already done to it."[9] That generation has passed. Grace period is over.

Nothing in the history of humankind has prepared us for this appalling event, but this single human generation now living will probably witness the disappearance of one third to one half of the Earth's rich and subtle forms of life, which have been evolving and blossoming for billions of years.[10] Jasper Carlton, the Earth First!er who founded the group's Biodiversity Task Force, an organization that litigates endangered species cases, has given this desperate state of affairs a graphic name — *biological meltdown.*[11]

The vast calculations of death confronting us in the form of this biological meltdown suggest its physical magnitude. Mere numbers, however, fail to convey how unprecedented the crisis is. Although mass extinctions are nothing new in the history of life on this planet, comparisons between these and the present spasm of extinction are inadequate in at least two important ways.

First, unlike previous biological cataclysms, which fell most heavily on larger animals high up on the food chain, the present crisis is sweeping away entire habitats. Biotopes — environmentally distinct regions — all over the world, from tropical and temperate forests to coral reefs and estuaries, are disintegrating in the wake of increasing human activity, especially industrialization — the panacea of politicians and economists everywhere. As a result, 20 percent of all terrestrial plant species may vanish within the next fifty years, an evolutionary milestone.[12] Because plants make up the foundation of entire biotic communities, their demise will certainly carry with it the extinction of an exponentially greater number of animal species — perhaps ten times as many faunal species for each type of plant eliminated.[13] Conceivably, the development of new species will also be forestalled by this. Even with plant life relatively intact, it took from 50,000 to 100,000 years after the dinosaur crash for biological diversity to begin to reestablish itself at its former richness.[14] Moreover, the resurrection of biological diversity assumes an intact zone of tropical forests to provide, as it has in the past, the genetic reseeding for new speciation after extinction.[15] Just the opposite is the case in the present biological meltdown: the tropical rain forests are disappearing more rapidly than any other biotope, ensuring that the Earth will remain a biological, if not a literal, desert for eons to come.

It is worth noting in passing the kind of world we are contemplating here. The environment of a postextinction landscape favors what biologists call r-selected creatures — that is, species that are highly mobile, adaptable, and opportunistic. In our world these are represented by rats, roaches, sparrows, gulls, and weeds. Regarding the children who will inherit this future r-selected world, ecologist Norman Myers mordantly suggests: "We might want to wish them luck."[16]

The second factor that differentiates the present pattern of extinction from previous ones is that it is in no sense natural. It is driven by human cultures and their values, which represent historical choices, not inevitabilities. Confusing history with nature has been a leitmotiv throughout the ages, and it has resurfaced in the present environmental debate with a vengeance. Humanist environmental writers such as Walter Truett Anderson, Andrew Bard Schmookler, Murray Bookchin, and Alston Chase, as well as blatant antienvironmentalists like Ron Arnold, insist that human control of the biosphere is somehow (we know not how) a natural, ineluctable consequence of evolution: "nature becoming aware of itself."[17]

If so, nature must surely be aghast at its own image. "Natural areas were not made less natural by human presence," Chase asserts about Yellowstone National Park, apparently blind to the roads, restaurants, and bullet-ridden grizzly bears that have increasingly marred the park during the last few decades of intense development.[18] Anderson generalizes the argument in *To Govern Evolution*, writing that "Earth itself brought forth human intelligence and . . . all the biopolitical events of our time . . . are part of nature.[19] Giving the ultimate secular sanction to extinction, pollution, and waste, Arnold claims that "humans and our disequilibrium are as much a part of the biological construction we call the biosphere as the birds or whales,"[20] making it a short step for him to do away with all commonsense distinctions between the natural and the artificial world: "Pollution is not, as we are so often told, a product of moral turpitude. It is an inevitable consequence of life at work. In a sensible world, industrial waste would not be banned but put to good use. The negative, unconstructive response of prohibition by law seems as idiotic as legislating against emissions of dung from cows."[21]

Understandably, Arnold does not go into detail about the "good use" to which industrial society's numberless toxins, carcinogens, and mutagens could be put. In any case, it is not quite clear what "good use" means to any of these writers, since for them anything humans do is natural: deforestation, water pollution, genocide, tyranny, thermonuclear warfare.

The argument that the environmental crisis is just another curlicue in the history of life on Earth is contradicted by the existence of numerous cultures that have developed a sustainable and harmonious relationship with their surroundings because they neither industrialized nor turned to monoculture nor presumed to take upon themselves the megalomaniacal task "to govern evolution": the Mbuti, the Penan, the !Kung, to name but a few. Out of some hidden source of wisdom these societies *chose* not to dominate nature. In the larger history of humanity, they are the norm and we are the exception. For very complex reasons, which have nothing to do with any putative superiority and everything to do with institutional power, our culture — the technological culture that now dominates much of the globe — regrettably set off on its own wayward path, the terminus of which seems to be our termination.

The biological meltdown is therefore not only a scientific description, but a crisis of values, often the most venal and profligate of values. For example, a major force behind the destruction of tropical rain forests, over 40 percent of which have already been razed, is the demand for cheap beef by the American fast food industry: the so-called hamburger connection. With the blessing of their governments and international financial institutions, Central and South American ranchers annually slash and burn swaths of rain forests the size of West Virginia to make way for cattle grazing. But the thin, lateritic soils of the tropical forests are fragile, and the cleared land can support cattle for only a few years before it is abandoned to erosion. All in all, the American consumer saves four or five pennies per pound of beef — a few pennies gained at the expense of innumerable species obliterated before they could even be named, and charged to the account of future generations that must suffer the consequences of the greenhouse effect, which follows hard upon deforestation.

As the bleak realities of the environmental crisis close in, people are resigning themselves to the fact that some of their more trivial cultural values will have to change. For this reason, governments and mainstream environmental groups generally restrict their efforts to the promotion of such unburdensome programs as recycling and energy conservation. But the biological meltdown is most directly the result of values fundamental to what we have come to recognize as culture under the regime of technological society: economic growth, "progress," property rights, consumerism, religious doctrines about humanity's dominion over nature, technocratic notions about achieving an optimum human existence at the expense of all other life-forms. These ideas have a long lineage, going back perhaps ten thousand years to the rise of urban centers, domestication, and the first political states during the Neolithic revolution, when agriculture first began to displace the hunter-gatherer way of life.[22] They are embedded in our understanding of civilization and the good life; and civilization, as the biological meltdown suggests, seems to require the progressive extirpation of life on this planet through habitat destruction, the production of toxic wastes, ozone depletion, and a thousand other affronts to the environment.

The ecocidal tendency of civilization is not a new thesis. In 1864 George Perkins Marsh wrote *Man and Nature*, universally acknowledged as the fountainhead of the conservation movement, in which he argued that lost civilizations of the past perished because they wasted their natural resources.[23] More than thirty years ago, in *Topsoil and Civilization*, Vernon Carter and Tom Dale presented a general theory of war, colonization, and the rise and fall of cultures from Sumeria to Rome, based on civilization's urge to deforest, overgraze, overhunt, and deplete through overfarming the lands it occupies (the application of this view to modern America was not lost on the authors either, even in the halcyon years of the 1950s). According to Carter and Dale, the results of this appetite for havoc are predictable:

One man has given a brief outline of history by saying that "civilized man has marched across the face of the earth and left a desert in his footprints." This statement may be somewhat of an exaggeration, but it is not without foundation. Civilized man has despoiled most of the lands on which he has lived for long. This is the main reason why his progressive civilizations have moved from place to place. It has been a chief cause for the decline of his civilizations in older settled regions. It has been a dominant factor in determining all trends in history.[24]

Canadian author Robert Paehlke has suggested that the time
has come to have environmentalism "without apocalypse,"
without the premise that the natural world is fundamentally
threatened by the interventions of human society: an "environmentalism without a millennial dimension . . . may turn out
to be a much more important movement than was anticipated
in the early years."[25] The suggestion seems to have come several millennia too late. We have yet to come to grips with this
"dominant factor" Carter and Dale mention: our culture is *lethal* and has been so for a very long time, seemingly from the
start, if they are to be believed. To James Lovelock's three
deadly *C*'s we need to add a fourth — civilization itself.

No Greek chorus of ecological warnings, however grim, can
adequately convey this cultural reappraisal compelled by the
biological meltdown. The morality play of Aldo Leopold's conversion prefigures on a personal level what is now beginning
to happen globally to the culture of technology as the environmental crisis moves from a future threat to a grievous reality.
Ecological decline is becoming the dominant theme of national
and international debate, often in a repentant atmosphere of
ashes and sackcloth, or at least for what passes as such among
politicians and national leaders. To give a conspicuous, if
slightly absurd, example, almost half of the final communiqué
issued by the 1989 economic summit of the world's seven largest industrial democracies concerned environmental issues,
warning of "an urgent need to safeguard the environment for
future generations."[26] In contrast, the summit of the year before had lavished a scant paragraph on the ecology. This concern was unexpected (some might say hypocritical), coming
from the same nations that for the past several decades have
financed the destruction of the Amazonian rain forests, depleted the ozone layer with refrigerators and hair spray, and
seemingly ensured vast climatic changes through their dirty
habits of production.

In some places in the world, ecological concerns have gone
beyond this kind of tokenism and seem to be driving political
events. The obvious example is the Green movement in Western Europe. Concern over nuclear accidents, pollution, and
Waldsterben — the death of forests from acid rain — has
brought Green party members into the Parliaments of most

West European countries to promote a far-reaching agenda for transforming industrial society and its intrusions on the natural world. As the German Green party program states: "The prevailing economic rationality must be replaced by a policy guided by long-term and ecological goals. We must stop the violation of nature in order to survive in it."[27]

In Eastern Europe the relationship between the environmental crisis and political change is even more striking. The rise of political opposition in the wonder year of 1989 is very much linked to discontent over central governments' insensitivity to environmental protection, an insensitivity that has left large areas of the Soviet Union, Poland, and Czechoslovakia some of the most polluted places on Earth. "Early opposition to the government's environmental policies helped to create the conditions in which the demands for greater democracy were framed," London University scholar Michael Redclift says of Hungary, and this also applies to the Baltic republics of Estonia, Lithuania, and Latvia.[28] With the Chernobyl accident, increases in infant mortality due to pollution, and forests sick with acid rain, East Europeans were forced to organize and speak out against their government's environmental policies even at the risk of reprisals. The example of the European Greens proves societies can begin to transform themselves to accommodate ecological balance. Unfortunately, it also suggests that they do so only *after* the environment becomes degraded virtually to the point of collapse, when there is very little left of the natural world to save.

This apparent shift in focus has caused some writers to call the waning years of the twentieth century the Age of Ecology.[29] Whether this is an expression of hope or alarm is not always clear, but it is apparent that this generation, whether it likes it or not, will come face-to-face with Leopold's choice. The history of the next ten years will probably document the unraveling of environmental processes that have been under way since the beginning of life on this planet. How nations respond to this calamity will say something about who they are as a people.

So far, the implications are less than flattering. Not only do the "solutions" of environmental policymakers lack the vision necessary to deal with the biological meltdown, they seem doomed to aggravate the situation when put into practice. To give an example, almost all national and international bodies dealing with the issue take it for granted that the way to stabilize ecological decline and population growth in the Third World is through technology transfer and modernization — in other words, replacing indigenous economies with market economies. Most environmental organizations have jumped onto the technology bandwagon more or less willingly, with the proviso that lending institutions link development loans to conservation efforts.[30]

Leaving aside the suspicious fact that technology transfer fits perfectly into the industrialized nations' goal of creating a global market, the strategy has one conspicuous shortcoming: it amounts to ecological suicide. If the worldwide coterie of polluters and mass consumers is joined by Nigeria, Brazil, Peru, Malaysia, and a dozen other Third World countries that retain at least a semblance of their indigenous, Earth-harmonious economies, there is very little doubt that life on this planet will soon become intolerable. For the rest of the world to use as much energy (not to mention consumer goods) per capita as the United States does, it would have to burn 300 percent more coal, 500 percent more petroleum, and 1,100 percent more natural gas.[31] What this would mean in terms of the greenhouse effect alone is not a comforting thought. The ecology of the planet is already coming undone from the production habits of that minority of countries that has industrialized; it cannot survive an India full of refrigerators.

Of course, the problem of Third World political economy is complex and directly related to the disruptions caused by colonialism and international markets in the first place. As sociologist William Catton says of the United Nations' hapless attempt to address the issue in its 1972 Conference on the Human Environment, "The luckier nations which happened to achieve industrial prodigality before the earth's savings became depleted had already infected the other nations with an insatiable desire to emulate that prodigality."[32] Nonetheless, from an ecological perspective — which in the long run is the only one that matters — industrial societies must be considered a fleeting, unpleasant mirage on the landscape rather than a vision of the future to be emulated.

The dilemma of technological culture is that its solutions inevitably raise problems more pressing than those it purports to solve. The environmental crisis makes this apparent as never before. A naive faith in technology, however, still pervades much of the environmental debate. In 1973 one author, anxious to discredit "ecocultists" and "technophobes," wrote the following with unfailing prophetic inaccuracy:

> There is little danger from a population explosion in the developing countries, for their population, hitherto kept in check by famine and disease, will stabilize as these countries industrialize, repeating the same patterns as observed in the industrialized countries some time ago. There is no threat of worldwide famine in the near future, because worldwide food production is keeping abreast of population. There is no reason to run out of energy; the Sun will shine for at least another ten billion years and its energy can be efficiently harnessed. There is little reason to run out of resources, for nonrenewable does not mean irreplaceable. Pollution is not an essential by-product of technology; it is an undesirable side product which can be eliminated by more and superior technology.[33]

Although every one of these rhapsodic assertions has been proved false over the past decade and a half, environmental policymakers continue to repeat them in one form or another, as if to cease would break the technological spell. Sadly, the mainstream environmental movement is often part of the chorus. When the executive directors of ten of the largest environmental organizations in the United States (the so-called Group of Ten, or, to radical environmentalists, the Gang of Ten) met in 1984 to formulate a political agenda, they sidestepped all discussion of the social implications of the environmental crisis. The resulting document, *An Environmental Agenda for the Future*, claimed that if its recommendations were followed they would ensure the continued march of economic growth with a healthy environment into the twenty-first century.[34] The agenda portrayed environmental degradation as a technical problem, a problem of resource management.

The environmental crisis simply belies this representation. As Langdon Winner writes in his evocative book, *The Whale and the Reactor,* in a society dominated by technology, "[t]o be realistic, to get things done, and to get on with one's career almost require that a person become an enemy of free humanity and a healthy biosphere."[35] The hope that our society can have the "benefits" of technology without its corresponding liabilities seems strangely out of place in a world where the intricate web of life itself is now being brought into confusion by the touch of technological development. Although the cost of technology can temporarily be transferred to the powerless, to other communities (human and nonhuman), or to the next generation, the environmental crisis guarantees that every one of us will pay in the end.

We must admit at least the possibility that dealing with the biological meltdown will require policies incompatible with modern industrial society as we know it. Based solely on ecological necessity, these policies might include an end to all commercial logging; the restoration of large wilderness areas on what is now developed land by removing roads, dams, and other technological intrusions; the reintroduction of large predators, such as grizzly bears and wolves, into areas where they have been extirpated; the banning of all pesticides and toxic wastes; the elimination of the automobile, coal-fired power plants, and manufacturing processes using petrochemicals; the end of monoculture and range cattle production; and, most important, the reduction of the human population to an ecologically sustainable level. It may require a stop to the exportation of technology to the Third World, and the deindustrialization of the First. It will certainly entail eradicating the relentless engine of environmental decline, the multinational corporation, whose sole purpose is to loot the Earth in search of an annual return on its capital. The crisis may at its worst conceivably incite armed intervention, "ecowars," against countries like Brazil whose deforestation projects threaten the stability of the world's climate.

Obviously, within the realm of contemporary politics, these solutions are not only unrealistic, but also seemingly unintelligible. That hardly matters. The biological meltdown is fast making the logic of industrial society irrelevant. Recently, Michael Soulé, founder of the Society of Conservation Biologists, made this chilling assessment of the status of the Earth's biosphere: "For the first time in hundreds of millions of years significant evolutionary change in most higher organisms is coming to a screeching halt. . . . Vertebrate evolution may be at an end."[36] Soulé is saying that humanity's disruption of the environment has been so systematic and profound that it has halted the same natural processes that have brought everything we know into existence, including our very bodies and minds.

Let that sink in. Soulé's statement may rank with the findings of Copernicus and Darwin in marking a shift in the way we understand our place in the world, one of those rare historical moments when the observations of science break into and disrupt the complacency of culture and realign patterns of thought. Although the concept of evolution is a relatively recent way of understanding our place in nature, the idea of a reciprocal relationship, whether hostile or benign, between human society and the processes of nature is central to what might be called the civilization complex — the interweaving of institutions, values, economics, populations, and the environment — that has dominated human affairs (and increasingly the ecology) since the Neolithic revolution ushered in sedentary agricultural communities some ten thousand years ago. Our society, industrial society, belongs to a continuum of ideas and values within the civilization complex, a continuum rudely shaken by Soulé's pronouncement. Only a hundred or so years after Darwin "discovered" our fundamental relationship to nature in terms of evolution, we are, according to Soulé, putting an end to it.

If Soulé is right, and there is every reason to believe he is, then nature as an entity distinct from culture has, like an errant moon, suddenly dropped out of our conceptual horizon. *"Vertebrate evolution may be at an end"* — this means the civilization complex has lost its reference point by overwhelming the natural processes it has always used to define itself. The otherness of nature is disappearing into the artificial world of technology. Not that nature will cease to be an object of discourse. Quite the contrary: as the environmental crisis worsens, we can expect increased attention directed at the ecological sciences, resource management, pollution control, and technological supervision of the reproduction of valued species, including Homo sapiens. This is already the case. But it only confirms the fact that the regime of technology has preempted natural processes to the point that they are almost entirely subordinated to culture. A living, breathing world has been transformed into what Martin Heidegger called the un-world, an ersatz environment "which is only supposed to be of use for the guarantee of the dominance of man whose effects are limited to judging whether something is important or un-important to life."[37]

Who will make these judgments now that human culture has, at least momentarily, swallowed up the natural world? A num-ber of thinkers have taken up the sociopolitical implications of this unworld in environmental disarray. Historian Arnold Toynbee writes that the ecological scarcity of the future will be so severe that "within each of the beleaguered 'developed' countries there will be a bitter struggle for control of their di-minished resources."[38] This conflict will inevitably lead, ac-cording to Toynbee, to the imposition of authoritarian regimes.

In *Ecology and the Politics of Scarcity*, political scientist Wil-liam Ophuls reaches a similar conclusion, stating that "in a situation of ecological scarcity . . . the individualistic basis of society, the concept of inalienable rights, the purely self-defined pursuit of happiness, liberty as maximum freedom of action, and laissez-faire itself all require abandonment if we wish to avoid inexorable environmental degradation and per-haps extinction as a civilization."[39]

Economist Robert Heilbroner sees this process as transcend-ing political distinctions between capitalist and socialist coun-tries, notwithstanding the recent braggadocio by conservative thinkers that "democratic" capitalism has triumphed over communism. Heilbroner suggests that the "exigencies of the future . . . point to the conclusion that only an authoritarian, or possibly only a revolutionary, regime will be capable of mounting the immense task of social reorganization needed to escape catastrophe."[40]

Implicit in these dismal vistas of the future is the establish-ment of ecological elites, a social phenomenon already observ-able. Power and status are increasingly measured not merely by economic control, but by control over the ecology. As the biology of the world becomes depauperate, access to clean water, fresh air, open wild spaces, and natural products is competing with ownership of German automobiles and Swiss watches as the index of privilege and power.[41] And since ecosystems, unlike status symbols, cannot simply be manufactured, the struggle for control over them is becoming the main preoccupation of political debate.

Just as the economic elite in our society influences the distribution of assets and the direction of the economy, the ecological elite into which it is developing will influence the course of evolution on this planet. The rise of the biotechnology industry makes such a conclusion unavoidable. In 1987, for example, the firm Advanced Genetic Sciences sprayed into the open environment millions of *Pseudomonas syringae* bacteria that had been genetically altered to prevent frost formation. The firm expects to earn up to $300 million a year from this patented life-form, called Frostban, mostly from sales to agribusiness, which naturally has an interest in preventing frost damage. The environmental effect, however, may be to allow non-frost-resistant plants to migrate north and displace native species. Moreover, the *P. syringae* bacterium is thought to be involved in raindrop formation, which may also be disrupted by Frostban. In other words, the entire landscape of the Northern Hemisphere may be altered as a result of this one company's marketing scheme.[42]

Even when a corporation decides to create a less exotic item not produced by genetic engineering, it is often indirectly determining what species will be exterminated to increase profits, which habitats will be sacrificed for economic growth, and whose children will be allocated the toxic water, poisoned food, and radioactive living space. The link between market economy and environmental decline is an issue that will not go away. We have yet to legitimize the right of people to live in a world of biological and habitat diversity. Conversely, we have taken only the first steps toward codifying the nature and extent of environmental crimes. At present a corporation — an inanimate, economic abstraction — has legal status and may destroy entire ecosystems under law, while the living animal and plant communities destroyed have no legal standing.[43]

That this situation is now becoming a concern suggests that environmentalism may well be the template through which we may finally perceive how power works in our society.

The bonds that hold a technological society together under an economic elite are tenuous at best, with the deep-seated conflicts among individuals, corporations, governments, and even generations held in check by a strange combination of state intimidation, promises of wealth, and threats of impoverishment. We can expect these conflicts to rise to the surface from the pressure of ecological collapse. Indeed, a recent study by the Institute for Environment and Development concludes that a great deal of social conflict and even political violence is already attributable to ecological decay.[44]

Consider, for instance, the generational conflicts that are being set in motion by the construction of nuclear power plants. The life span of a nuclear reactor is about thirty years, after which the installation must be dismantled at the cost of anywhere from $50 million to $3 billion. There are 84 reactors in the United States alone, 380 worldwide. Dismantling just one large reactor will produce some eighteen thousand cubic meters of low-level radioactive waste — enough to fill a football stadium to the height of ten feet. The volume of contaminated concrete and steel from all American plants will be enough to build a radioactive wall ten feet high and three feet wide from New York to Washington, D.C., if such were wanted. As to high-level radioactive waste, there is still no safe, practical way to deal with it after four decades of the nuclear age.[45]

None of the cost of this cleanup has been internalized by the nuclear power industry — that is, it has not been factored into the price of electricity sold. Future generations, therefore, will have to pay dearly for this "inexhaustible" source of energy, ironically without ever having used a kilowatt of electricity produced by nuclear power. And this is just a monetary calculation; it says nothing about the degradation in physical and genetic health that will result from the inevitable accidents and miscalculations of the nuclear power industry.

The Faustian bargain our parents made to obtain nuclear power may very easily set the next several generations against those who profited from the nuclear Mephistopheles, perhaps in tangible ways. A generation facing a moribund world of ecological scarcity may simply deny social security benefits to an older generation that plundered the Earth and left its children to pay the economic and ecological debts. Ecological scarcity may make the expropriation of the relatively more affluent prior generation the social norm.

Unfortunately, this is not the mere speculation of doom-sayers. In some parts of the world it is a harrowing reality. Thirty years ago, a hunter-gatherer tribe of northern Uganda called the Ik was forced from its native lands by the government into a barren, mountainous region subject to drought and desertification. Living a scavenger existence among the rocky outcroppings, the Ik soon found that caring for the young and the old was a luxury they could not afford. Ik mothers fed their children for a short time, after which they abused them, beat them, laughed at their injuries, and finally drove them from the family — at three years old. The children formed gangs that competed with each other for scraps of food. In the end they had a revenge of sorts. When their parents grew too old to care for themselves, there was no one willing to look after them. In fact, it was considered foolish.

An anthropologist who lived among the Ik recounts a story that expresses the utter breakdown of social bonds in that society. After a raid by a hostile tribe, the Ik decided to flee and build a village elsewhere. A sick old man tried to follow the others as best he could by crawling on his belly. The anthropologist asked one youth who the old man was. After indifferently stepping over the crawling figure, the boy said, "Oh, that's no one, that's my father." The anthropologist bribed the boy to carry his father, but when everyone started laughing at him, he dropped the burden and went forward on his own.[46]

We might ask if the story of the Ik father is not a parable for the fate this generation is making for itself by bringing on the biological meltdown. When various authorities from a variety of disciplines reach similar conclusions about this unprecedented problem, it suggests, at the very least, that the environmental crisis has made our culture obsolescent in ways we have yet to contemplate, with our timid rhetoric about alternate energy sources, recycling, and appropriate technology. Such is the scope of the environmental crisis that it makes us question our entire history on Earth, back to the origins of civilization. People in the future may very well look back and wonder how the last several generations could have gotten caught up in such minor distractions as two world wars, space flight, and the nuclear arms race.

Paul Ehrlich puts it bluntly: "Extrapolations of current trends in the reduction of diversity imply a denouement for civilization within the next 100 years comparable to nuclear winter."[47] Ehrlich is too cautious. Modern society's confrontation with nature's limits has probably already let loose forces of cultural change that ensure the breakdown of a cluster of concepts representing the core of the civilization complex — progress, hierarchy, order, work, humankind's dominion over nature — in the following way.

From its origins, civilization defined itself in relation to the natural world. By dividing the world between cultivated lands and wilderness, *civilized* people became *citizens* (the two words are cognate), with an allegiance to a politically ordered space distinct from the "disorder" of wild nature. The distinction between the natural and the cultural world enforced by civilization generated a number of concepts that have dominated human thought, with differing emphasis and varying forms, ever since.

When the privileged speakers of our society such as politicians, economists, and religious leaders talk about progress, for instance, they have always already presumed that the undisturbed processes of nature are somehow stagnant or defective or detrimental and must be improved by human intervention. In short, there is an unspoken representation of nature in any appeal to progress. The representation seems unassailably correct to us, caught up in the civilization complex as we are, but even a brief look at primal cultures, which reject the notion of nature as deficient, suggests how arbitrary this view is. It goes without saying that our ideas about progress have changed drastically through history and have been used to justify a variety of different behaviors — from cultivating a field to building an atomic bomb to cutting down rain forests in order to produce cheaper hamburgers. What progress means is endlessly variable, as are the behaviors it is used to validate. But whatever its use or particular form, progress always carries with it a representation of nature, a socially defined view of how the nonhuman world relates to the human world.

But what will be the meaning of progress when progress itself leads to the end of the natural processes from which culture distinguishes itself? At the end point of civilization's progress is the termination of evolution, the disappearance of nature into the artifacts of culture. What will it mean to progress from there, except to see the whole language of progress as a sham?

What will be the meaning of "order" to a people whose political institutions, even when they were democratic, turned them into ecological refugees, citizens of the unworld of environmental paucity?

What will "God" mean to a generation condemned by the antinature of prevailing religious doctrines to be the poor who inherited an impoverished Earth?

When the paradigmatic ideas of an age lose their grip, they are perceived as what they always were: not truths, but *values*, cloaked in a language that made them appear natural, universal, unquestionable, inevitable. Roland Barthes calls this type of discourse myth. Mythic discourse, in this sense, must "suggest and mimic a universal order" to disguise the values that empower whatever group is dominant enough to impose its linguistic will on a culture.[48] When, for whatever reason, the myth is no longer taken seriously, the disguise becomes painfully obvious — as has happened with the concept of the divine origin of kings in pagan society and the concept of the divine right of kings in feudal Christian society. We read about these ideas and can only smile at the gullibility of the cultures that allowed their rulers to weave such self-serving fictions into the fabric of society.

And yet, as the environmental crisis focuses attention on the values that gave it birth, will our references to mass democracy, free markets, technological advancement, and scientific objectivity also be exposed as myth? Will we suddenly, to our chagrin, see the core concepts of our culture as "alibis" that institutional power has always used to gain control over the politics, economy, and finally the ecology of the world?

The ability to perceive the fiction of the myth is central to our historical sense. It is what distinguishes the past, with its obviously self-serving mythic discourse, from the self-evident correctness of the present and its ideas. If, therefore, the environmental crisis is causing us to reexamine and reject the accepted values of the civilization complex in its entirety, a unique event is taking place: the passing of civilization into history.

There have, of course, always been shifts and discontinuities in history. Michel Foucault has convincingly argued that discontinuity is the stuff of history, rather than some presumed development that has inevitably and mysteriously guided events to produce us, the self-proclaimed pinnacle of evolution.[49] But never has the rupture been so complete as to sever all continuity and reduce the civilization complex itself to a historical artifact. Just such a breach, however, may be heralded in Soulé's statement about the biological meltdown, forcing us to admit what thinkers in the tradition of Rousseau and Thoreau have long suggested: that civilization is a fake, a vast pyramid scheme in which privileged groups use such concepts as "progress" to control nature and human nature for their own benefit.

This generation, therefore, may be living in civilization's terminal culture — in both senses of the world. The regime of technological culture is terminal in that it is lethal to the ecology on which it depends; and it is terminal in the sense that it is ending as the biological meltdown reveals its myths, passing into history, as surely as the Bronze Age did with its buxom goddesses and aristocratic warriors.

Endings, however, change people. What the dying green fire was to Leopold, the biological meltdown is to a growing number of environmental activists, who see the crisis as too imposing to be dealt with in a business-as-usual fashion. "Our job is to save the building blocks," Dave Foreman has said of radical environmentalism, "and to make sure there are grizzly bears and great blue whales and rain forests and redwoods somewhere, so that in the final thrashing of the industrial monster, everything else that's good on this planet isn't destroyed."[50]

Of course, as Langdon Winner has pointed out, basing one's social philosophy on the probability of an ecocatastrophe has its drawbacks: "What if new data indicate the emergency wasn't what you said it was? Are you then obliged to apologize and fall silent?"[51] Certainly most radical environmentalists would be willing to fall silent under those circumstances, but redeeming data about industrial society and its abuse of the ecology do not at the moment seem to be forthcoming. It is true that the predictions of imminent social debacle made by some environmentalists in the early 1970s did not come to pass in this country (though elsewhere in the world, as in northern Africa, for instance, they have), prompting one writer to proclaim, "Doomsday has been cancelled."[52] We now know that it was merely postponed; the ecocatastrophe of biological meltdown is an undeniable scientific fact upon which rests an equally undeniable sociopolitical predicament.

Unfortunately, not even the most scrupulously empirical findings of science can convince some people that industrial society is a threat to the health of the biosphere. Donald Hodel, the flannel-shirted secretary of the interior under Reagan and worthy successor to James Watt, assured the nation that the answer to the threat of ultraviolet-radiation-induced skin cancer due to atmospheric ozone depletion was sunglasses and sunscreen. In a long and belligerent article in *Newsweek*, Gregg Easterbrook discounted the tragic consequences of the 1989 Alaska oil spill with the bland explanation: "Conceptually, what Exxon did was reposition a natural contaminant from inside a rock formation to the surface of a water body, where natural forces (wave action, bacteria, sunlight) immediately began acting in opposition to the intrusion."[53] To be sure, these are burlesque examples. But they embody the method by which industrial society conceptualizes environmental degradation: either it does not exist, or there are technological answers to these technologically caused problems. Impatience with doomsaying is strong in our culture, especially when backed up by economic self-interest, as is usually the case. And as the environmental crisis worsens, the voices for more development only seem to be growing louder, the call for technological answers more shrill, the disrespect for the natural world and its defenders more frenzied.

Curiously, the impetus for the radical environmental movement, at least in this country, was not solely a response to the smug advocates of wilderness destruction and industrial development. Rather, it was by all accounts also a reaction to a less benighted position, one that raised the hopes of many young environmental activists in the 1960s and 1970s only to dash them in a welter of compromise, bureaucratic politicking, and an obsession with attaining respectability and thus the favor of the powers that be. In short, the mainstream, reformist environmental movement, embodied in national groups like the Sierra Club and the Wilderness Society, ensured an explosion of radical environmental forces by anxiously trying to restrain them.

CHAPTER 3

THE RISE AND FALL
OF REFORM ENVIRONMENTALISM:
AN UNEXPURGATED HISTORY

Subversive elements plan to make American children live in an environment that is good for them.

— *Mississippi delegate to the 1970*
Continental Congress of the Daughters
of the American Revolution

I think the Wilderness Society, Sierra Club, Audubon Society, and all the others should combine and hire Lee Iacocca to run them.

— *Mike Roselle,*
Earth First! cofounder

The Sierra Club is becoming like Velveeta: everything must be processed.

— *David Brower*

APRIL 22, 1970: EARTH DAY. It was one of the most remarkable public events in American political history. Two hundred fifty thousand people gathered in Washington, D.C., to voice their support for decisive action on environmental protection. One hundred thousand New Yorkers walked down Fifth Avenue in an eerie, silent requiem to ecosystems despoiled by industrial pollution. At 1,500 campuses and 10,000 schools across the nation, students and teachers observed the occasion with

teach-ins on environmental issues, putting knowledgeable
speakers in such demand that in some cases they had to fly
from state to state or even coast to coast to make their engage-
ments.[1] Both houses of Congress recessed to allow members to
join their constituencies in observing the event, though with a
few notable exceptions most national politicians, wary of this
uncharted political sea, chose to watch the spectacle unfold on
television, from the relative safety of their homes.[2] But even
this minor disappointment was turned to the environmentalists' favor, by Scott Lang, president of Harvard's Environmental Law Society, who assured the press that most politicians
were not particularly welcome anyway, since "we wanted informed people."[3]

Informed people were theirs for the asking. Population biologist Paul Ehrlich, biologist Barry Commoner, biologist Rene
Dubos, consumer advocate Ralph Nader, all gave major addresses to inform and exhort Americans in what amounted to
the equivalent of a national town meeting on America's environmental future.

Even in a time of mass protests against the Vietnam War and
racial injustice, Earth Day represented an impressive display
of public support for a political ideal — the preservation of
America's deteriorating environment. Sustained by that good-
will, the mood of the environmental movement radiated optimism, if not euphoria. Local environmental action groups were
springing up all over the country. To accommodate the flood
of new activists, the Sierra Club used the occasion to publish
four hundred thousand copies of a handbook, with the over-
stated title of *Ecotactics*, in which Sierra Club executive director Michael McCloskey applauded the environmental
movement's sudden leap into the political arena, "because that
is how lasting improvements can be secured in our society."[4]
The ebullience that many environmentalists felt at the time
was best expressed in a speech to a Denver crowd delivered by
the man who had originated the idea of an Earth Day, Wisconsin senator Gaylord Nelson: "Earth Day may be a turning point
in American history. It may be the birth of a new American
ethic that rejects the frontier philosophy that the continent was
put here for our plunder, and accepts the idea that even urban-

ized, affluent, mobile societies are interdependent with the fragile, life-sustaining systems of the air, the water, the land."[5]

As subsequent events would prove, the Athena-like birth of a new ecological ethic anticipated by Nelson was not to be. But it might have been, and Nelson had good reason for thinking it was imminent.

On the spring morning of Earth Day the American environmental movement was riding high. The last few years of the 1960s had brought environmentalists a number of stunning political and legal successes, with prospects of many more on the horizon. First and foremost was the passage of the National Environmental Policy Act of 1969. Signed on January 1, 1970, by President Richard Nixon as his first official act of what he called the new "environmental decade," NEPA was a blueprint for achieving goals of environmental quality and the text for a whole new vocabulary of federal land use requirements, such as the now-famous environmental impact statement. The act also led to the creation in 1970 of the Presidential Council on Environmental Quality and eventually the Environmental Protection Agency, which consolidated a sweeping range of powers formerly held by the Departments of the Interior, of Agriculture, and of Health, Education and Welfare, and by other executive arms, whose bickering forestalled the implementation of environmental laws. The leaders of several national environmental organizations gave testimony and lobbied Congress in support of the act.

Less spectacular, but in its own way equally satisfying to the environmental community, was the Endangered Species Conservation Act of 1969 (not to be confused with its more muscular descendant, the Endangered Species Act of 1973). The National Audubon Society, Defenders of Wildlife, the National Wildlife Federation, and the Sierra Club were able to overcome the usually powerful coalition of trophy hunters, furriers, and other animal-product exporters and get the bill passed almost unanimously. It mandated, for the first time in American history, the listing of species threatened with extinction. Although only foreign wildlife shipped in or out of the country fell under the protection provisions of the law, it nonetheless set the stage for the more comprehensive bill of 1973.

In the first roll-call vote in the House in the 1970s, the environmental community was also able to beat back the perversely named National Forest Timber Conservation and Management Act, a bill sponsored by the timber industry, which tried to use the housing shortage of the time as an excuse to propose intensive and unsustainable logging of the national forests.

On the legal front, environmentalists were just beginning to savor the implications of the *Parker* case. The Forest Service, at the behest of the timber industry, had drawn up plans to log East Meadow Creek, a roadless area adjacent to a designated wilderness in the White River National Forest, in Colorado. This would have made East Meadow Creek ineligible for wilderness status and protection under the 1964 Wilderness Act. Clif Merritt, the Wilderness Society western regional representative, and Tony Ruckel, a young, environmentally minded criminal lawyer, brought suit against the Forest Service, arguing that the agency could not develop areas eligible for inclusion in the wilderness system until the president and Congress acted on the agency's recommendations to exclude them.[6] The federal court agreed with the environmentalists, and the Supreme Court refused to review the ruling. The *Parker* case seemed to ensure that roadless areas adjacent to designated wilderness would not be eliminated from possible wilderness designation by a preemptive strike on the Forest Service's part.

This was just one of many suits brought by environmentalists, who had begun to realize that the federal courts were the real battleground for shaping environmental policy. By 1971 the Natural Resources Defense Council was bringing suit after suit on environmental issues, and the Sierra Club had established its Legal Defense Fund. Litigation would play an increasingly significant role in enforcing the regulatory minutiae that seemed to be the new currency of environmental protection. In 1967 a Sierra Club staff member wrote, "Last year, the New York lawyers began joining the Club at such a rate that I was afraid we were going to become the New York Bar Association."[7] Soon most of the national leadership would be attorneys, a fact that for better or worse would irrevocably change the complexion of the environmental movement.[8]

The movement's new political clout was reflected in its growing membership rolls. Under the vigorous leadership of David Brower, the Sierra Club had grown sevenfold in a decade, from 16,066 in 1960 to 114,336 in 1970.[9] It would continue to grow dramatically throughout the seventies and on into the eighties, buoyed by the so-called Watt boom, an influx of people frightened into environmental activism by the retrograde policies of President Reagan's maladroit and messianic secretary of the interior, James Watt. Other groups like the Wilderness Society, Defenders of Wildlife, and the National Audubon Society were experiencing a similar membership explosion.

Politicians could no longer afford to ignore the growing bloc of environmentally minded voters. Even President Nixon, the politician who a decade earlier had shown his support for the pesticide industry by eating four highly publicized helpings of DDT-treated cranberry sauce,[10] had begun to make ecological noises to attract the environmental vote, if not to distract attention from his convulsive Indochina policy. Ironically, in light of the cranberry sauce affair, he also contributed a quote to the back of the paperback release of Rachel Carson's *Silent Spring* — the book that exposed the pesticide problem — calling on America to restore "the purity of its air, its waters, and our living environment." Somewhat unsure of the political implications of the Earth Day festivities, however, Nixon cautiously relayed his environmental sympathies, such as they were, through an aide.

Yes, Earth Day represented the high point of the reform environmental movement. It was all downhill from there.

Although by any standard the environmental movement was a political success, the national environmental leadership had begun to discern a number of problems — or, for the more paranoid among them, threats. A lingering fear had taken shape that the environmental movement was being infiltrated by undesirable elements who sought revolutionary changes in society. Michael McCloskey of the Sierra Club reported ominously to the board that "our very success in fueling the environmental awakening is raising implications that it is well for us to understand."[11] Lawyer, duck hunter, and Sierra Club president Philip Berry spelled out one of these implications, as he saw it: "We welcome real converts, but the growing popularity of our cause has attracted some whose motives must be questioned." Among these suspect converts, Berry urged, were "anarchists voicing legitimate concerns about the environment for the ulterior purpose of attacking democratic institutions."[12]

It should be noted that at the time the Sierra Club was very much the liberal cutting edge of the environmental movement, with three quarters of its membership joining specifically because of the club's conservation agenda.[13] The other national environmental organizations attracted a more conservative clientele, or at least one less given to political engagement. Most environmentalists of that era were decidedly more interested in goose hunting than social revolution.

The environmental movement as a whole was very much a Republican, white, middle-class affair, having little spiritual affinity with the growing protest movements in the country. To use the late Abbie Hoffman's oxymoron, it was a hotbed of repose. In a 1977 survey of its readership, *Audubon*, the official and picturesque publication of the National Audubon Society, found that the average income of its readers was $35,708, 40 percent were in professional or technical occupations, 26 percent had top or middle-management jobs, 43 percent had attended graduate school, and almost 60 percent were male.[14] Even today, when presumably they should know better, a large segment of Sierra Club members, perhaps one third, vote Republican.[15] In fact, in 1986 the club hired the conservative Republican Doug Wheeler to be its executive director and receive the position's $100,000-a-year salary. Dave Foreman, a founder of Earth First!, sums up the character of the reform environmental movement from its origins: "The early conservation movement in the United States was a child — and no bastard child — of the Establishment."[16]

Earth Day forced that child to do some introspection. The movement's sudden emergence as the boisterous theater of cultural discontent confused and discomfited its longtime conservative supporters, many of whom took refuge in the apolitical complexities of the Environmental Defense Fund's economic analyses or, at the other extreme, the Sierra Club's sumptuous outings to Kenya, Peru, and Nepal. The subsequent history of the environmental movement has been influenced in large part by the awkwardness these mainstream supporters felt with the adversarial role their cause was suddenly assuming.

There was at the time little basis for this angst. Both the traditional and new left eschewed the environmental movement in general and Earth Day in particular. Except for a few renegades like Paul Booth, the Students for a Democratic Society boycotted Earth Day teach-ins as a "distraction" from the antiwar movement. Black leaders and militants also embraced the distraction theory. "The nation's concern with the environment," said Richard Hatcher, the black mayor of Gary, Indiana, "has done what George Wallace was unable to do: distract the nation from the human problems of black and brown Americans."[17] Robert Chrisman, the editor of *Black Scholar*, went so far as to call ecology "a racist shuck," excoriating environmentalists as the vanguard of "reactionary primitivism."[18] Unions were suspicious of the supposed elitism of environmentalists and worried that increased environmental protection would be exacted at the cost of unemployment, as a number of business leaders threatened. Traditional East Coast liberals disputed the relevance of protecting wilderness in an age of racism, capitalism, and Nixon. One liberal publication admonished that "the nation is now in a self-gratifying frenzy over ecology."[19]

Nevertheless, voices were beginning to emerge from within the environmental community itself that had something significant to say about social change and ecological decline. Barry Commoner, whose bespectacled face had graced the cover of *Time* a few months earlier, sounded this theme of social transformation and envisioned Earth Day as an opportunity to reflect on the course our technological culture was taking. "Those who are already convinced that our social system is in need of radical revision," he wrote, "will welcome this opportunity to discuss the prospect."[20] Expressing apprehension over the possibility of violent revolution over ecological scarcity, Gaylord Nelson suggested that "the growing concerns of our young people outline the need for some radical changes in our national habits."[21] More adventurous thinkers like Murray Bookchin predicted, and called for, the end to industrial society and its hierarchical system of governance. A

somewhat crude Marxist perspective on the environmental debate was given in James Ridgeway's *Politics of Ecology* and
Barry Weisberg's *Beyond Repair: The Ecology of Capitalism*,
both of which attacked the mainstream environmental movement for its links to the corporations causing ecological deterioration.[22]

But these voices fell on deaf ears. The leadership of the national environmental organizations considered them a conspiracy of malcontents and pop theorists rather than a promising
expansion of the environmental debate. The divergent perspectives coincidentally appeared side by side a month before
Earth Day in the form of two articles published in the Wilderness Society's periodical *Living Wilderness*. One article, by bot-
any professor Edward Clebsch, soberly endorsed a long-range
approach to environmental problems, expressing the hope that
"the Teach-in will plant the seeds for continued growth and
maturity of environmental concerns," which succeeding generations would harvest into effective reforms.[23] The other, by
Douglas Scott, the cochairman of Environmental Action for
Survival, portrayed Earth Day as "youth on the march" and
exhorted: "We will stop the destruction of this planet even at
the cost of our own futures, careers, and blood."[24]

In Scott's revolutionary, quasi-Jeffersonian vision, Earth Day
represented an opportunity to make the environmental movement a force for social change that could help avert an ecological disaster, the biological meltdown we are now facing. But
the opportunity, if it existed, was squandered. Every April Gaylord Nelson, now chairman of the Wilderness Society, is asked
whatever happened to Earth Day. He has replied sedately that
Earth Day only "gave an opportunity for [environmentalism]
to express itself."[25] Sadly, the environmental movement's national leadership, increasingly entrenched in Washington and
aloof from grass-roots activists, refused to listen to an important part of that expression, choosing instead to champion liberal reform to the exclusion of fundamental changes in our
society's relationship to the natural world. We will never know
if the American public was ready for this radical reappraisal,
but at the very least it would be more receptive to changes now
that they are absolutely essential had the environmentalist
leadership discussed the possibility twenty years ago. As if to

symbolize the direction the mainstream environmental movement would choose, the militant Scott eventually took a job as the Sierra Club's conservation director in Washington and would play a major role in the movement's withdrawal into middle-class respectability.

The national leadership was particularly anxious to present the environmental movement as a credible, professional, long-range affair, not a spasm of antiauthoritarianism. "We're afraid of this becoming too fashionable," fretted Dennis Hayes, national coordinator of the Earth Day's campus teach-in program, "of its being dismissed as a fad."[26] Ironically, Hayes went on to head the short-lived Solar Energy Research Institute, with its distinctly faddish rhetoric about alternative energy as a cure for the ills of industrial society. Even ten years later Brock Evans, director of the Sierra Club's Washington office, still felt the need to assert in print: "We are not a fad. We are here to stay."[27] The elusive goal of credibility loomed so large in the leadership's mind that it became a standard of comparison among the groups. The Sierra Club's McCloskey proudly maintained that "with Earth Day . . . the Club was better positioned than most of the organizations to move with greater assurance and professionalism into advancing an environmental agenda."[28]

These concerns were a response to a common criticism from both the right and the left at the time. Conservative economist Milton Friedman, with the same degree of inaccuracy found in many of his economic forecasts, predicted that the environmental movement was a mere passing fancy of the American public that would vanish as ignominiously as the war on poverty.[29] In a corresponding fit of clairvoyance gone astray from the liberal side of the political spectrum, the editors at the *New Republic* (when the magazine *was* liberal) suggested that environmentalism was a "craze" whose only real impact would be to bolster the political fortunes of the Nixon administration.[30]

Much of this criticism was seemingly directed at the type of protests environmentalism was producing among the young: a guerrilla theater of car burials, dump-ins, and mock trials of industrial polluters. Apparently dissent was significant only if it followed the somber lead of the antiwar and civil rights movements. One incident in particular captures mainstream environmentalism's sudden obsession with respectability. Casting about for a demon of revolution and faddism to exorcise, the national environmental leadership found one within its own ranks: David Brower, executive director of the Sierra Club during the sixties. Even to his detractors "a combination poet, naturalist, and politician,"[31] the tall, white-haired Brower seemed more in the mold of John Muir and Aldo Leopold than that of the lawyers and real estate investors who were beginning to predominate on the club's board of directors. With only a few lapses Brower had attempted to steer the Sierra Club down a path of uncompromising defense of the environment. If that meant conflict with government agencies and industries — and it did — then Brower was prepared for it.

The same could not be said of the conservative members of the Sierra Club board. Suspicious of Brower's aggressive book publishing and media campaigns (which produced such classics as Paul Ehrlich's *Population Bomb*) and angry at his insubordinate opposition to the Diablo Canyon nuclear power plant, these forces united into the Concerned Members for Conservation faction within the club in order to oust Brower. (Pro-Brower forces said the group's acronym, CMC, stood for Conservatives for Minimal Conservation.) The best of these conservatives thought a more nonconfrontational stance was the proper strategy for the club to take to reach its goals; the worst, bitten by the worm of credibility, wanted to curry favor with the industries and government agencies Brower opposed.

The mastermind behind the anti-Brower forces was Richard Leonard, attorney and former Sierra Club president, who faulted Brower because he "impugned the motives of Forest Service people, Park Service people, congressmen."[32] He and his associates wanted the club to follow the "mature" course of moving closer to government agencies and industry.[33] Using Brower's alleged mismanagement of club funds as a pretext (Brower was fond of saying "It's nice to be in the black, but better for the world to be in the green"), the CMC conservatives were able to force Brower off the board after a 1969 election gave them a majority of seats.

Having polished off Brower, the new leadership was free to reorganize the Sierra Club after its own image: that is, a consumer-oriented corporate bureaucracy. It consulted Ike Livermore, secretary of resources for California under then-governor Ronald Reagan, for recommendations on carrying out this restructuring, which eventually included instituting a conservative financial and publications policy and hiring a paid president, as most of the other environmental organizations had already done. The club also made plans for increasing its small staff in Washington, where the real action was for the environmental professional of the seventies.

For his part, Brower went on to found the more militant, grass-roots-based Friends of the Earth. But in 1986, history repeated itself, and he was ousted from the board by a conservative clique who wanted to move the organization to Washington. Brower, nothing if not persistent, then formed another grass-roots activist group, the Earth Island Institute, with which he remains — for the time being, at least.

Brower was not the only environmental leader to fall victim to the movement's raging moderates. Sydney Howe, president of the Conservation Foundation, was fired early in 1973 after he had incurred the wrath of conservative businessmen on the board by trying to make the foundation more responsive to grass-roots activism. Thereupon, the environmental advocacy of the Conservation Foundation dwindled into neutral economic analyses of resource consumption. The foundation reached its low point in 1977 with the publication of *Business and Environment: Toward Common Ground*, which, in what sounded like a parody of moderate environmentalism, called for "reasoned discussion" between business and environmentalists to take the place of "name-calling, agitation . . . caricature . . . and simplification of issues."[34] In that same year, the foundation's president, William Reilly, declared momentously that "the environmental rally is over"; in other words, environmentalists would have to learn to work with industry.[35]

The Brower and Howe incidents reflected what was happening to the environmental movement as a whole. It was becoming a career endeavor for professionals rather than a calling for those committed to the environment. This was perhaps to a degree unavoidable as the successes of environmentalists led to the codification of the issues into law, shifting the struggle from legislation to administration, from local communities to the federal courts. As has already been mentioned, the most obvious result of this change was that more and more lawyers were taking their place as leaders of large environmental organizations. The less obvious result was that environmental activism was slowly sinking into the murky world of the *Federal Register*, administrative hearings, and settlement negotiations. As it seemed to Douglas Scott, the "romantic days" when an embattled band of amateur environmentalists could take on industry and the federal government without the help of a lawyer were over.[36]

But the change in the environmental movement went far beyond its adaptation to the legal culture of national politics. Professionalism struck at the heart of what it meant to be an environmentalist. The founders of the American conservation movement, people like John Muir, Aldo Leopold, and Robert Marshall, had been impassioned amateurs, motivated by a great devotion to the land, not a desire for career advancement. Because to these lay activists environmentalism was a love, not a labor, they were free to demand whatever they felt was necessary for the protection of the wild, regardless of how their views sat with people of money and influence. The result was what would later be called a Deep Ecology perspective on environmental issues. These early conservationists believed, with greater or lesser consistency and clarity and at times significant lapses, that the natural world was there for its own sake, that it had its own inherent value quite apart from the commodity interests of mankind.[37] More than that, they were willing to articulate this heartfelt position even when the logic of industrial society insisted that there were, according to Gifford Pinchot, founder of the Forest Service, "only people and resources." This ecological sensibility found perhaps its most graceful expression in Leopold's land ethic: a thing is right when it tends to preserve the integrity, stability, and beauty of the biotic community. But it can also be heard in Marshall's declaration that there is only one hope of repulsing the tyrannical ambition of civilization to conquer every niche on the Earth — those "spirited people who will fight for the freedom of the wilderness."[38] Or in the dedicated work of thousands of other unheralded conservationists who placed the integrity of the natural world above the calculus of economics and politics.

The new environmental professionals were different from these "spirited people" in a number of ways. They looked at the environmental movement not as a cause so much as an opportunity to build a career. Before the midseventies, environmental leaders typically worked their way up to a position of authority by being volunteer grass-roots activists, going to local hearings, passing out flyers, and visiting the wild areas that needed protection. By the close of the decade the large organizations were no longer looking to the grass roots, but rather were recruiting outside "experts" with the financial and managerial skills necessary to run their growing business concerns. Even a progressive, action-oriented group like Greenpeace had taken on a corporate personality, a process that Greenpeace cofounder Robert Hunter defended: "If we were going to hope to generate the kind of money we needed, we had no choice but to adopt a successful corporate model. If there were to be budgets, someone with a professional background was going to have to implement them and ride herd on everyone involved."[39] In 1986 the Sierra Club's outgoing executive director, McCloskey, said he wanted his successor to be "a person who is strong in finance and budgets, who can offer entrepreneurial leadership, who is alert to changes in the marketplace."[40] If John Muir had been subject to these criteria, he would not have been hired to lead the Sierra Club, the organization he brought into being.

McCloskey was describing a professional who had spent six or seven years of his life in college and graduate school to get an M.B.A. or law degree and who presumably expected a return on his investment of time, money, and energy. The large environmental organizations provided. By 1985 the Sierra Club and the Wilderness Society were offering their executive directors a salary of between $70,000 and $90,000. Audubon could go above $100,000. The well-funded and conservative National Wildlife Federation bestowed on its leader, Jay Hair, a salary in the $120,000 range, a $15,000 expense account, a car and expenses, and a fully furnished apartment in Washington.[41]

The mainstream organizations defended their high salaries by saying they were necessary to attract the kind of leadership qualified to run what amounted to multimillion-dollar corporations. "We have two hundred and forty employees in data processing alone," says Robert Hattoy, Sierra Club's Southern California representative. "There has to be somebody in the structure who can run it all, and I want him to be top-notch."[42] From an organizational standpoint this may make sense — the Sierra Club's annual budget is $23 million and rising, while even the relatively small Wilderness Society has an $8 million budget, the handling of which requires a great deal of financial expertise.[43] Nevertheless, working in a milieu of corporate high finance was bound to change the relationship between environmentalists and their vocation. As Lisa Finaldi, chair of the Radioactive Waste Campaign, puts it: "It's becoming just another business."[44]

A business that provided jobs, not a little prestige, and, increasingly, access to high places. Starting in the early 1970s the major environmental organizations began to cluster in Washington. The Sierra Club staff presence increased from seven in 1970 to seventeen in 1987. The 1987 *National Journal* list of organizations with the best access to the capital's decision makers included the National Wildlife Federation, the Wilderness Society, and the Sierra Club. This mass exodus to Washington created what has been called "the Potomac conservationist,"[45] an environmental professional whose contact with the movement takes place almost entirely through the dense medium of lobbying efforts, congressional hearings, and legislative digests.

Access to high places gave environmental leaders in Washington another powerful motivation for working in the environmental movement distinct from any desire to protect the natural world: the prospect of getting a position in an administration that wanted to appear friendly to the environmental cause. Thus, Rupert Cutler, assistant executive director of the Wilderness Society, was appointed to several resource commissions by the governor of Michigan, "where he acquired a 'better' understanding of all sides in environmental disputes."[46] Cutler finally hit the big time when President Jimmy Carter made him assistant secretary of agriculture. Carter also appointed James Mooreman, head of the Sierra Club's Legal Defense Fund, assistant U.S. attorney general. At present, William Reilly, former head of the Conservation Foundation and the World Wildlife Fund, runs the Environmental Protection

Agency under George Bush. Even the notorious Dave Foreman admits that while he was a lobbyist for the Wilderness Society he wistfully aspired to becoming secretary of the interior some- day — a prospect that must send shivers down the spine of re- source industry executives.[47]

Inevitably, the possibility of crossover into government office affected the kind of stands the national environmental leaders were willing to take. They began to formulate policy with an eye to the fact that if their demands alienated or embarrassed government leaders by being too "extreme," they might be passed over when it came time for a new administration to fill the government's ever-increasing need for environmental ad- ministrators. Moderation and compromise became the neces- sary tools of the ambitious environmental professional.

But even without these venal motivations, there was a gen- eral feeling among professional environmentalists that their ef- fectiveness — however that was calibrated — depended on a public image of moderation and compromise calculated not to earn the disfavor of government and business leaders. As Eliot Porter, Sierra Club board member, friend of Brower, and wil- derness photographer, once chided the board, "Many among us believe that only by compromise and accommodation can the club retain its influential position with the government. . . . I say that compromise and accommodation with industry and private interests and as well with bureaucratic agencies will destroy the influence and standing of the club."[48]

In the stampede for influence and credibility, Porter's views lost out. The tendency toward accommodation was clearly ev- ident in the environmental movement by the end of the sev- enties. "Conservationists have got to learn to work with industry," declared Don Naish, Audubon's chairman of sanc- tuaries and nature centers.[49] For Naish, this meant allowing Mobil Oil to drill under Audubon's Baker bird sanctuary in Michigan, a plan that prompted the *Detroit Free Press* to call the organization "the Oilubon Society."[50] Larry Moss, western representative for the Wilderness Society, expressed a similar cosmopolitan desire for accommodation with industry, stating that "not all disagreement on environmental issues is absolute. Often the parties misapprehend each other's objectives; or they mistake the nature of the industrial or environmental theology;

. . . or they let animosity and bitterness stand between them and a solution they can accept."[51] Apparently, for the environmental professional there were no fundamental differences between the goals of conservationists and industrialists, only misunderstandings and mistakes. This, unfortunately, was rapidly becoming the case, and not due to any moderation on the part of industry.

The National Association of Environmental Professionals, which was formed in 1977, supported this kind of accommodation. Throwing its weight into the ill-starred "environmental mediation movement" — to use a name that suggests a degree of prominence it never attained — it expressed its desire to avoid the "excesses" of citizen participation and adversarial politics by encouraging compromises and negotiated settlements, an attitude often called the rule of reason — at least by those who got their way. The environmental mediation movement supported the efforts of groups like Resolve, the Center of Environmental Conflict Resolution, which tried to arbitrate environmental disagreements without recourse to the legal system.[52] There was a flurry of such mediation between environmentalists and industry at the end of the 1970s involving national coal policy and toxic waste disposal, but it led to nothing. With the election of Reagan, business leaders realized they no longer had to bother with environmentalists and left them and the rule of reason alone at the negotiating table.

Some of what might be called the sociological implications of this professionalization of environmentalists were easy to see. Automobile ads, for example, began to appear in the magazines of most of the large environmental organizations, which disturbed some readers but, if the advertising agencies' demographers were correct, met the needs of most.[53] However, a more subtle, more important implication was first mentioned by a Norwegian philosopher in a small article written thousands of miles from the Washington scene. In 1973, in "The Shallow and the Deep, Long-Range Ecology Movement," Arne Naess suggested that two distinct environmental movements were emerging from the contemporary maelstrom of interest in ecology.[54] The one, presided over by the professionals, was large, bureaucratic, and shallow in the sense that it merely sought reforms of pollution and resource depletion. The other, less influential movement was deep in that it contemplated a fundamental change in the way our culture related to the natural world. This Deep Ecology movement was an heir to the environmental sensibility of lay activists like Muir and Leopold. "There are political potentials in this movement which should not be overlooked and which have little to do with pollution and resource depletion," wrote Naess, as it turned out, quite prophetically. For a decade later Deep Ecology would become the banner under which radical environmentalism rallied its forces, using civil disobedience and ecotage to attack government policies toward the wilderness and the natural world.[55]

The peculiar fruit of the shallow, professional environmental movement became evident in the late seventies during the struggle to make a comprehensive decision as to which public lands should be protected in their natural condition as wilderness. In this one issue the new moderation, the crossover into government service, the willingness to compromise with industry, all played a part in revealing what the mainstream environmental movement had become.

The battle began with Rupert Cutler, former executive at the Wilderness Society, who was encouraged by his associates in the environmental movement to apply for the position of assistant secretary of agriculture in the Carter administration. Cutler did not need much of a push: he went to Washington and "lobbied for the job on his own."[56] Secretary of Agriculture Bob Bergland was impressed by Cutler's background in resource management, but he was worried the powerful timber industry lobby would block the appointment of the former environmental leader (who had already confidently sold his home in Michigan and moved to Washington). Thus he took Cutler to a meeting with a group of timber industry officials at a hotel near O'Hare Airport, in Chicago, where Cutler expressed his sympathy for the officials' complaint that their industry faced legal and political uncertainty in attempting to log areas that were eligible for wilderness designation but still unprotected. Translated, this meant that environmentalists, mostly on a local level, were successfully bringing lawsuits to keep pristine areas pristine until a political decision could be made about their ultimate fate. The meeting apparently soothed the industry's fears, and Cutler was confirmed on April 18, 1977.

Cutler immediately moved to clear up the uncertainty by instituting an inventory of all national forests eligible for wilderness, at the completion of which the Forest Service would propose which wildlands would be protected and which would be opened to exploitation. This second Roadless Area Review and Evaluation (it was the inadequacy of the first that led to the troublesome litigation that industry complained of), or RARE II, identified 62 million acres in national forestland eligible for wilderness protection. The resource industry lobbied the Forest Service hard to have as little acreage as possible proposed as wilderness, using its own employees in letter-writing campaigns and issuing warnings that "locking up" too much wilderness would threaten the country's security and prosperity.

At the time there was an unwritten rule among the national environmental organizations: they would all speak with one voice on conservation issues, even when there was a diversity of opinion among their membership. It was felt that in this way they could present a unified front and enhance their influence. Therefore, the major groups reached a consensus by accepting the lowest common denominator among them. Beating back the protests of "extremists" among the grass roots, they requested that a modest one third of the roadless areas be designated wilderness.

They didn't get even that. In the end the Forest Service accommodated the resource industry and proposed that only 15 million acres be protected, about 24 percent of the total. Of this, almost 5 million acres were in Alaska, lands that conservationists had expected to be protected anyway through the pending Alaska Lands bill. The additional 11 million acres the service put into the "further planning" category included areas in Alaska and Wyoming where, according to geologists, large oil and gas deposits existed, virtually ensuring that these lands too would be developed, as the Department of Energy was already advocating. In the final tally of RARE II, therefore, 36 million acres of roadless areas would immediately be opened to the resource industry, with another 11 million possibly, if not likely, to be added. In all, 77 percent of America's remaining wilderness areas would receive no protection and probably would be developed. The Carter administration accepted the Forest Service's proposal.

It was immediately apparent that the RARE II process, beyond its stinginess, suffered from a number of serious legal flaws. First, the original figure of 62 million acres grossly underestimated the number of acres eligible for protection. In Oregon alone conservationists estimated that the Forest Service overlooked approximately 1 million acres qualifying as wilderness under the service's own standards. Second, those standards themselves were too restrictive and left out areas worthy of being considered for protection. Lawrence K. Karlton, the U.S. District Court judge who would preside over a case challenging the legality of RARE II, hypothesized that had the agency reviewed the Grand Canyon for wilderness status, it might have come up with an evaluation like "Canyon, with river, little vegetation." Third, and most important, the environmental impact statement the Forest Service submitted for the areas to be developed was hopelessly biased in favor of industry. The service provided a wealth of information on resource output and development potential but almost nothing about wilderness values, such as scenic landmarks or rare species endangered by development. It neglected to examine the economic and environmental benefits of wilderness status, including tourism and sales of recreational equipment. It failed to consider the obvious option of increasing resource development in areas already despoiled instead of allowing industry to move into pristine areas.

The resource industry was ecstatic. The Forest Service braced for the inevitable lawsuits. Grass-roots activists girded their loins. And the large environmental organizations — did nothing. According to Douglas Scott, the national environmental leadership did not feel it was politically prudent to oppose President Carter, because of his support for the ample Alaska wilderness bill. In the arena of political horse trading in which the Potomac conservationists dwelt, one favor had to be repaid with another, even if, as Scott admitted, "some wilderness quality had to be sacrificed." [57]

But the national leadership was worse than quiescent. In an

attempt to impress upon Congress that the environmental movement was reasonable and would not sabotage the RARE II process, as the resource industry had predicted, several large organizations attempted to dissuade grass-roots activists from challenging RARE II in court. In particular, Sierra Club and Wilderness Society national staff members tried their best to prevent the irrepressible Huey Johnson, chief of California's Resources Agency, from bringing suit against the federal government.[58] The organizations were not afraid Johnson would lose; on the contrary, they were convinced he would win and thus anger some powerful senator or congressman whose political friendship they might have to cultivate in the future.[59] One Wilderness Society staffer bluntly described the inversion of values that had overtaken the Potomac conservationists: "Those of us in Washington were plotting on how to keep the grassroots in line."[60]

The RARE II debacle was testimony to the paradoxical success of the reform environmental movement. It demonstrated the extent to which the national environmental organizations had become an accepted part of the political process — so much so that they could be taken for granted by avowedly pro-environment politicians. It showed they could work with industry, avoid conflict, shun immoderate demands, strategize on a national level, and play the sophisticated role of a high-powered interest group.

It was also damning evidence of their growing irrelevancy when it came to defending the environment from a mounting siege of governmental and corporate exploitation. Even by their own negligible standards the national environmental organizations had gained nothing by being reasonable in the RARE II process. Compromise designed to make modest environmental gains politically possible was at least a legitimate, if uninspiring, tactic for environmentalists to take. But the professional environmentalists in Washington seemed to have abandoned the idea of making any progress in favor of propitiating business and government interests — and to prevent the menacing possibility they inevitably referred to as backlash.

Like the youth movement, the women's movement, and rock and roll, the reform environmental movement suffered from its own successes. It entered the seventies as a vague critic of our society and exited as an institution, wrapped in the consumerism and political ambitions it once condemned. In their drive to win credibility with the government agencies and corporations that made public lands policy, the new professional environmentalists seemed to have wandered into the ambiguous world of George Orwell's *Animal Farm*, where it was increasingly difficult to tell the farmers from the pigs.

At the conclusion of the RARE II process, one such aspiring professional, a Washington lobbyist for the Wilderness Society, lifted his cowboy boots onto his desk in his office just down the street from the Capitol, took out a Stroh's, and reflected on what was happening to the environmental movement. As a result of these reflections, he would later call some friends who had also worked on RARE II and who seemed equally uneasy with the role the large environmental organizations had played. Bitter and exhausted, they decided to take a trip into the wilderness they loved and for which they had presumably been fighting.

When they returned, the environmental movement would be changed forever.

CHAPTER 4

———

EARTH FIRST!

———

So, from the vast sea of raging moderation, irresponsible compromise, knee-jerk rhetorical Sierra Club dogma, and un-
knowing (ok, sometimes knowing) duplicity in the systematic
destruction of the Earth, a small seed of sanity sprouts: Earth
First!

> — *Howie Wolke,*
> *Earth First! cofounder*

DAVE FOREMAN left his position with the Wilderness Society
in Washington and returned to his old job as the society's
Southwest representative in the small ranching community of
Glenwood, New Mexico. But the bad taste of RARE II followed
him even there. Although he had advocated moderation and
concessions while in Washington, he received several death
threats from local residents who were apparently convinced
that any type of environmental protection was un-American,
not to mention unprofitable. Foreman began to wonder how he
could have ever worried about the environmental movement
appearing too extreme in light of this kind of prodevelopment
zealotry. In fact, he was beginning to think that the entire
moderate strategy of the national organizations was miscon-
ceived.

He was not alone. A number of his friends who had worked
on RARE II were having the same feelings of disillusionment
and exasperation with the reform environmental movement
and its idée fixe, credibility. With death threats and President
Reagan's antienvironmental furies in the air, it seemed to them
as good a time as any to disappear into the wilderness for a

while with like-minded people, to commiserate, to complain, perchance to dream of a new vision for the environmental movement emerging from the ruins of RARE II.

Superficially, the five activists who gathered at Foreman's home seemed to have little in common except perhaps the fullness of their beards. In his early thirties, Foreman had been a Young American for Freedom, a Goldwater supporter, a farrier, a marine officer recruit who went AWOL and wound up in the stockade for a month because, he says, "I couldn't take orders very well." His roots in the West went deep — his family had been among the first Anglo pioneers who settled New Mexico — and this tradition was reflected in his love of the desert and his quasilibertarian values. Foreman was good at telling stories around the campfire in a quavery, Southwest accent, an ability he would later cultivate to become an accomplished and fiery speech giver.

His friend Howie Wolke came to the West via New Hampshire and the quintessentially East Coast state of New Jersey, where he was born. Settling in the oil boom town of Jackson, Wyoming, he studied forestry, was a bouncer, and worked for a while in the oil fields detonating test charges with a seismographic team. But he found his real vocation working for David Brower's fledgling organization, the Friends of the Earth. Paid seventy-five dollars a month, he was the organization's most active representative in Wyoming, attending public hearings on wilderness issues, talking with the press, appealing timber sales, and organizing local support. When the staff decided to cut his already paltry salary, he resigned. His stint with moderate environmentalism had come to an end while he was still in his twenties.

Wolke brought along Mike Roselle, a friend from Jackson. Roselle was a tall, gangly, keen-witted oil field roughneck, with a long history of radical politics. His first arrest came for passing out antiwar leaflets during a be-in in Los Angeles in 1969, when he was thirteen. A self-described "early Dead Head," he ran away from his home in Texas at sixteen and for a short while became active with the Yippies, Abbie Hoffman and Jerry Rubin's media-hungry counterculture organization. Unhappy with the misuse of funds and political opportunism he witnessed in the group, Roselle joined up with A. J. Weberman and Dana Beale, who had split from the Yippies to form the Zippies, so called because they aimed to put the zip back in the counterculture movement. They failed, the Vietnam War ended, and Roselle grew weary of the paranoia and backbiting of the protest movement. After meeting Wolke in a café in Jackson, he turned his considerable organizing skills to saving wilderness.

Bart Koehler was a Wilderness Society staffer from Wyoming who had introduced Wolke to Foreman. He was never much enamored with the strategy of moderation, and his controversial stands on the environment were often quoted in local papers. Yet he was often politically adroit enough to get his proposals adopted, and the preservation of some choice Wyoming wilderness areas was due to his efforts. Also a talented singer and songwriter, Koehler recognized a need to use music in the environmental movement the way the civil rights and antiwar movements did. After RARE II he left the Wilderness Society in disgust. He would later become director of the Southeast Alaska Conservation Council.

Finally, there was Ron Kezar, a longtime member of the Sierra Club and seasonal worker for the U.S. Park Service. He had been trained as a librarian, and he was, in addition, an expert on the history of American military strategy, although his stint in the armed services was as unpleasant as Foreman's. Kezar was an accomplished peak bagger, and his name can be found on numerous summits throughout the Southwest. During his peregrinations, he had seen firsthand the severe environmental damage caused by cattle grazing, clear-cutting, and off-road vehicles.

The five environmentalists decided to hike the Pinacate Desert, in Mexico, a coastal barrens along the Gulf of California in the rain shadow of the Baja's Sierra San Pedro Mártir. Abbey had described it in one of his works as "the wildest, least developed part of Mexico, and therefore the best."[1] Being Abbey fans, they followed this recommendation and were rewarded with a wilderness of arroyos and rolling hills, mesquite, saguaros, coatimundi, kit foxes, and the untameable, unkillable javelina — the animal Foreman says he can closely identify with.

They spent a week in the desert. Amid the drinking, story-telling, and moon howling, the conversations kept returning to the same disgruntled themes: the lack of vision in the environmental movement, the ineffectiveness of its moderate stance, the estrangement between its professional leadership and grass-roots activists, the extremism of industry and government opposition to environmental protection, the crisis of wilderness destruction as a result of unfettered industrial development. They shared their admiration for the characters in Abbey's novel *The Monkey Wrench Gang*, the neo-Luddite rebels with an ecological cause who scoffed at the convoluted tactics of institutionalized environmentalism and instead took direct action, in the form of ecotage, to protect the environment.

In this way it gradually became clear to the five activists that to get the environmental movement out of its doldrums and cope with the environmental crisis, a radical, no-compromise voice was desperately needed[2] — a group that would display the same fervor and unruliness as Abbey's fictional band of ecoraiders. It would have to be made up of grass-roots activists, impassioned amateurs in the tradition of John Muir, rather than a professional, bureaucratic hierarchy that could be beguiled by the world of politics. It would need to take uncompromising, militant stands in defense of the environment and wilderness, refusing to let economic or political considerations water down its ecological agenda, even if that earned it the dreaded label "extremist." Finally, its members would have to carry out direct action to defend threatened natural areas, using the tactics of the civil rights and antiwar movements: guerrilla theater and civil disobedience, and, if necessary, monkeywrenching.

On April 4, 1980, having stopped off on their way home at a bar in the border town of San Luis Río Colorado, the five men decided it was time. Wolke and Koehler had already quit their jobs with mainstream environmental groups, Foreman was on the verge of quitting his, and Roselle, as he puts it, "didn't have a job to quit."[3] They agreed to form this radical environmental group themselves. Foreman came up with the name, Earth First!. Roselle designed the logo: a green fist in a circle to represent, he says, "the Earth, the cycle of life, and the coffee stain on an environmental impact statement."[4] They agreed that their motto would be No compromise in defense of Mother Earth.

As if to solemnize their commitment to ecological defiance, they decided to disregard artificial political boundaries and smuggle some of their favorite Mexican beer, Pacifico, back into the States. While Foreman, Roselle, Wolke, and Koehler climbed over a border fence with the contraband, Kezar drove the car through customs. But by the time he arrived to pick up his friends, they had already drunk all the beer. The impatience of the new radical environmental movement was unmistakable from the very start.

"The people who started Earth First!," Foreman would later say, "decided there was a need for a radical wing that would make the Sierra Club look moderate. Someone has to say what needs to be said, and do what needs to be done and take the kinds of strong actions . . . to dramatize it."[5] The statement sums up the twofold purpose of Earth First! as conceived by its founders. On the one hand, it would help make the mainstream environmental groups operate more effectively by making them appear reasonable in comparison. On the other, it would strive to be a force in its own right, taking whatever actions within its means that were necessary to protect the ecology, irrespective of the mainstream environmental movement's agenda or the niceties of politics or even the constraints of the law.

In the beginning there seems to have been an emphasis on the first of these aims. But as Earth First! grew in size and self-assurance, the second, ultimately more interesting objective began to take precedence in the thinking of most Earth First!ers. As Wolke explained a few years later: "Earth First! proposals and tactics make sense. . . . Who gives a damn if a bureaucrat thinks we're unrealistic? In a world where it is possible that *Homo sapiens* will drive nearly half the species on this planet to extinction by early in the 21st century, the Earth First! whole ecosystem approach to land preservation is the ONLY approach that really makes sense."[6]

This "whole ecosystem approach" involved a new way of

framing the environmental issue. For obvious political reasons and less evident cultural ones, the mainstream environmental movement concentrated its efforts on environmental health hazards to people caused by air, water, and pesticide pollution. Organizations like the Sierra Club had as members and clientele people who were worried about the effects of toxic waste, radiation, and smog. The question of keeping natural areas pristine for the benefit of the nonhuman creatures that dwelt there was considered somewhat ethereal and elitist. Lester Brown, founder of the Worldwatch Institute, sums up this perspective in suggesting that the purpose of environmentalism is "making industrialism safe for human life."[7]

The founders of Earth First! turned this thinking on its head. Wilderness, big wilderness whose ecological equilibrium was still undisturbed by industrial society, became their central concern — the basic unit, so to speak, of radical environmentalism. To a degree this priority was grounded on the scientifically sound premise that since all parts of the environment are ultimately connected, any particular component, including that relatively expendable part called humanity, can be secure only if the entire ecosystem remains healthy. Keeping pollution under control — that is, within politically determined standards — did nothing to ensure that the more subtle environmental imbalances caused by industrial development and overpopulation would not also come back to afflict human welfare in insidious ways. The unforeseen link between refrigerator coolant, atmospheric ozone depletion, and skin cancer induced by ultraviolet radiation demonstrates the point. Ecologist Frank Egler states the case for prudence in tinkering with the natural functioning of ecosystems with the statement "Nature is not only more complex than we think, but it is more complex than we can ever think."[8]

But Earth First!'s emphasis on ecosystems went far beyond a more sympathetic awareness of the role of ecology in human welfare. Although there were any number of pragmatic, social reasons for protecting as much of the natural world as possible, Earth First! stood for the more radical proposition that the natural world should be preserved *for its own sake*, not for the sake of any real or imagined benefits to humanity. "A grizzly bear snuffling along Pelican Creek in Yellowstone National Park with her two cubs has a life just as full of meaning and dignity to her as my life is to me," Foreman asserts. "A Goodding's onion, an endangered species in the Gila that's threatened with clear-cut logging, has a history, has a pedigree on this planet just as long as mine is, and who's to say I have a right to be here and it doesn't?"[9] For most radical environmentalists the same biological egalitarianism extended to all the natural world, in all its manifold shapes and forms.

With this perspective Earth First! transcended the environmental movement's reformist program and embarked, with tentative if noisy feet, upon a larger agenda of ethical and cultural defiance. The founders of Earth First! were not going to limit themselves to lobbying for stronger air-quality standards, more scenic hiking trails, or better-managed national parks. They had a more ambitious goal: restoring the natural world to its wild state. "Wilderness is the essence of everything we're after," proclaims Foreman. "We aren't an environmental group. Environmental groups worry about environmental health hazards to human beings, they worry about clean air and water for the benefit of people and ask us why we're so wrapped up in something as irrelevant and tangential and elitist as wilderness. Well, I can tell you a wolf or a redwood or a grizzly bear doesn't think wilderness is elitist. Wilderness is the essence of everything. It's the real world."[10]

The idea of putting the integrity of ecosystems above economic and political considerations, a position that in its academic setting was known as biocentrism, or more generally Deep Ecology, was in a broad sense a reprise of Aldo Leopold's land ethic. "Muir and Leopold are the old-time religion for us," says Roselle.[11] Earth First!, however, was able to dramatize this ethic in forceful, unapologetic, and often humorous ways — as its first public act demonstrated. A few weeks after returning from Mexico, Foreman, along with ten people who had already converted to the radical environmental cause, hiked a mile or two into New Mexico's Gila Wilderness to the ghost town of Cooney to erect a plaque in honor of an Apache warrior who obliterated a mining camp there a hundred years earlier. The plaque read:

VICTORIO

*Outstanding Preservationist
and Great American*

This monument celebrates the 100th Anniversary
of the great Apache chief, Victorio's, raid on the
Cooney mining camp near Mogollon, New Mexico,
on April 28, 1880. Victorio strove to protect these
mountains from mining and other destructive activities of the white race. The present Gila Wilderness is partly a fruit of his efforts.

ERECTED BY

THE NEW MEXICO PATRIOTIC

HERATIGE [*sic*] SOCIETY

The plaque was at once sarcastic and earnest, a foretaste of
the radical environmental style of protest. Although it appeared to poke fun at the ludicrous monuments to the triumph
of European culture and "progress" that are particularly prev-
alent in the western United States, it also seemed to embody
the serious doubts a growing number of people, particularly in
the ranks of the environmental movement, were having about
the legitimacy of industrial society in the age of Three Mile
Island and Love Canal. The ethics of biocentrism necessitated
siding with the Indians and their basically Earth-harmonious
way of life over Western culture and its foolhardy exploitation
of nature, for these ethics implied a radical reappraisal of history. If the portrayal of an Indian massacre as an environmental victory shocked the values of the society that eventually
won the conflict, Earth First! was willing to take that iconoclastic step, even at this early stage of its evolution. And with
this step radical environmentalism, at least in America, eventually wandered toward a far-reaching critique of civilization
and of the view that humans have the right to dominate nature.
As one of the Victorio raid celebrants put it in a newspaper
article about the plaque: "We're concerned about people, but
it's Earth first."[12]

If there was ever any doubt that Earth First! took this sentiment seriously, it was quickly dispelled. Shortly after the

Mexico trip Foreman began publishing the *Earth First!*
Newsletter, a two-page photocopied offering produced in his
parents' home and later in the office of book publisher Ken
Sanders. The publication would soon blossom into the journal
Earth First!, a ranting, ungrammatical, and insightful forum
on environmental concerns not covered elsewhere: obscure
concerns such as the greenhouse effect, acid rain, the destruction of tropical rain forests, and, of course, ecotage. The first
issue of the newsletter announced Earth First!'s national wilderness proposal, which called for a system of "ecological preserves" within which "the developments of man will be
obliterated."[13] It dwarfed anything the reform environmental
movement had ever contemplated. As refined over the next few
years, the Earth First! Wilderness Preserve System demanded
wilderness protection for vast areas of the United States, particularly in the western states. Almost one half of Nevada, for
instance, some thirty million acres, would be declared "off-
limits to industrial human civilization, as preserves for the
free-flow of natural processes."[14] Similar acreages were demanded for Idaho, California, the Dakotas, Utah, and Oregon.

Not only was the size beyond anything the environmental
movement had ever had the temerity to demand, but the type
of wilderness regime envisioned was also more rigorous than
the rather capricious management of wilderness undertaken by
the federal government. The preamble to the proposal expressed the biocentric outlook that "the central idea of Earth
First! is that humans have no divine right to subdue the Earth,
that we are merely one of several million forms of life on this
planet. We reject even the notion of benevolent stewardship as
that implies dominance. Instead we believe, as did Aldo Leopold, that we should be plain citizens of the land community."[15] Wilderness in this land community meant no
permanent human habitation (except, in some cases, indigenous peoples with traditional life-styles); no use of mechanized
equipment or vehicles; no roads; no logging, mining, water
diversion, industrial activity, agriculture, or grazing; no use of
artificial chemical substances; no suppression of wildfires; no
overflights by aircraft; no priority given to the safety and con-
venience of human visitors over the functioning of the ecosystem. As a lagniappe to old-style environmentalism the proposal

also stated, perhaps tongue in cheek, that all this would be done "without significant impact on the economy."[16] For the next, more radical generation of Earth First!ers, sparing the economy would, at any rate, not be considered a virtue.

Even more visionary than these land community guidelines was the demand for the *restoration* of developed and degraded areas to a more or less natural state. This would require the removal of exotic species; reintroduction of extirpated species (such as grizzly bears and jaguarundi); and the dismantling, removal, or destruction of dams, roads, power lines, and the other intrusions of industrial society. In this way Earth First! was asserting the heretofore unheard-of possibility that environmentalism could mean more than just preservation of the tattered remnants of lost wilderness. It could take the initiative and demand the re-creation of despoiled ecosystems.

Indeed, restoration ecology would later become a movement of sorts and an accepted — perhaps too accepted — part of re-form environmentalism's agenda, popularized by John Berger's 1985 book, *Restoring the Earth*. The restoration ecologists soon began to work with the resource industry as a kind of sorcerer's apprentice, cleaning up the aftermath of mining, drilling, and logging operations. At a conference of restoration ecologists in early 1988, Foreman warned that an uncritical attitude toward the resource industry would give it a "license to kill," making restoration ecology a mere pretext for more development. "It's not enough to save the remaining 10% of wilderness that remains," he urged the conference. "It's time to restore it, to take it back."[17] Needless to say, with this view of restoration Earth First! was never in any danger of finding favor with industry officials.

William Tucker, a tireless voice among the splenetic ranks of antienvironmental writers, expressed the conventional view of wildlands preservation when he wrote in 1982: "The wilderness concept appears valid if it is recognized for what it is — an attempt to create what are essentially 'ecological museums' in scenic and biologically significant areas of these lands. But 'wilderness,' in the hands of environmentalists, has become an all-purpose tool for stopping economic activity as well."[18] A number of environmental organizations hotly denied Tucker's accusation, tacitly accepting his parsimonious view of wilderness. As its first wilderness proposal showed, Earth First! was not among them. Its followers believed it was the dead artifacts of technology that belonged in a museum, not wilderness, not "the real world."

The founders of Earth First! were optimistic that people were ready to listen to their militant ecological message. With their audacious wilderness proposal in hand, Foreman, Koehler, and Kezar went on a cross-country road show, speaking at college campuses and meeting halls, attracting audiences that numbered from the dozens to the hundreds. The road show was a mixture of populism, protest, humor, and ecological agitation, with Koehler making music and the group trying to make operating expenses by selling bumper stickers with such messages as "Rednecks for Wilderness," "Malthus Was Right," "Building Chaos out of Anarchy for a Better Future," and the Shakespearean "Out, Damned Watt!"[19] Foreman, for his part, made speeches, passionate speeches about radical environmentalism's vision of a world of big wilderness, which often ended with him jumping up and down onstage. The road show was repeated countless times over the years, and many Earth First!ers would later say that they were brought into the movement by Foreman's ability to rabble-rouse for the environment.

The message struck a chord. Within a year of Earth First!'s founding, its membership, as measured by subscriptions to its newly established newsletter, soared to more than 1,500, making Earth First! perhaps the fastest-growing environmental group in history.[20] It has not stopped growing since then, attracting an unusual coalition of cowboy types, hippies, former businesspeople, students, scientists, and academicians that numbered about 10,000 by 1989. Earth First! sympathizers in the traditional environmental organizations are estimated to be many times that figure.[21]

The reason was clear: the ecological extremism that moderate organizations feared would alienate them from business and government leaders was simply not considered a vice among many grass-roots environmentalists acquainted firsthand with the decimation taking place in America's wildlands. A growing number of activists were coming to the conclusion that the human race, not to mention that irresponsible fragment of it that managed corporate enterprises, had gone too

far in exploiting nature.[22] To the chagrin of the national organizations, their greatest anxiety instantly became Earth First!'s
major appeal. One activist describes the difference this way:
"The major environmental groups still believe that man's use
of the natural world is its highest and best purpose. They're
just arguing about whether backpacking is better than mining.
Whereas Earth First! is saying that the natural world for its
own sake is the highest and best use of this world. . . . I joined
Earth First! because I was angry, and there are other angry
people in it, and we don't accept the fact that we can't win."[23]

As the Victorio incident suggests, Earth First! had from its
beginning a flair for dramatizing this anger toward the mega-
lomania of industrial society. This industrial chauvinism made
an easy target. Barely a year after Earth First! was formed, the
notorious plastic crack at Glen Canyon Dam revealed the
group's ecological discontent. A while later a particularly en-
terprising group of Earth First!ers, who happened to be experienced rock climbers, rappeled down the three-hundred-foot
face of the Elwha Dam, north of Washington's Olympic Mountains, painting a hundred-foot crack and the words "Elwha be
free." The statement they sent to the media read: "The dams
on the Elwha stand as monuments to human folly and greed.
. . . The dams must come down!"[24] A number of other dams,
including the O'Shaughnessy (Hetch Hetchy) Dam in Yosemite,
which John Muir had opposed, also suffered the indignity of
becoming billboards for radical environmental sentiments.

This type of protest was more than just playing to the media.
It expanded the universe of thinkable thoughts about environmental policy. Thus, in 1986, none other than Donald Hodel,
secretary of the interior during Reagan's second term, publicly
suggested that the O'Shaughnessy Dam, which supplies water
to San Francisco, be removed to restore the Hetch Hetchy Valley to its original, pristine condition. In one of the archetypical
battles in the history of the conservation movement, John Muir
had spent the last years of his life in a bitter struggle to rally
the public against the dam and, failing to succeed (as legend
has it), died of a broken heart. Hodel probably had his own
perverse reasons for making this proposition — namely, to put
the San Francisco–based Sierra Club on the spot. Nevertheless,
the idea of removing a dam would never have received any

public attention, as it subsequently did in a number of publications, even as a juvenile ploy by the Reagan administration,
had it not been for Earth First!'s imaginative protests.

On a less monumental scale, Earth First! seemed to have the
ability to discomfit the powerful and complacent — a virtue
with which the media could easily identify. This ability took a
literal form in 1981 when James Watt traveled to Wyoming,
his home state and an Earth First! stronghold, to attend the
Western Governors' Conference in Jackson. As he left the meeting Watt was greeted by 350 protesters, among them Howie
Wolke. Watt turned his back on the environmentalists and began shaking hands with twenty or so rancher supporters of his,
who tried unsuccessfully to drown out the protesters with the
horns of their four-wheel-drive vehicles. Watt biographer Ron
Arnold described the scene in terms that cannot be improved
upon for sheer fantasy and servility: "It was a triumph. . . .
His big cowboy hat hid his bald pate and gave Watt a photo-
genic appeal that shocked network cameramen. One was heard
to say, 'Boy, those environmentalists better start praying if
Watt ever buys contacts and a wig.' "[25] Watt did not buy a wig,
and Wolke did not say his prayers. Instead, he walked over to
the secretary, pushed through his Secret Service bodyguards,
grabbed Watt's hand, and, crushing it, said: "Mr. Secretary,
I'm Howie Wolke and I organized the anti-Watt rally over
there." The agents separated the men and hustled Wolke aside.

Thus was official Washington introduced to the new radical
environmental movement.

But Earth First! had to go beyond symbolism and gestures if it
was to fulfill its stated objective of protecting the environment
when the political system failed to do so. The opportunity came
in the summer of 1982 over an ill-conceived plan to drill for oil
in a remote and majestic basin in the Gros Ventre Range of
northwestern Wyoming.

The Gros Ventre, French for "Big Belly," was a half-million
acres of de facto wilderness belonging to an area known to
ecologists as the Greater Yellowstone ecosystem — North
America's temperate-forest equivalent of the Amazon basin.
Nowhere else in America is there such a diversity and abundance of wildlife, including moose, grizzly bear, black bear,

wolverines, coyotes, and cougars. The area also contains one of the largest populations on Earth of elk and bighorn sheep. For more than fifty years conservationists had recommended the Gros Ventre for wilderness status, but in the antienvironmental euphoria of the Reagan Revolution, Getty Oil Company requested permission to build a seven-mile-long road into the heart of the range and begin exploratory drilling in an alpine saddle called Little Granite Creek.

It was not quite clear why. The Minerals Mining Service labeled data on the oil and gas potential of the proposed fields "inconclusive," and in these places Getty had only a one-in-twenty chance of finding gas or oil. The optimum amount of oil projected to be there was, moreover, trifling, having the potential to supply America's energy needs for a day or two at best. Apparently Getty thought the risk worthwhile in light of tax benefits available if the exploratory wells were dry.

In contrast, the reason the Reagan administration granted the company's request for a permit was crystal clear, if somewhat Machiavellian. Like most of Reagan's appointees in the Interior and Agriculture departments, John Crowell, assistant secretary of agriculture in charge of the Forest Service, had close ties with the resource industry. He had in fact been the general counsel of the Louisiana-Pacific Corporation, the largest purchaser of timber from the national forests — experience that hardly reassured environmentalists, especially when the corporation's president, Harry Merlo, asserted that Crowell was merely "on loan to Washington."[26] While Crowell was acting as its attorney, Louisiana-Pacific was found guilty of violating antitrust laws by colluding with a Japanese firm to put smaller timber companies out of business. He was also with the company when it engaged in fraud and market manipulation in a takeover of the Fibreboard Corporation, preparing one of the incriminating letters in the case.[27] Crowell denied any knowledge of illegal action at his Senate confirmation hearings. Wilderness protection was anathema to Crowell, who wanted to keep public lands out of the wilderness system so they could be put to their "highest and best purpose" — economic exploitation by private commodity interests such as his former employer. To do so, Crowell, like so many officials who had overseen the Forest Service before him, apparently was

hoping to invoke the purity doctrine in order to keep the Gros
Ventre available to corporate appropriation.

This doctrine was developed by the Forest Service after the
passage of the 1964 Wilderness Act as a way to limit the total
acreage of public lands receiving wilderness protection. In its
own, arbitrary reading of the Wilderness Act, the service
treated areas with any kind of development, no matter how
insignificant, as ineligible for wilderness designation because
they were not "pure." Thus the service might argue (and did)
that an old, abandoned remnant of a jeep road disqualified an
otherwise pristine tract of land from inclusion in the wilderness system. Forest Service Director of Recreation Richard
Costley, the fatefully named creator of the purity doctrine, was
frank about whose interests the Forest Service was protecting
with this construct:

> The timber industry does not have the credibility or the mus-
> cle to stop these ill-advised [wilderness] proposals. . . . In
> my judgement the best opportunity — by far — for us to keep
> wilderness classification action sound and in balance is for
> us to make sure that the public comes to realize . . . [wil-
> derness] is EXPENSIVE. It is expensive not only in terms of re-
> source opportunities foregone; it is expensive in management
> costs.[28]

It was not a large step from using the purity doctrine to deny
developed areas wilderness protection to taking the initiative
and making areas impure in order to prevent their inclusion as
wilderness. The Gros Ventre was an example of such a step.
Crowell, and of course Watt, realized that allowing Getty to
build a road and drill in the area would be a preemptive strike
against wilderness designation. The Gros Ventre with oil wells
would no longer qualify for wilderness protection and would
become open for logging, mining, or commercialized recreation.

What Crowell did not realize was the degree of local opposition, or the determination of the fledgling radical environmental movement. The Teton County Chamber of Commerce
immediately came out against the drilling. The leading local
environmental group, the Jackson Hole Alliance for Responsible Planning, was less firm, however; some of its members ar-

gued that they should give in on the Little Granite Creek well so that they could concentrate their efforts against a well proposed close by, in Cache Creek. That changed when Wolke and Roselle marched into an alliance meeting and challenged the members to take a stand against big oil. The alliance eventually registered its opposition. The governor of Wyoming, Ed Herschler, made a direct request to the federal government that the drilling permit be denied. Nevertheless, Watt signed the papers granting Getty permission to bulldoze seven miles into the Little Granite Creek ridge and sink an exploratory gas well. Getty laid down survey stakes in anticipation.

It was not going to be that easy, however. Although the local environmental groups had basically given up on opposing the road except in spirit, Earth First! decided to make it, in Foreman's words, "an OMDB issue: over my dead body."[29] Plans were made to hold the annual Round River Rendezvous, Earth First!'s festival-like gathering named after Leopold's paradoxical metaphor for the ecology, in Little Granite Creek, with the promises that militant environmentalists would "occupy the Gros Ventre from snowmelt to snowfall next summer to stop Watt and Getty" and that "they will not pass."[30]

Getty did not pass. On July 4, 1982, five hundred Earth First!ers and other environmental activists gathered in Little Granite Creek and held a rally against Getty. There was a great deal of tension in the air. Sometime before the rally, ecoteurs had pulled up the survey stakes to the proposed road, costing the company about five thousand dollars. When Getty sent out more surveyors, the stakes were pulled out again. More disconcerting for the company, some of the expensive seismological equipment Getty had brought into the area was destroyed. Although the police had a good idea who had carried out the ecotage, the local district attorney expressed his belief that no jury in the county would convict the culprits. Edward Abbey, speaking at the rally, was told about the ecotage and said, "I'm not advocating illegal activity, unless you're accompanied by your parents, or at night."[31]

The same day several hundred Earth First!ers began a blockade of the access route into Little Granite Creek, bringing construction to a halt. Never before had the resource industry, used to having its way on public lands, faced this kind of militant opposition. The radical environmental harassment slowed progress on Getty's road, and an administrative appeal filed by Bart Koehler finally stopped it. The Interior Board of Land Appeals vacated Getty's drilling permit and ordered a new environmental impact statement that considered a no-drilling alternative. Eventually the Gros Ventre was designated a wilderness by Congress, ensuring once and for all that Little Granite Creek would remain as it had been for millennia.

The Little Granite Creek episode suggested the importance of Earth First! not only as an alternative model for environmental activism, but also as a new cultural force. Earth First! had demonstrated that it could embody a belief in biocentrism merely talked about by scholars and ethicists. This viewpoint had offered what many found a theoretically appealing alternative to the domination of nature that modern society presupposes, but radical environmentalists gave it flesh and blood, put it into practice, and, at least in those wild areas on the margins of civilization, triumphed.

About this time, with the success of environmental sabotage against Getty in mind, Foreman began to conceive of writing a book on the subject of ecotage, a how-to manual that radical environmentalists could use in fighting their own personal war against the industrialization of wilderness. "We knew that a lot of ecotage was going on at the time," says Roselle, "but it was being reported as 'mindless vandalism.' Earth First! brought it out of the closet to be reported for what it was."[32]

Tentatively called *Ecodefense: A Handbook on the Militant Defense of the Earth*, the publication was to be a radical environmental version of William Powell's *Anarchist Cookbook*. In its final form, brought out by Foreman's own Ned Ludd Books (suitably named after the nineteenth-century British worker who destroyed supposedly labor-saving machinery), *Ecodefense: A Field Guide to Monkeywrenching* gave practical, detailed instructions on how to decommission bulldozers, pull out survey stakes, spike trees, and generally harass and delay resource industry plans. It was an immediate success; dog-eared copies of it could be found in the backpacks of young environmental militants literally throughout the world. This kind of popularity led Oregon's Willamette National Forest supervisor Michael Kerrick to denounce the book in a white paper presented at a congressional hearing, in which he peevishly threatened to "close the entire [national forest logging] area to unauthorized entry" if the ecotage described in the book took place.[33] As good as his word, Kerrick soon thereafter introduced the controversial and legally questionable policy of closing national forests to the public whenever environmental protests were expected.

It is no exaggeration to say, therefore, that *Ecodefense* changed forever the way public lands policy was made in this country and perhaps even abroad. Ecotage was, as Getty learned, a new factor in making environmental policy.

A number of years after the Little Granite Creek episode, Geoff Webb of the Friends of the Earth defended moderate environmentalism's nonconfrontational strategy, in contrast to Earth First!'s militant stance, by claiming that radical environmentalists were "hard-pressed to point to anything themselves they've accomplished. They're basically just doing guerrilla theater."[34] On the contrary, Earth First!ers could happily point to a quarter-million acres in Wyoming preserved as wilderness due to their commitment to direct action, including ecotage. "It was," says Roselle with justifiable pride, "*our* victory."[35]

CHAPTER 5

ESCALATIONS

It's time for a warrior society to rise up out of the Earth and throw itself in front of the juggernaut of destruction, to be antibodies against the human pox that's ravaging this precious beautiful planet.

— *Dave Foreman,*
Earth First! cofounder

THE LUSH, CHIAROSCURO forest of southwestern Oregon's Kalmiopsis roadless area seems an unlikely place for a clash of worldviews. Undisturbed by the icy assaults and retreats of glaciers, these stands of Douglas fir, cedar, and sugar pine are thought to have held their peaceful vigil over the area since the Pliocene Epoch some five million years ago — when the ancestors of humankind were still scurrying on all fours a hemisphere away. Remnant of a more verdant period in Earth's history, the Kalmiopsis represents the heart of a vast *Urwald*, or virgin forest, that once stretched from Alaska to central California and, according to some ecologists, may have been the place where coniferous trees first evolved. As that primeval forest dwindled in the face of climatic changes and industrial economy introduced by European settlers, its unique biota — including such rare or endangered species as the pine marten, the Pacific salamander, and the elusive spotted owl — sought refuge in the Kalmiopsis, where a subtle mosaic of ecological processes, from two-hundred-foot-tall trees to colonies of mycorrhizal fungi at their roots, remained intact. Remote and rugged, the Kalmiopsis is not often visited by people, and only now are ecologists beginning to piece together the forest's complex and often mysterious relationship with the biosphere as a whole: through its ability to assimilate greenhouse gases, stabilize the runoff from rainstorms, and provide habitat for anadromous fish, like salmon, that live in the ocean but spawn in the clean, cool streams associated with virgin forest.

Civilizations in the Old World from antiquity to medieval times were put to the sword for control of ancient, old-growth forests such as these; the Sumerian cultural hero Gilgamesh hewed them down to "establish his name";[1] and, as George Perkins Marsh recognized over a century ago in *Man and Nature*, when these timberlands disappear, the societies that destroy them inevitably sink into poverty and chaos.[2]

In the spring of 1983, with snow still on the ground, the millennia-old solitude of the Kalmiopsis was broken by men who had something on their minds other than the forest's intricate beauty. A road-building crew was working its way along the Silver Creek drainage beneath Bald Mountain toward a timber sale, led by a bulldozer.

It was a depressingly familiar example of the Forest Service's acquiescing to the economic desires of the timber industry rather than considering the environmental welfare of the American public as a whole. In 1936 the venerable Robert Marshall, as Forest Service recreation director, recommended that more than a million acres of the Kalmiopsis, in the Siskiyou National Forest, be preserved in their natural state as a wilderness park. This was before the idea of wilderness designation was enshrined by the 1964 Wilderness Act. Through administrative designations several hundred thousand acres were kept from the logger's blade for the next three decades. By 1964, however, with the passage of the Wilderness Act, Marshall's successors at the Forest Service had reduced that amount to a mere 77,000 acres, which did receive wilderness protection in that year. The race was then on for the hundreds of thousands of pristine acres in the Kalmiopsis still unprotected.

The timber industry exerted all the political pressure it could muster on the receptive senator Mark Hatfield of Oregon, who promised, "Not one more acre of wilderness will be added to the Kalmiopsis."[3] The Forest Service worked to make Hatfield's promise a reality by approving timber sales and punching roads into virgin stands surrounding the protected wilderness. Just as it had in the Gros Ventre, the service planned to invoke the purity doctrine to disqualify the area for wilderness status before environmentalists and public sentiment moved Congress to "lock it up." The Bald Mountain road was part of a plan to build more than seventy miles of roads into the area, effectively cutting off the northern part of the Kalmiopsis from wilderness consideration.[4] The local Rogue River Chapter of the Sierra Club, with very little support from state and national levels, appealed the sale and lost. It sought a court injunction and lost. The mainstream environmental groups seemed resigned to the fact that Marshall's dream of a greater Kalmiopsis wilderness would never come to pass.

The timber industry was particularly eager to carve up the Kalmiopsis and make it available for commercial logging because old-growth stands yield a higher volume of timber per acre than second-growth forests, with a tremendous savings in per-unit labor costs. Moreover, the range of wood products that can be made from old growth is much greater than what second growth yields. For these reasons anywhere from 90 to 95 percent of old-growth forests (depending on one's definition) has already been cut down over the past hundred years and replaced by a second-growth harvest regime with forty- to eighty-year rotations, preventing the return of old growth even where it is possible and driving toward extinction those creatures, such as the spotted owl, dependent on older trees.[5] Because they have already overharvested old growth, timber companies are now in the process of retooling their mills to accept smaller, second-growth trees in lieu of large-saw timber. They argue that they need to cut the last of the profitable old growth on public lands to finance the retooling process made necessary in the first place by their own overharvesting.

On the morning of April 27, 1983, however, this economy of paradox was temporarily halted. As the driver Les Moore settled into the cab of his Plumley Construction Company bulldozer and revved up the engine, he watched dumbfounded as four men walked out of the woods and took their places in front of the blade.

"Shut 'er down," said one. "We ain't moving."

It was Mike Roselle of Earth First!, with a fellow Earth First!er from Wyoming, Kevin Everhart, and two local activists, Steve Marsden and Pedro Tama. Roselle and Everhart had been alerted to the Forest Service's plans by an anonymous letter (from, it turned out, a Forest Service soil biologist sympathetic to Earth First!) telling them that one of the country's most beautiful old-growth forests was about to be destroyed. When the pipes in their rented house in Goose, Wyoming, had burst and caused an ice sheet to form on their floor, they had figured it was as good a time as any to begin an Earth First! campaign in Oregon. They had driven to Grants Pass in Roselle's "Lumbago," a dilapidated motor home, and attended a meeting of dispirited local environmentalists. Roselle and Everhart had suggested they physically block the road but received no support. "Well, if no one else will," Roselle had said, "we'll just do it by ourselves." At this point Marsden and Tama had decided to join the out-of-state Earth First!ers.

Moore leapt off his machine, cursing the environmentalists as communists, among other things, but suddenly thought better of it. His fellow crew members were a quarter mile away and all the protesters were over six feet tall, with Roselle and Marsden at six five and wearing cowboy hats and boots. Moore got back into his machine and used the blade to dislodge some rocks from the high side of the road cut; the rocks rolled off the berm toward their feet. But the protesters held their ground, and Moore finally gave up. The four men hung an Earth First! banner on the blade of the captured bulldozer and waited in the cold until the sheriff arrived three hours later and carted them off for a night in jail.

During the next several months, wave after wave of protesters inspired by Roselle and company blockaded the road, resulting in forty-four arrests and slowing the bulldozer's progress to a snail's pace. The confrontation was not always peaceful. On May 5, Fred Brown, a new bulldozer operator even less genteel than Moore, charged five protesters several times, screaming the threat "If you don't get out of the way, I'm going to kill you!" Doug Norlen, a twenty-year-old business major from the University of Oregon who had neglected his accounting studies to join the Kalmiopsis campaign, had his foot run over; tread marks were left on his boot. His friend Diana Warren was knocked down and buried almost up to her neck in the mud dredged up by the bulldozer's blade.

Two days later, on May 7, Dave Foreman, along with David Willis, a handicapped Earth First!er confined to a wheelchair, took up a position on an access road ten miles from the construction site in order to keep the work crew out. The oxymoronically named Les Moore entered the picture again at this point, driving a Plumley Company truck with five crew members. While a sheriff's deputy looked on, Moore began pushing Foreman back, going faster and faster until Foreman slipped and went down under the truck. Holding on to the bumper, Foreman seriously injured his leg as he was dragged over the rough road. Moore jumped out of the truck and shouted at the prostrate environmentalist, "You dirty communist bastard! Why don't you go back to Russia?" "But, Les, I'm a registered Republican," was Foreman's reply, which at the time was true.

Having watched the whole assault, the deputy rushed in to do his duty and arrest the guilty party. He handcuffed Foreman and took him away.

While the blockade was under way, Earth First! in conjunction with the Oregon Natural Resources Council filed a suit against the Forest Service, claiming the Bald Mountain road was illegal because the environmental impact statement that had been filed (such a statement was required by RARE II and Huey Johnson's ground-breaking suit, *California* v. *Block*) was inadequate. In July, Federal District Judge James Redden ruled for the environmentalists. The road building came to a halt.[6]

The road, or what is left of it after erosion caused by the rainy climate, now ends where the last group of protesters had stood with a banner that read "AMERICAN WILDERNESS, LOVE IT OR LEAVE IT ALONE" — at the brink of the West's largest and most diverse old-growth forest. The Forest Service closed the road to the public, affixing the sign No Trespassing by Order of the USFS. Radical environmentalists suggested that the ruins of the Bald Mountain road be declared a national monument, a tangible reminder of the mismanagement of public lands by the agency charged with their protection.[7]

"We came out to Oregon on a mission to get arrested saving old growth," recalls Roselle. "We wanted to start the war. We knew this was the first volley in the nonviolent wilderness war."[8]

It was indeed. The blockade at Bald Mountain inspired protests throughout the West over Forest Service timber policy, focusing on the cutting of old-growth forests like the Kalmiopsis. Although a definition for old growth has eluded foresters, biologists, and environmentalists alike, who have used such indices as a tree's diameter at breast height or age, the *qualities* of an old-growth forest have never been in dispute. They include a full canopy, a variety in the ages of trees, a large amount of deadfall and snags, and the presence of a number of indicator species, such as the spotted owl, that require older trees. In other words, old-growth forests develop certain characteristics that managed forests do not — characteristics that, taken together, represent what we often mean by the word "wilderness." These characteristics are part of the cycle of natural successions that such management techniques as clearcutting disrupt or destroy. To find the natural world one merely has to go to an old-growth forest, assuming they survive the present onslaught of deforestation.

Some moderate environmentalists consider the radicals' preoccupation with wilderness elitist. But this focus on wilderness embraces the broadest, most fundamental questions for an industrial society at the end of the twentieth century: Are we going to leave some places wild enough to support the natural diversity of life left to us by our parents, or will development completely undermine and replace the natural world with a managed landscape? Managed by whom? What right does this generation have to deprive the next of large, biologically diverse ecosystems enjoyed by most people for most of history? And is it, in particular, right to do so for our own comfort and for the profit of a few?

Lofty as these questions are, they became an issue for very concrete, identifiable, and even mundane reasons: the particular mind-set and economics of the timber industry and the dereliction of the agency whose duty it is to supervise the national forests, the U.S. Forest Service.

"California will for centuries have virgin forest, perhaps till the end of Time," remarked one overly optimistic observer in the 1880s.[9] Unfortunately, the end of time came about fifty years later, when most of the ancient forests in California and the Pacific Northwest in general had disappeared under the blade. Once the cut-and-run logging of the late nineteenth century became unfeasible for lack of easily accessible stands, timber companies began to follow European methods of forestry and planted tree farms. The harvesting regime that resulted involved the use of even-age monoculture (the replanting of one species only, all cut at the same time), herbicides, short rotation periods, and clear-cutting, a practice that, as explained by Bob Watson, a timber manager for a southern Oregon mill, "leaves the forest as bare as a timber yard."[10] The intricate living web of life the ancient forests represent was being replaced by tree plantations that were as unnatural and ecologically jejune as midwestern cornfields. Tree farming manages the forest for the single purpose of producing board feet. Wildlife diversity, water purity, long-term soil productivity, and such unquantifiable qualities as beauty and solitude all fall by the wayside. They persist, if at all, only as a deviation from the forester's plan.

A few farsighted timber companies rejected this method of logging, but by the 1980s, with the rise of merger mania, they were on their way out. Companies that harvested on a longer-term, sustainable basis found themselves cash-poor but rich in assets and thus vulnerable to hostile takeover in the stock market. This is exactly what happened to Northern California's Pacific Lumber Company in 1986, when the New York–based Maxxam Corporation under the leadership of billionaire Charles Hurwitz took control of the prudent 120-year-old company, financing the takeover with a $754 million junk-bond debt. To pay off the debt, the new management began a massive liquidation of the company's assets — in this case, more than three hundred square miles of forest, including the largest privately owned stands of *Sequoia sempervirens*, or redwoods, in the world.[11] Some of these trees have stood since the time of Christ, are three hundred feet tall, and have trunks the size of a two-car garage. The rush to raise capital has meant the doubling of harvest rates, from 170 million board feet in 1984–85 to 350 million in 1988–89, causing alarm even among usually probusiness loggers, who realize they and their community are going to be left without an economic base in fifteen years and who lament the passing of the sensible former management. In its 1981 proxy statement, for example, Pacific Lumber stated that the "stewardship of scarce resources such as timber [has] a duty to use resources wisely."[12]

There have been five federal investigations of Hurwitz, a man who oversees a vast natural resources empire and is noted for his own version of the Golden Rule: "The man with the gold rules."[13] The investigations have included a criminal allegation that Hurwitz put together a secret group of inside traders, including former arbitrageur Ivan Boesky, to buy Pacific Lumber in violation of Security and Exchange Commission laws. But the cutting continues unabated and has reached a pace unseen since the San Francisco earthquake of 1906 sparked a huge demand for lumber.

To ward off raiders like Hurwitz, companies that once had acted relatively responsibly have been forced to make extravagant increases in their harvests in an attempt to maximize short-term profits. The Plum Creek Timber Company of Roslyn, Washington, is an example. Faced with a takeover by Burlington Resources in 1988, it began logging its 155,000-acre holdings in Douglas fir, hemlock, and other evergreens in the Eastern Cascades at a rate that will leave no standing commercial timber by the end of the next decade. To further increase short-term profit the company is exporting almost half of the harvest as raw logs to Japan, taking jobs away from local mills.[14]

The frenzy for short-term profits and the forest management it produces are bad enough if carried out on company-owned land, much of which was granted by the federal government to the timber companies in their prior incarnation as railroad companies during the nineteenth century.[15] Ecological degradation of such private land eventually ripples out to affect everyone. Even worse is that the practice of tree farming, through the Forest Service's timber sale policy, has found its way into America's public forests.

It did not have to be so. In the 1970s a series of cases struck down the use of clear-cutting in national forests, starting with the 1973 *Monongahela* case in West Virginia, which held that the practice violated the Organic Act of 1897.[16] Subsequent cases in Alaska and Texas also found this method of logging illegal, under the Multiple Use–Sustained Yield Act and the National Environmental Policy Act.[17] It seemed that if timber companies wanted to continue logging on public lands they would have to do so using environmentally sound methods, such as the selective-cut, all-species, all-ages management used by Orville Camp and other members of Oregon's Forest Farmer's Association.[18] If such had been the case, the United States would still have expansive areas of primeval forests like the Kalmiopsis intact.

Unfortunately, however, under timber industry pressure, in 1976 Congress passed the National Forest Management Act, which legalized clear-cutting and allowed the Forest Service to replicate the kind of monoculture management of private tree plantations on public lands, bringing along with it pesticide use, animal control, and the inevitable decline in natural diversity.

The introduction of timber corporation management into our national forests not only poisoned the landscape with herbicides, it also poisoned the political process involved in making land policy. Since the passage of the Wilderness Act in 1964, the forest-products industry has been adamantly opposed to wilderness (and hence old-growth) protection. Joe Hinson, a forest-products spokesman, sums up the industry's attitude when he says, "Wilderness is like herpes. Once you got it, it's forever."[19] It is, of course, the right of people like Hinson to believe anything they want, but timber corporations have used their vast financial resources — often garnered from taxpayer-subsidized timber sales — to lobby Congress and bully a submissive Forest Service. If the timber and other resource lobbies had gotten everything they wanted over the past three decades, today there would be no Wilderness Act protecting any areas in their natural state; most of the redwoods of Northern California would have been cut and turned into hot tubs; the last remnants of old-growth forest would have been logged; the Grand Canyon would be dammed; and oil wells would mar the Pacific coast from San Diego to Seattle. This is hardly the vision of the country most Americans desire.

More important, this prospect would produce ecological havoc if carried out, since large wilderness areas are necessary to prevent extinctions.[20] Preoccupied with economic considerations, the timber industry has shown very little appreciation of the ecological importance of the public lands to which it has gained access. Sometimes this urge to develop pristine land takes on almost messianic proportions, as it does for H. D. Bennett, a timber industry executive from Virginia, who says: "We have the directive from God: Have dominion over the earth, replenish it, and subdue it. God has not given us these resources so we can merely watch their ecological changes occur."[21] More commonly, however, it is not God but Mammon that motivates the timber industry. The almost preternatural greed of some executives in the industry was epitomized by the now infamous (among environmentalists) comment of Harry Merlo, president of Louisiana-Pacific: "It always annoys me to leave anything on the ground when we log our own land. We don't log to a twelve-inch top; we don't log to a ten-inch top or an eight-inch top. We log to infinity, because it's out there and it's ours and we want all of it now."[22] Such rapacity is hard to comprehend.

The paucity of understanding in the industry about the ecological necessity of large, undisturbed forests is undeniable. The former executive vice president of the Southern Oregon Timber Industries Association, for instance, does not see why we need to protect any more land at all, since "within a hundred miles of southern Oregon there are two million acres of wilderness, national parks and national monuments. How can any one person see two million acres of wilderness?"[23]

In 1987 the timber industry mounted a campaign of sorts to get these and similar ideas across to the public. They were spurred on by Ron Arnold, executive director of the Center for the Defense of Free Enterprise, who was making the rounds at timber industry association meetings, spreading the message of "industrial activism." In his book *Ecology Wars* and in numerous articles, Arnold had developed a theory that environmentalism had succeeded because of its "archetype manipulation" (as well as fifteen separate tactics he enumerated) against "father figures" like big business.[24] Therefore, he argued, industry should form activist groups that would "evoke powerful archetypes such as the sanctity of the family, the virtue of the closeknit community, the natural wisdom of the rural dweller and many others I'm sure you can think of," in order to win public support for wilderness destruction.[25] "Neglect this message," Arnold urged, "and be destroyed. Attend to it and survive."[26]

The industry attended. Using a multimillion-dollar television ad campaign in the Pacific Northwest, timber companies zeroed in on the issue of jobs, arguing that the forests have to be cut down to keep the economy growing and the American dream intact. As the battle for old growth heated up, this argument often succeeded in turning workers and communities against environmentalists. Some workers have become the antienvironmental activists Arnold envisioned, organizing protests in southern Oregon and packing Fish and Wildlife hearings to oppose listing the spotted owl as endangered.[27] Corporate scapegoating of environmentalism apparently even incited a fanatic to kill several spotted owls and attach monkeywrenches to the corpses in a macabre and criminal fulfillment of Arnold's call for archetype manipulation.[28] Anti-ecology activism has at times taken the timber companies into strange territory, as when industry representatives in Laytonville, California, unsuccessfully attempted to force the local school board to ban Dr. Seuss's story "The Lorax" in a second-grade class because it "unfairly portrays the timber industry as a force for deforestation and the looting of the wildlife habitat."[29]

Arnold's Jungian psychology aside, the facts indicate that the local economy in the Pacific Northwest, where the old-growth controversy rages, has been more affected by lumber imports from Canada, the export of raw timber to Japan, automation in the mills, and the movement of corporations to the southern states than it has by timber being "locked up" as wilderness.[30] The accelerated harvests and export policies of large corporate timber companies virtually ensure higher unemployment in the long run. In the short term, many timber companies are intentionally abandoning the small communities that contributed to their success in the Pacific Northwest and moving to the South or abroad in order to maximize profits. Louisiana-Pacific, for instance, closed five California mills in the late eighties and began building twelve mills in Mexico to process its redwood harvest, using cheaper labor. In light of this, the argument that environmentalists are costing the industry jobs is beginning to wear thin, even among workers with little sympathy for ecological causes.

Corporate irresponsibility toward the environment should come as no surprise to anyone but the naive. For this very reason, public resources are put in the ultimate charge of agencies like the Forest Service and not private, profit-seeking entities. But since the days of Robert Marshall's visionary wilderness proposals, the Forest Service has inexorably fallen under the influence of business interests, especially during the Reagan years and the tenure of John Crowell as assistant secretary of agriculture with authority over the service.

The quirks of history seem to have conspired to make it so. The Forest Service was founded amid a national panic over a nonexistent timber famine, the idée fixe of its founder and first chief, Gifford Pinchot, who went so far as to write with jittery pen that the "United States has already crossed the verge of a timber famine so severe that the blighting effects will be felt in every household in the land."[31] Thus for him the mission of the service was evident: "Forestry is Tree Farming. . . . The purpose of Forestry, then, is to make the forest produce the largest possible amount of whatever crop or service will be most useful."[32] The Forest Service began with this utilitarian orientation, and, as David Clary points out in *Timber and the Forest Service*, it has never looked back: "Pinchot left behind him an organization that was thoroughly dominated by foresters with an outlook all their own. They were on a righteous crusade to guarantee more wood for the nation and to prevent timber famine."[33]

The crusade has marched blindly into the present crisis of habitat loss and biological meltdown. By the 1980s John Crowell was using the giant Forplan computer system in Fort Collins, Colorado, to calculate and propose huge timber outputs: "I think before the turn of the century we've got to be managing the National Forests for 20–25 billion [board feet]."[34] As a point of comparison, this would be more than double the production of 1976 and a fifteenfold increase from four decades before. Along with this intensive cutting come 10,000 miles of new roads a year (bringing the grand total in 1989 to 350,000 miles in the national forest system, approximately fourteen times the circumference of the Earth), which further fragments the forests and allows increasing numbers of recreationists access. Such unrealistic cutting plans provoked opposition even within the service itself. "We can physically do it," says Northwest Regional forester James F. Torrence about his region's 4-billion-board-foot harvest plan. "But we can't do it for the 10-year life of the plans."[35] Chris Maser, a wildlife biologist with the Bureau of Land Management in Oregon, also criticizes the Forest Service's intensive harvesting plans for their unsustainability, saying, "I know of no nation, no people that have maintained their forests beyond three rotations. We're only now cutting the second rotation, and the forest is not producing as it did."[36]

The Forest Service was a misnomer from its beginning. It was not interested in forests per se, the living ecosystems that hold together the web of life in the temperate zone, but in forest *products*. This is clear from the record of Forest Service opposition to every major prowilderness initiative in the last thirty years. The practical implications of this bias were candidly admitted in 1984 by Reid Jackson, the Bridger-Teton National Forest supervisor, who wrote, "We have a responsibility to keep the Louisiana-Pacific mill [in Dubois, Wyoming] in business."[37]

As a matter of fact, since 1960 and the passage of the Multiple Use–Sustained Yield Act, it has by law specifically *not* been the responsibility of the Forest Service to keep timber companies in business, but rather to ensure that logging in our national forests can be carried out judiciously enough to last "in perpetuity" without damage to recreational, wildlife, scenic, and other values. Environmentalists asked Crowell to fire Jackson for gross misconduct, but, not surprisingly, they received no response. Crowell had himself made similar comments, to the effect that the service should allow logging "at levels greater than is economically efficient for the purpose of aiding dependent industries in nearby communities"[38] — in other words, the timber industry.

As a result of this attitude, over the years the Forest Service has become the conduit of huge subsidies, both direct and indirect, to the timber industry, mostly through deficit timber sales.[39] Often the deficits are a result of the Forest Service's use of taxpayer money to build expensive logging roads by means of which the companies can reach remote or marginally profitable stands of timber. In a case of insult being added to injury, the public is thus forced not only to suffer the deforestation of a national treasure for the private profit of business, but also actually to finance it.

Congress deserves most of the blame for this state of affairs, since it passed the Knutson-Vandenberg Act and the Brush Disposal Act, which allow the Forest Service to keep a portion of timber sale receipts whether the sales are profitable or not. This gives Forest Service supervisors the incentive to cut more and more of the forest in order to build up their own budgets. At times Congress has all but mandated below-cost sales through special legislation. The worst case of this is in the Tongass National Forest of southeastern Alaska, a coastal coniferous rain forest whose seventeen million acres dwarf all other national forests and represent America's largest refuge of old-growth Sitka spruce, western hemlock, and cedar. To promote settlement of the former Alaska Territory and help rebuild Japan's post–World War II economy, the government granted fifty-year contracts and other special dispensations in the early sixties to two multinational timber companies, Louisiana-Pacific and a Japanese consortium, the Alaska Pulp Company. (These are the two companies that were convicted of antitrust violations while Crowell was general counsel to the former.) Today, old-growth trees that bring a profit to the companies of between $600 and $1,000 each are being sold to them by the Forest Service for less than $2 a tree. The result has been both a $312 million deficit from timber sales since 1970 and, more important, a loss of perhaps 50 percent of the old growth in the area, threatening the populations of grizzly bear, black-tailed deer, and moose, which depend on its cover in winter.

In *Reforming the Forest Service*, Randal O'Toole argues that these kinds of deficit sales, and the budgetary incentives that produce them, are the primary problem with the Forest Service. He therefore suggests that the agency be funded from its net income from all fees (including a new recreational fee for hikers and backpackers), so that the agency will have no inducement to make the 20 percent or so of total timber sales that lose money. The proposal makes sense as far as it goes, though special action would still be necessary to protect old growth, which is highly profitable. But it fails to take into consideration the timber-famine ethos in which the Forest Service was born and bred. In the Tongass, for instance, the agency went above and beyond the imprudence of the Congress and has actually built roads into areas for sales that have yet to be made — a practice called preroading. The desire of the Forest Service to develop wilderness seems to be a compulsion that transcends even its own budgetary well-being. It is a philosophy, a self-imposed mission.

The imperative to produce lumber has tainted every aspect of the Forest Service, undermining its credibility even among its own employees. This became particularly clear in the controversy over the spotted owl, a threatened species dependent on old-growth forests. The Forest Service has refused to follow the recommendations of its own biologists to list the owl as endangered, because listing will close large numbers of forests to logging operations. Apparently, pressure on Forest Service biologists to manipulate data to indicate that increased harvesting is called for is not uncommon.[40]

This kind of unprofessional conduct has recently led some Forest Service employees to form a dissident group within the agency. In a remarkable letter to Forest Service chief Dale Robertson, one of these dissidents, Jeff DeBonis, Willamette National Forest timber sale planner, called on his boss to "forge a new resource ethic by publicly endorsing an alignment with the worldwide environmental community." He further exhorted: "Let us start erring on the side of resource protection instead of resource extraction. Let's go to court defending the environmental 'moral high ground.' "[41] When the letter was made public, timber industry officials requested that DeBonis be reprimanded.

In a moment of insight into the founding of the Forest Service, Gifford Pinchot wrote a letter to himself, often called the Magna Carta of the agency, in which he said: "In the administration of the Forest Reserves it must be clearly borne in mind that all land is to be devoted to the most productive use for the permanent good of the whole people. . . . Where conflicting interests must be reconciled, the question will always be decided from the standpoint of the greatest good of the greatest number in the long run."[42] Almost a century later, in what may become the Magna Carta for a new, environmentally responsible Forest Service, DeBonis's letter laments just how far the agency has strayed from its democratic ideal:

> We delude ourselves in thinking that we are somehow in the "middle" between the environmentalists and the timber industry. . . . we ally ourselves with the timber industry and think that the "environmentalists" are somehow obstructing us with their numerous appeals and lawsuits. . . . The fact is, environmentalists are winning appeals and court cases because *we* have broken the law. . . . We are the obstructionists, in our insistence on promoting the greedy, insatiable appetite of the large corporate timber industry we serve so well.[43]

So much for the greatest good for the greatest number.

A powerful industry shielded by an administrative agency unresponsive to reform and motivated by ideas applicable to the ecological Dark Ages — this is the background of the wilderness war. In this light it is not only understandable that conflict between grass-roots environmentalists and commodity interests should escalate, it is surprising that more Americans are not up in arms over the plundering of public lands for private profit.

Radical environmentalists, however, did react. Shortly after the Kalmiopsis blockade, twenty members of Earth First! and other local activist groups sat on boxes of dynamite that were going to be used to blast a hillside into gravel for a road into the Middle Santiam Cathedral Forest, in Oregon's Willamette National Forest. Five were arrested. A month later fifteen protesters, Roselle among them, blockaded a logging road into the nearby Pyramid Creek sale. Nevertheless, despite additional continued opposition in the form of civil disobedience, the road crept inexorably toward the sale. As a last-ditch effort, Roselle sneaked into the stand one night and spiked it. He sent a letter to the timber company announcing the spiking, wished them good luck in finding the nails, and signed it "the Bonnie Abbzug Feminist Garden Party" — a reference to the voluptuous ecoteur in *The Monkey Wrench Gang*. The authorities caught neither the allusion nor the tree spiker.[44]

As more old-growth timber sales proceeded in the Middle Santiam, some of the protesters felt a sense of urgency and were growing dissatisfied with road blockades, which stopped the bulldozers only for the time it took the sheriff's deputies to arrive and make arrests. They wanted to find a more effective method. Two of these activists, Mike Jakubal and Ron Huber, came up with a novel approach to the problem: tree sitting.

Their idea originated, innocently enough, around a campfire in the Middle Santiam in the summer of 1985. Jakubal, a twenty-four-year-old rock climber, and Huber, a twenty-eight-year-old from Maryland, were venting their frustration with the unsuccessful campaign to prevent Willamette Industries from clear-cutting an area they called Millennium Grove in honor of the longevity of the trees there, some of which sprouted around the time of the fall of Rome. Jakubal had already earned himself a reputation as a walking action, and he would play an important part in forming an even more radical faction of Earth First!. Huber was also anxious to get involved in some direct action that went beyond symbolism. They asked each other what skills they had to attract public attention and make the campaign work. They had heard about Australian environmentalists scurrying up trees to prevent cutting, but the trees there were much smaller and easy to get into, unlike the giants of the Pacific Northwest. Jakubal said offhandedly: "I'm a rock climber, but we're not defending cliffs." A wicked idea flashed into their mind. Predictably, it was going to cost the timber industry money.

A few days later Jakubal was eighty feet up a huge Douglas fir scheduled to be clear-cut. He had driven a series of eight-inch pinions into the wood and worked his way up. When the loggers arrived in the morning for work, they were flabbergasted to find a protester sitting on a plywood platform he had hauled up with the help of friends. Jakubal explained to the loggers that he was going to be there for a while.

The foreman called the authorities. When the deputy arrived he asked the tree sitter for his name. "Doug Fir," Jakubal replied. The deputy dutifully, if somewhat obtusely, put the name into his report.

Jakubal had enough food and water for a week-long vigil. But when he came down that evening to walk around, a cagey deputy who had hidden nearby was waiting for him. Doug Fir was arrested after only one day.

Huber was more fortunate, however. He also climbed one of the giant conifers, which he dubbed Yggdrasil, the Old Norse name for the mythical tree that held up the world. On his makeshift platform he hung an American flag and a home-made banner: "ECOTOPIA IS RISING." He also attached ropes to nearby trees using grappling hooks, making it difficult for the loggers to cut them down without jerking his platform to the ground.

This time the law enforcement included some top brass: Carla Jones, Forest Service investigator; Jim Christiansen, special agent-in-charge; and David Olsen, the bedraggled forest ranger who had been forced to deal with growing protests over old-growth timber sales in his district. Soon the media was there also.

"Cut this tree here," Huber shouted, pointing to one of the cedars at the end of a grappling line, "and this platform I'm on is gonna bite the dust!"

A logger started his chain saw and approached Huber's tree. He sliced out a wedge of tree flesh with a sweep of the blade, and a plume of sawdust shot out in protest. Huber held up a heavy jar of Cornnuts, pointed at the logger below, and made the cutthroat sign. The authorities and the logger got the message.

After a month of threats and cajolery, consultations with higher-ups (both in Washington, D.C., and in the tree), and more threats, an exasperated Christiansen had a construction crane brought in from Portland. For three hours Huber and two deputies struggled in an aerial ballet before the officers pulled him into the basket and brought him down. Handcuffed in the backseat of the sheriff's car, Huber watched as the loggers girdled his tree and knocked in an iron wedge. Yggdrasil shivered and twisted and fell to the ground. When the tree was finally cut down, it fell at a cost of several hundred thousand dollars in extra security, time, and trouble, perhaps the most expensive tree ever put into a mill.

Huber later defended his actions by expressing his sense of

urgency over the destruction of wilderness: "I'm saying, take
the law into your own hands. That's all you have to do. If you
just go by their laws, then down come the trees, up goes the
slash in smoke. Instead of having this gorgeous jungle of vines
and mushrooms, chipmunks and squirrels and birds and fun-
gus and bacteria and old-growth trees holding the whole world
up, you'll have crispy critters."[45]

Since Huber's vigil at Millennium Grove there have been
dozens of tree sitting protests, most notably in the fight to preserve California's redwoods from the Maxxam Corporation. Although the trees in question are on privately owned company
land, Earth First!ers Darryl Cherney and Greg King argue that
they are a national treasure that should not be destroyed in the
pursuit of Wall Street investment strategies. Putting the campaign in a larger perspective, Cherney says, "One thing human
beings have never done is we've never assessed how many trees
we can cut down before we should stop. We have to account
for regeneration, of course, but can we cut down 75 percent of
the trees, 60 percent? What amount of trees is necessary to
sustain life on the planet? I don't think anybody really knows
the answer to that question and that really scares me."[46]

Radical environmentalists have carried out tree sits and road
blockades against Maxxam, but the trees continue to fall. For
this reason the Pacific Northwest has experienced an enormous
increase in incidents of ecotage. In Whatcom County, Washington, several hundred thousand dollars' worth of damage was
done to logging equipment in the spring of 1989 alone. Tree
spiking in particular is rampant. But King, who once dangled
on a line a hundred feet above a major highway in Northern
California to hang a banner calling for old-growth protection,
believes even ecotage cannot overcome the economics of old-
growth logging. "Tree spiking won't work against these people.
They'll get the spikes out whatever the cost. There's simply too
much profit in old-growth redwood."[47] Many activists in the
old-growth campaign are therefore now forming coalitions
with timber workers and introducing a ground-breaking ballot
initiative in California banning old-growth cutting in what
they believe is the only way to combat the industry's extraordinary economic power.

Others have gone in the opposite direction. For Mike Jakubal, Earth First! was still too enmeshed in America's corporate middle-class culture to form an effective opposition to the destruction of wilderness. Having no background in the mainstream environmental movement, as the founders of Earth First! did, he and other second-generation Earth First!ers want radical environmentalism to advocate a broader opposition to capitalism and its consumer culture, along the lines of the anarchist critique in publications like the journal *Fifth Estate*. According to Jakubal, limiting radical environmentalism to wilderness issues "can only lead to fragmentary and temporary solutions. At worst, it subverts and delays the genuinely radical transformation — which can only be termed revolutionary — required to save wilderness and everything else."[48] This criticism sounds very much like an echo of what Murray Bookchin and the young radicals were saying about the mainstream environmental movement during the early 1970s.

The results of this perspective were Stumps Suck! and later Live Wild or Die!, which were never intended as organizations (though the Forest Service and media took them as such) but merely sobriquets under which the anarcho-environmentalists could distinguish their activities from Earth First!'s.[49] And those activities were distinguishable by their irreverence, brashness, and hostility. At a conference of the Western Forestry and Conservation Association (a pro-industry group) in Seattle, anarcho-environmentalists under the name Revolutionary Ecoterrorist Pie Brigade threw pies at industry spokesmen, took over the dais, and raised a banner that made this suggestion to the participants: "GO CLEAR-CUT IN HELL!"

Some Earth First!ers have criticized this kind of protest as infantile, claiming that the freewheeling approach of Live Wild or Die! cannot mount campaigns, and campaigns are the only way to win on the old-growth issue. Nonetheless, the anarcho-environmentalists do seem to have made some members of Earth First! more militant. This became evident in a protest on July 6, 1988, when 120 Earth First!ers fresh from their annual rendezvous descended on Washington's Okanogan National Forest supervisor's office, which resulted in several hours of guerrilla theater, defacement of property, and disagreeable pranks like placing cow pies over the building's air conditioners.*

There is no doubt that environmentalists and the timber industry are now at each other's throats over the old-growth issue. Radical environmentalists are taking more confrontational actions, while the industry has turned up the heat on its rhetoric, casually recommending physical violence against protesters. Editor of *Forest Industries* David Pease, for instance, urged his readers to deal with Earth First!ers in the following way: "Nuke 'em — you have my vote."[50] Some timber workers have followed Pease's advice, in spirit at least. Environmentalists have received death threats and had their cars vandalized. One protester eighty feet up in a Douglas fir had the tree all but cut out from under him by an irate logger.

The tragedy here is that, at one level at least, such confrontation is completely unnecessary. The forest-products industry insists that all it wants is a reasonable policy on old-growth logging. Since timber interests have already taken between 90 and 95 percent of this unrenewable resource, what could possibly be more reasonable than to ask that they take no more and adopt a sustainable, ecologically sound method of forestry? For decades such a method, all-age management, has been successfully practiced in Switzerland, where steep slopes and fragile soils make clear-cutting unacceptable. As described by forestry professor Rudolf Becking, in all-age management

> you thin young stands out, harvest a few big trees, and create a space for the young stands to grow. You work in all size classes. You cut some noncommercial timber; you cut some commercial timber. . . . [U]nder even-age management we have always relied on computerized yield tables. We rely on the table to tell us how the stand should grow, but we have lost touch with the stand itself. In all-age management there is no such thing. You have to establish empirically what changes you can expect from the forest, to see how far you can push the productivity of the forest before it stabilizes on

---

* One of the participants in the incident was Mike Fain, an undercover FBI agent who, using the assumed name of Mike Tait, infiltrated Earth First! and later assisted in the felony arrest of Foreman and several other radical environmentalists for allegedly conspiring to cut off electricity to three nuclear power facilities in the West. Fain reportedly took part in some of the property damage.

your sustained-yield cut. . . . You have to learn the limits of
the natural system, and you try to maintain that system. . . . The forester has not only to mark the timber, he
has to reason out which tree to cut. And he marks which direction it has to go. He has to do it in such a way that his
first concern is the replacement, not to lose the growing
stock.[51]

Foresters in Switzerland are held in high esteem for the service they perform in promoting the continuity of the community. They are, in fact, elected to represent the entire
community, rather than appointed for political reasons, as is
often the case in the Forest Service hierarchy.

Orville Camp developed a variant on all-age management
that is called natural selection forest management, a method
more sensitive to the wilderness values that are lacking in
Swiss forests. It includes emphasizing the ecological stability
(and hence the health) of the forest by taking care to maintain
adequate habitats for all natural species of plants and animals
found in a forest community. By sustaining its diversity the
forest can yield not only timber for sawlogs but also a variety
of renewable (and marketable) products like fish, venison, and
edible plants. For Camp, forestry is a way of life, not just an
industry in the limited sense:

> Understanding the forest as a living ecosystem with its own
> set of natural checks and balances is the first step toward
> sensible management of your forest land. Once you begin to
> see the forest as a whole and observe its complex interdepen-
> dencies, you quickly see the ecological inadequacy of har-
> vesting trees on the basis of a monocultural model.
> Preserving the forest environment becomes a primary goal
> not only to benefit ecological health but also because it is
> more profitable in the long term as well.[52]

Had America's timber industry adopted this form of forestry
it might today be capable of supporting communities for the
long term instead of hastening an ecological decline that will
impoverish us all. Had the Forest Service done the same, our
national forests would still be intact ecosystems rather than
tree plantations run for private profit. There would have been

no occasion for the wilderness war now under way, and deeper questions about what responsibilities our society has toward nature and future generations could be addressed in a thoughtful atmosphere more appropriate to a national debate of this significance than is the present climate of acrimony.

But perhaps a showdown between radical environmentalists and the resource industry is inescapable, and the present escalation is just a prelude to a more intense conflict. Even if the timber industry wanted to shift to a more responsible form of forestry, it might prove impossible in an economic system that requires constant growth and a national ethos that celebrates increased consumption. The United States is not Switzerland. If Jakubal is right, the problem is not the timber industry, however greedy, shortsighted, and reckless it indubitably is, but industrial society as a whole. For the present, prudence suggests that it is enough to call for the end to old-growth logging and the protection of all remaining de facto wilderness. But the wilderness war has prompted many radical environmentalists to sharpen their appreciation for the scope of their own ecological imperative. What started as an attempt to shake up the mainstream environmental movement seems to have expanded to shaking up the entire culture — or even the world.

CHAPTER 6

THE GREEN WORLD

The inroads Greens have made into German politics are a populist reaction to what is basically an unlivable European environment. The only problem with the Greens is that their defense of the natural world started too late, only after they no longer had anything natural to defend.

— Jesse ("Lone Wolf") Hardin,
Earth First! poet

You build this dam, we will go to war, and you will die.

— Kayapo Indian,
Brazil

SEVERAL YEARS before Earth First!'s desert genesis, Paul Watson, one of the founders of the Canadian-based group Greenpeace, was charging across the ice floes in the frigid Atlantic swells off the coast of Labrador. The sea was pitching so violently that at times he found himself surrounded by twelve-foot-high walls of ice, and both his friends behind him and his adversaries in front of him disappeared from view. But Watson was intent on moving forward; as he had told reporters a few days before, "This year we are determined to physically stop the [seal] hunt. Some of us may not be coming back."[1]

Watson carried out his first prediction and almost fell victim to the second.

Sweaty and out of breath, he reached the bloody ice of the hunting fields, where one of the sealers had just bashed an in-

fant harp seal on the skull with his hakapik, the spiked club
sealers use, and was leaning over the carcass to skin it. Watson
grabbed the hakapik and threw it into the ocean. When the
sealer went to retrieve it, Watson threw the seal pelt into the
ocean also. He then handcuffed himself to a bale of pelts about
to be hauled up onto the sealers' ship, the *Martin Karlsen*,
thinking the crew would have to abandon their operations until
he was cut loose or risk killing him.

They risked killing him. Cheered on by the sealers, the winch-
man hauled in the cable attached to the bale of pelts, dragging
the burly, boyish-faced Watson across the ice and slush and
lifting him up against the steel hull of the ship ten feet into the
air. Then the line slackened, and Watson was plunged into
the frigid waters. Again he was hoisted up and again dipped
like a tea bag into the sea. On the fourth ride, Watson broke
free and fell helplessly into the water, immobilized by the cold.
He would have drowned had his friends from Greenpeace not
arrived and pulled him to safety.

Several months later Greenpeace's board of directors met in
Vancouver to discuss Watson and his death-defying effort in
defense of seals, an exploit that had attracted international
news coverage (upstaged a bit by the unexpected arrival on the
scene of animal rights advocate and sex symbol Brigitte
Bardot). The result: they expelled him from the organization.
It seems that by throwing the sealer's hakapik into the ocean
he had broken Canadian law and violated Greenpeace's nonviolent code. The real reason for the expulsion was that Watson's activism had become an irritant to a board that, like its
counterparts in the United States, was becoming increasingly
preoccupied with credibility and budgets as the organization
grew in size and influence. Like David Brower and Dave Foreman, Watson had become too radical for the mainstream environmental movement, even in its more strident incarnation
as Greenpeace, a group he had helped create and had worked
for without pay for seven years.

Shortly thereafter the twenty-five-year-old merchant marine
and another disgruntled Greenpeace activist, Al "Jet" Johnson,
started the short-lived group Earth Force, which ceased to
exist before it could carry out its plans to stop the ivory

trade.* Undaunted, Watson created a new organization, based in his hometown of Vancouver, which successfully put into practice his militant environmental views: the Sea Shepherd Conservation Society. With a $120,000 grant from Cleveland Amory's Fund for Animals and a $50,000 grant from Great Britain's Royal Society for Prevention of Cruelty to Animals, Watson bought a weather-beaten fishing trawler in 1979 and christened it the *Sea Shepherd*, "the flagship of Gaia's [the Greek word for "Earth"] whale navy," as he described it.[2] Watson planned to use the ship to take direct action in defense of threatened marine mammals around the world without the bureaucratic restraints of Greenpeace and the mainstream environmental movement.

Watson's sense of ecological mission came out of an experience he had back in the spring of 1973, at Wounded Knee, South Dakota. Declaring the reemergence of the Independent Oglala Sioux Nation, armed members of the American Indian Movement were occupying the Sioux reservation to protest government policy toward the Indians. Watson, who as a young radical supported black power, red power, the antiwar protests, and almost any other counterculture movement, slipped past armored vehicles and machine-gun-toting National Guardsmen besieging Wounded Knee in order to offer his services to the Indian cause as a medical aide. When the occupation ended, Watson was initiated into the tribe as a warrior-brother. He was guided by two medicine men, one of whom was the grandson of the legendary Black Elk, on a spirit journey, which he later described to a journalist:

> I suddenly saw myself in a grassy, rolling field, gazing into the eyes of a wolf. The wolf looked at me, then into a pond, and walked away. When I told the Sioux what had happened, they gave me my Indian name: Gray Wolf Clear Water. Then I went back into the vision, and saw a buffalo standing on a ridge. It began to speak to me. And as it told me that I must protect the buffalo of the sea, an arrow came and struck it in

---

* A decade later, in 1989, the international community, including many African nations, finally proposed just such a ban, in response to the precipitous decline in elephant population caused by poaching.

the back. Attached to the arrow was a cord, symbolic of a harpoon.[3]

Gray Wolf Clear Water was aware that the buffalo had a special resonance for the Sioux, who had gone to war with the doomed general George Custer in part to protect the dwindling buffalo herds on which they depended from the depredations of the whites. Watson saw his commitment to protect whales, the buffalo of the sea, as the modern-day equivalent of the Sioux's war to save the bison.

With this shamanistic tenor and his connections with animal rights groups like the Fund for Animals, Watson brought a perspective to the radical environmental movement that was in some ways very distinct from that of Earth First!. While Earth First! emphasized the protection and restoration of wilderness and habitat, the Sea Shepherds championed individual endangered species such as whales, seals, and timber wolves. Many of those who participated in the *Sea Shepherd*'s subsequent voyages were active in the animal rights movement, which in Britain in particular was also turning to militant actions, such as the ransacking of laboratories engaged in vivisection. The animal rights movement was generally less interested in ecological relationships than in what it saw as the moral obligation humans had not to cause suffering to animals. Such an obligation was almost by definition limited to sentient animals and seemed to exclude the wild Goodding's onion in Foreman's biocentric embrace and the rivers and ecosystems whose elemental dignity Earth First!'s Deep Ecology philosophy asserted.

Theoretical considerations aside, most animal rights activists and radical environmentalists have found enough intellectual overlap to be able to work together on environmental concerns. This alliance apparently made the FBI think it was necessary to sow dissension between the two groups by sending a letter to the journal *Earth First!* in March 1989 that purported to be from a radical environmentalist and that called on Earth First!ers to poison wild horses and burros, a position that touches perversely upon an important ecological concern (horses and burros are introduced species to the Americas) but is unacceptable to animal rights advocates.[4] Needless to say, radical environmentalists do not support the use of poison.

Although influenced by the animal rights movement, Watson was equally at home with Earth First!'s whole-ecosystem approach and in fact later declared himself an Earth First!er after "that dust-eating, river-loving, land-lubber Abbey gave me a subscription [to the *Earth First!* journal] and drafted me."[5] For Watson, the Sea Shepherd Society was meant to be "the navy of Mother Earth, and Earth First! the army."[6]

The Sea Shepherd Society decided to wage its naval war to save the environment using five simple guidelines: Sea Shepherd crew members cannot use weapons; they cannot use explosives; they cannot undertake any action that could result in a physical injury to humans; they must take responsibility for their actions; and they must accept moral and legal consequences for their actions.[7] The guidelines did not exclude property damage in pursuit of ecological goals. As Watson would later write, "Pardon me for my old-fashion ways, I believe that respect for life takes precedence over respect for property which is used to take life."[8]

Watson made that abundantly clear during his first Sea Shepherd expedition, in July 1979. The Sea Shepherds had learned that a ship called the *Sierra* was engaged in illegal whaling operations along the west coast of Africa, sailing out of Portugal under contract with a Japanese company dealing in gourmet foods. With an international crew of eighteen conservationists (including Watson), most of whom had never been to sea before, the *Sea Shepherd* began a search of the waters between the Azores and the Portuguese coast where the pirate whaler was rumored to be. Miraculously, Watson found the *Sierra,* only because he paused for several hours to let a vast herd of migrating loggerhead turtles swim past; this took on significance for Watson when he learned that on the day he left port a medicine man at Wounded Knee had told Watson's friend David Garrick that "Gray Wolf will find the enemy, and be led to the enemy by the turtle."[9]

Watson hesitated to go through with his plan to ram the *Sierra,* because the seas were rough and some of the *Sierra's* thirty-nine crew members, mostly black South Africans, would surely have lost their life in the encounter. Instead he followed the ship to the Portuguese port of Leixões, taking pictures and sizing it up for an attack. Watson advised his crew that if they had any qualms about facing imprisonment, injury, or death they should disembark at port now. Fifteen chose to do so. Only Watson's Australian chief engineer, Peter Woof, and Jerry Doran from Hawaii stayed on. After a warning brush along the pirate ship's prow, the undermanned *Sea Shepherd* charged full speed ahead into the *Sierra*, retreated, and charged again, cutting a gaping hole in her port side and staving in forty-five feet of hull. The crippled whaler, its illegal cargo of whale meat visible through the gash, limped into port.

Unfortunately for Watson, the *Sea Shepherd* was pursued by a Portuguese destroyer and confiscated. When Watson refused to sign the notification of a $950,000 suit brought against him by the owners of the *Sierra,* his passport was confiscated by the authorities, and he had to slip out of the country using his merchant marine papers. After it became clear that his ship would be turned over to the pirate whaling company, Watson sneaked back into Portugal and scuttled the *Sea Shepherd* himself. The reoutfitted *Sierra* also wound up on the bottom of the sea, sunk by a magnetic mine a few months later.

The *Sea Shepherd's* actions brought international attention to the problem of unregulated whaling. In Norway authorities began an investigation of Forretnings Bank when it was discovered that it had acquired part ownership in the pirate operation, contrary to Norwegian law. In Japan, Taiyo Fishing Corporation, another investor in the *Sierra,* also became the object of an inquiry. The South African government began a crackdown on pirate whalers operating out of its country.

Watson's swashbuckling environmentalism won his new organization instant notoriety. Warner Brothers Studios paid Watson an advance for a film adaptation of the Sea Shepherds' exploits, a project that never got off the ground, but the advance nevertheless enabled him to buy a new ship, the *Sea Shepherd II.* Over the years the Sea Shepherds participated in a variety of campaigns, from stopping seal hunts along the Labrador coast to interfering with British Columbia's wolf-eradication plans to chasing off Japanese fishing fleets, using highly destructive drift nets in the North Pacific. By the late

1980s the society's membership climbed to more than twelve thousand, the majority of whom were "women fed up with the timidity of most environmental groups," according to Scott Trimingham, Sea Shepherd president and editor of its newsletter.[10]

But like Earth First!, the Sea Shepherd Society not only attracted media; its militant activities also succeeded in influencing the environmental movement as a whole. The best example is its most well known action, the 1986 raid on Reykjavík.

In 1986 a four-year moratorium on all commercial whaling was about to go into effect in accordance with a plan formulated by the International Whaling Commission, the body that regulates whaling worldwide. The respite was intended to give the world's dwindling population of whales a chance to recover and to allow time to develop a satisfactory data base for determining a sustainable hunting quota for any future whaling, if such were possible. Several nations that still engaged in whaling objected to the ban, and one, Iceland, used its Viking ingenuity to circumvent it.

Under pressure from the wealthy Jon Loftson — owner of Iceland's only whaling company, with the inauspicious name of Whales Limited — the Icelandic government announced plans to begin a four-year study of whale populations, which would involve the killing of several thousand fin, sei, and minke whales "for research purposes." Whales Limited was hired to carry out this research whaling and would be allowed to sell the "by-products" of the research, such as whale meat and oil, to Japan for millions of dollars. No one for a second believed this was anything but an attempt to continue commercial whaling under the guise of scientific research. But the IWC's moratorium pertained only to commercial whaling, not research. Simply by announcing that its hunt was for research purposes, Iceland found it could keep alive a moribund industry for a few more years. Other whaling nations, including Japan and Norway, seeing an opportunity, hastily announced their desire to add to the body of scientific knowledge about cetaceans in a similarly lethal fashion. The whales of the Earth, it seemed, were about to be researched to death.

Mainstream environmental groups tried to get American secretary of commerce Malcolm Baldrige to declare a boycott of Icelandic fish products, Iceland's major export to the United States, in response to its violation of the IWC moratorium, at least in spirit. But Iceland was the site of a strategically located NATO base, manned almost exclusively by Americans, and neither Baldrige nor his chief executive, Ronald Reagan, was about to let environmentalist opposition to Iceland's destruction of whales jeopardize the military's ability to destroy the Russian Leviathan. The United States also did not want to become embroiled in a dispute with the country that was about to host the Reagan-Gorbachev summit. Lobbying efforts to get Baldrige to act against Japan for buying the products of Iceland's research whaling also failed. A short time later Baldrige fell from a horse and was killed, tempting radical environmentalists to suggest some mysterious providence was at work.

Nevertheless, the research whaling began in earnest in the summer. This was unacceptable to Rod Coronado, a skinny, soft-spoken Californian who had signed on as a *Sea Shepherd II* crew member during its antiwhaling campaign in the Faeroe Islands, south of Iceland, where he had been beaten and jailed by police. Coronado was a supporter of Earth First! and an avid reader of Edward Abbey's works and Foreman's recently released monkeywrenching manual, *Ecodefense*. He had, in fact, painted "Earth First!" in giant silver letters inside the stack of the *Sea Shepherd II* during the Faeroe campaign, so "no pilot or seagull could escape the message."[11] On the return voyage Coronado approached Watson with a plan to disrupt Iceland's research whaling. Watson asked if Coronado could carry out the plan while operating within the Sea Shepherd Society's guidelines, and when he answered yes, the captain of the Sea Shepherds gave him his backing.

With a copy of *Ecodefense* among his belongings, Coronado and fellow Sea Shepherd David Howitt, a lanky, vegetarian Cornishman who, like Coronado, was in his early twenties, flew to Iceland in October and took jobs at a fish factory. After several weeks of reconnaissance they set out on the stormy night of November 8, 1986, to the whale-processing plant fifty miles north of Reykjavík on the narrow Hvalfjord — "the Fjord of the Whale." The two Sea Shepherds spent the next eight hours destroying the facility's refrigeration system, dismantling diesel engines, demolishing its laboratory, and pouring acid onto computer files. The damage was later estimated at almost $2 million.

Half their plan was now complete. From Hvalfjord, Coronado and Howitt drove down to Reykjavík harbor, where the four-vessel whaling fleet was docked. They boarded two of the ships and opened their sea-valve flanges, allowing the cold waters of the North Atlantic to rush in. The ecoteurs left the third ship unharmed because a sleeping guard was on board. The fourth was in dry dock. By the time they traveled the thirty miles to the airport and boarded a plane, the two ships were at the bottom of the harbor — another $2.8 million in damage added to the Sea Shepherds' stay in Iceland.

Not surprisingly, the Sea Shepherds' raid was denounced by the mainstream environmental movement. Greenpeace International likened it to a terrorist attack in a letter to the Icelandic government and in an interview with NBC News. The largest newspaper in British Columbia, the *Sun,* virtually called for Watson's arrest, asking in conclusion the melodramatic question "Is Vancouver to become a sanctuary for international terrorists?"[12] While avoiding charges of terrorism, several mainstream environmental leaders did comment that ecotage of this sort would in any case do nothing to stop whaling in the long run.

The two sunken ships in Reykjavík harbor were raised shortly after being scuttled but did not take part in subsequent seasons of "research," since, despite cosmetic repairs, they were no longer seaworthy. Moreover, the impact of the Sea Shepherds' action went far beyond the disabling of two ships. It is no exaggeration to say that the raid on Reykjavík persuaded many Icelanders to change their views about whaling and for the first time generated a debate about the way environmental policy was being made in their country.

On the night of the raid a television interview of a hooded Icelander was broadcast on the Reykjavík evening news. He claimed to have helped the Sea Shepherds with the logistics of the raid, though the Sea Shepherds deny that any Icelanders were involved in the operation.[13] Whether or not it was true, the declaration by an Icelander that environmental concerns had prompted him to help foreigners attack Icelandic property gave many people in the largely homogeneous nation reason to reflect. Iceland is a sparsely populated country with an almost nonexistent crime rate and a great deal of social cohesion. That one of their own would assist the Sea Shepherds caused many Icelanders to forget the patriotic ire raised by talks of boycotts and seriously question their country's association with this disreputable use of science — all the more so since it was for the profit of one rich citizen, Loftson, in a society that prided itself on its egalitarianism. The issue of whaling thus seemed to many to go to the heart of what Icelandic society stood for.

Younger people were in the forefront of questioning how environmental policy was being formulated in their country. This led to the rise of Iceland's first activist environmental group, the antiwhaling Hvalvinurfelag ("Friends of the Whale"), founded by Magnus Skarphedinsson. Its first public action came in 1987, when members chained themselves to the masts of the two undamaged whaling ships to prevent them from leaving port. The good-natured Icelandic police apparently had read the weather forecast and made no effort to remove the protesters, who gave up after a squall set in. It was not much of a protest, but as a cultural matter it was an extraordinary event, the first instance of environmental civil disobedience in a country noted for its political equanimity, not to say complaisance. This ecological awakening was proof that radical environmentalism was affecting people in ways the leaders of the mainstream environmental movement never dreamed of.

Despite its militancy — or perhaps because of it — the Sea Shepherds were able to win the support of a number of people, including celebrities, who might otherwise have been reluctant to endorse ecotage. When Watson was arrested in 1983 for interfering with Canada's seal hunt, his ten-thousand-dollar bail was posted by actor Mike Farrell of the television series *M★A★S★H*, who not coincidentally is a spokesman for the animal rights group People for the Ethical Treatment of Animals. Maxwell Gail of the *Barney Miller* series did a commercial for the Sea Shepherds that aired on local stations in California. In the strangest instance yet of Hollywood's embracing radical environmentalism, actor Harvey Korman appeared on the TV quiz show *Animal Crack-Ups*, which donates the winnings of its celebrity panel to environmental and animal rights groups, and played for Watson's organization. Charges that the Sea Shepherd Society was a terrorist organization were not, apparently, being taken seriously by society at large.

In a curious postscript to the Reykjavík incident, Watson flew to Iceland in 1988 to turn himself in to the authorities, in accordance with the Sea Shepherd guideline of accepting the moral and legal consequences for one's actions and not unaware of how embarrassing his presence would be to the Icelandic government. Although the authorities had threatened to extradite him, once he was within their jurisdiction they wanted nothing to do with the possible bad publicity a trial would focus on their whaling policy. Watson was held without charge for twenty-two hours and then expelled without cause, an unprecedented event in liberal-minded Scandinavia, as many unfavorable editorials in the Icelandic press pointed out. The government also became the object of indignant commentaries for arresting several journalists who tried to interview Watson. Gray Wolf Clear Water, it seems, had struck again.

On the other side of the world, in the dwindling subtropical rain forests of southeastern Australia, another radical environmental awakening was taking place at about the time the Sea Shepherd Society and Earth First! got started, bringing an additional perspective to the movement. The story here begins in medias res, as hundreds of young protesters who had blockaded a timber road were running from police through the rain forest near Terania Creek, New South Wales, an area called the Big Scrub. At this moment one of them, a back-to-the-land advocate named John Seed, had a revelation of sorts that would influence the course of Australian environmentalism: "I realized then through all this chaos that I was part of the rain forest — that I was the rain forest defending herself."[14]

Seed was among several hundred protesters who lived near the Big Scrub, a fragment of a once-mighty primeval forest that covered Australia before it split off from the Gondwanaland supercontinent (which also included South America, Africa, Madagascar, India, and Antarctica) one hundred million years ago and slowly drifted toward cooler, southern climes. When the Australian Forestry Commission decided in 1979 to permit fifty thousand acres of the forest to be logged, environmental-

ists filed petitions and appeals and, just as usually happens in
America, lost. Receiving lukewarm support from the Sierra
Club—like Australian Conservation Foundation, local activists
decided to take direct action: three hundred environmentalists
blockaded the timber road being punched into the area, lying
down in front of the equipment, climbing trees marked for fell-
ing, and tying the trees together with cables. The scene had a
surrealistic air about it as a squad of police one hundred strong
escorted the rumbling road-building machinery through the
primeval forest half-light, harassed at every turn by protesters.
It presaged the kind of militarization of the wilderness that the
United States and other countries would eventually experience.

Dozens of people were arrested for trespassing and obstruc-
tion, Seed among them. When he was haled before a New
South Wales court, he pleaded innocent by reason of environmentalism: "I respectfully submit, Your Worship, that the defendants in front of this court were a key to saving rainforests.
In the light of the ecological evidence, and the expressed desire
of the people of this state, I suggest we should be receiving
medals, not the maximum penalty under the law."[15] When
charges against Seed were in fact dropped three years later, he
wrote the police commissioner that he refused to allow the case
to be dismissed, because he wanted to cross-examine the arresting constables to make sure they did not make a similar
mistake in the future.

The Big Scrub protests touched upon a number of environmental issues, most of which were framed by protesters using
the traditional arguments of the mainstream conservationist
movement. But for Seed the fight was no longer just for rational forest management policies or local control of resources;
it was a question of self-defense, of identification with the natural world, which was under attack on all sides by industrial
society.

The environmental protesters eventually won out against the
developers, and the government preserved some half-million
acres of the Big Scrub as national parks. But this was not sufficient for the growing number of Australian radical environmentalists. "For every [acre] of rain forest we preserved this
way," said Seed, "another hundred were destroyed someplace
else."[16] For many of the protesters a more far-reaching change

was called for, a new way of seeing humanity's place in nature, an environmental movement with a spiritual, rather than political, basis.

The word "spiritual" is problematic here, since it has become closely associated with New Age ideology and its patina of Eastern religiosity. It is true that most of the people involved in the Big Scrub protests lived in a community founded after an "Aquarius Festival" was held there in 1973, and Buddhism had an important influence on Seed's thinking. But the New Age doctrine that humanity was entering an era of enlightened (and total) stewardship of the Earth was the furthest thing from the Australian activists' mind as they set about battling bulldozers, loggers, and police. At a 1983 environmental conference held at the University of Melbourne, Seed reflected the more sober mood of radical environmentalism in saying, "Change is still possible, but not likely."[17] He even once suggested, as if to have fun with New Age optimism, that in lieu of nuclear arms the great powers should develop biological weapons lethal only to humans so that in the coming Third World War humanity would limit the apocalypse to itself and spare the rest of the biosphere.[18]

Seed's vision of an environmental movement based on an identification with nature was strengthened by his study of Deep Ecology in the writings of Arne Naess, the Norwegian philosopher who coined the term, and the Americans Bill Devall and George Sessions, all of whom had an important influence on Earth First!'s ecological sensibility. For Seed the real environmental goal was biocentrism, a recognition that humans are not "the crown of creation, the source of all value, the measure of all things."[19]

Like Foreman, Bart Koehler, and Ron Kezar, Seed and his friends took their vision of environmentalism on the road, forming what he called a Nomadic Action Group (NAG) to nag politicians and environmentalists into taking action on behalf of wilderness. In 1984 he even joined up with Earth First! in America on one of its later road shows, where he made the issue of rain forest preservation a priority of many Earth First!ers, including Mike Roselle and Randall Hayes,[20] who subsequently helped organize a successful boycott of Burger King for its use of cheap beef raised on cutover tropical forests.

Seed also began holding a series of what he called Councils of All Beings in Australia and around the world. The councils originated from discussions between Seed and Joanna Macy, an Australian antinuclear activist. They were conceived as despair workshops in which environmentalists would have a chance to shed their identification with purely human problems and develop a greater empathy with nonhuman nature under siege. The councils were intended "to allow people to grieve for the ecological destruction going on and for their sense of isolation from the natural world — something our anthropocentric culture consciously tries to suppress."[21] The point, however, was not self-involvement but a higher degree of commitment: "If we embark upon such an inner voyage, we may find . . . that our actions on behalf of the environment are purified and strengthened by the experience."[22]

Members of the Australian environmental movement were responsive to the ideas of Deep Ecology as articulated by Seed, no doubt because their country, like America, was still vast enough to allow for encounters with big wilderness. The natural world was an intense, tangible reality, not a theoretical issue involving resource depletion and land management. They began using "Earth First!" as their rallying cry and soon proved themselves among the most creative environmental activists in the world, developing methods of protests, such as chaining themselves to logging equipment and tree sitting, that were later used elsewhere.*

Shortly after the Big Scrub victory, the Australian Earth First!ers undertook a campaign to prevent road building in the Daintree rain forest of the Cape York Peninsula, in northern Queensland. A number of protesters spent several days buried up to their neck or chained to logs in front of bulldozers and backhoes. One self-interred protester, Graham Innes, gave the backhoe operator trying to unearth him a righteous, Jonsonian tongue-lashing: "Sir, you are stripping the Earth of her mantle and she will die. . . . I know that in your heart, you know it to be so. Go home, Sir. Go home."[23]

Because the backhoe operators of Australia were not going

---

* By American Earth First!ers in Millennium Grove and the Bald Mountain road blockade in the Kalmiopsis; in the latter demonstration, protesters used a manual written by the organizers of a dam blockade in Tasmania.

home, even in the face of civil disobedience, radical environmentalists soon embraced the use of ecotage. Since the early 1980s they have caused hundreds of thousands of dollars in damage to bulldozers and logging equipment annually, using techniques familiar to American Earth First!ers and helped along by the presence of Foreman's ubiquitous *Ecodefense.*

Seed's revelation that he was the rain forest defending herself led him to found the Rainforest Information Centre, which helped to make rain forest destruction the global issue it is today and inspired the establishment of other rain forest organizations. One of these was Randall Hayes's Rainforest Action Network, which worked closely with Seed and attracted the support of David Brower and Roselle. The work of the center put Seed in touch with the environmental struggles of indigenous people throughout the world. Among these was the Koroga tribe, which inhabits the Solomon Islands, a chain of quiescent volcanoes east of New Guinea noted for its superb lagoons and a startling array of forest types. The traditional lands of the Koroga were being logged by the multinational Lever Brothers firm. A war party of Koroga took the law into their own hands and attacked a Lever Brothers logging camp, burning houses, vehicles, and timber machinery. When Seed visited the islands in 1983, he found that Premier Tausinga and his wife, who had the biblical first names Job and Ruth, were more than just a little sympathetic to his radical environmental outlook. Tausinga was in the habit of attending meetings with timber companies wearing a Rainforest Information Centre T-shirt that had the words "Save Our Trees" blazoned over an image of a human-shaped tree cut and bleeding at the neck — not the sort of picture calculated to put a timber industry representative at ease at the negotiating table. Tausinga agreed to become Earth First!'s contact in the Solomon Islands. After only three years in existence the environmental group that started with five malcontents could claim (and did at every opportunity) that it had a premier as one of its representatives.

Tausinga demonstrated his radical environmental temperament in a letter to Lever Brothers, which admonished: "Any attempts by us or others of defiance against your unjust, oppressive and illegal activities will not be regarded as an in-

fringement or breach of the peace or rule of law, but as
retaliation against your violation of our privacy and our rights
and absolute intention to protect our customary land."[24] Indeed, the displacement of indigenous peoples caused by deforestation was leading many tribes to become radicalized in this
way. In 1980 a hundred Indian tribes in the Amazon basin of
Brazil banded together into the Union of Indigenous Nations,
whose actions stretched from lobbying the Brazilian Congress
to doing war dances outside the presidential palace as a warning that violence would ensue if the government went through
with a plan to dump radioactive waste on Indian land. And
violence has broken out on a number of occasions. In one vivid
incident, in January 1984 a band of Piromasco Indians, painted
red and firing poison-tipped arrows, attacked a Shell Oil work
crew drilling an exploratory well on their traditional hunting
grounds in the Peruvian Amazon. Less dramatic but no less
violent confrontations are not uncommon.

Seed was impressed with the fact that for tribal peoples, defense of their environment and their existence as a people were
one and the same thing, a position very close to the Deep Ecology vision he espoused. Hunter-gatherer peoples, like the
Penan in the Malaysian provinces on the island of Borneo, embodied in their culture an attitude toward the environment
that accepted natural cycles and that saw nonhuman beings as
part of an extended family of beings all sharing a place, rather
than as inferior creatures to be dominated or destroyed at will.
Seed found this an attractive model for modern society to use
in learning to reinhabit the natural world — a model that was
disappearing before his eyes as multinational firms plied the
Malaysian government with money to allow them access to the
Penan's timber-rich ancestral lands. Seed became a tireless
supporter of the Penan's resistance, which involved road blockades by blowpipe-wielding tribesmen, lobbying efforts, and
ecotage. The Penan's continued environmental insurgency contributed to a political crisis in August 1987, when environmental activists charged that officials high up in the Malaysian
government secretly owned stock in the timber companies that
were logging tribal lands. Prime Minister Mahathir Bin Mohamed invoked an emergency Internal Security Act permitting
the arrest of several dozen Penan and environmental activists

in Malaysia's Friends of the Earth, the closure of three newspapers, the banning of all public rallies, and the suppression of timber-road blockades. Once again radical environmental action was playing an important role in social ferment.

The importance of tribal peoples' perspective toward the natural world has not been much appreciated by the mainstream environmental movement, which generally sees wilderness as a recreation resource to be managed rather than an indispensable component of human cultures. In contrast, radical environmentalists like Seed and Roselle have looked upon the understanding of tribal, or "customary," culture as essential for learning to reinhabit the natural world after the inevitable collapse of industrialism. Roselle, who visited the Penan in 1989 in his capacity as Rainforest Action Network tropical timber campaign director, makes the interesting point that throughout its history civilization has always been able to perceive its roots in nature, if only by way of contrast, through the existence of tribal cultures. But with the destruction of the rain forests and their inhabitants, even this last tenuous link is being severed. "You hear about the death of nature and it's true," Roselle says, "but nature will be able to reconstitute itself once the top of the food chain is lopped off — meaning us. But what also is going on right now is the death of customary law, the tribal way of existence. Tribal peoples have always acted as a link back to a sustainable way of life in nature. When they're gone we're going to lose our reference point, something that's never happened before in the history of civilization. That's why it's critical to start with the millions of tribal people still left in the world and build up from there."[25] According to Roselle, as customary cultures are displaced by industrial development, the opportunity to rebuild a sustainable culture will vanish by the end of the century. We will be left with a global Ruhrgebiet — Germany's industrial heartland — with no connection to the natural world, no way back.

The relationship between ecology and society adumbrated by Roselle was a theme of radical environmentalists everywhere. But nowhere was it felt so acutely as in industrialized Europe, the home of the Ruhrgebiet, with the emergence of the Greens. Unlike radical environmentalists in North America, Australia, and the Third World, environmentalists on the Continent were able to mobilize protesters in the tens of thousands, even hundreds of thousands, against their government's environmental and energy policies, in what often turned out to be violent confrontations. Eventually they gathered enough support to enter the arena of electoral politics and send representatives to the Parliaments of several European nations, as well as to the joint European Parliament, with far-reaching proposals to transform the consumer societies of the Western democracies into something more compatible with ecological limits. The European environmentalists of the early 1980s were willing and able to embrace the call for fundamental social change, from which the more cautious American environmental leaders recoiled in the early 1970s.

They virtually had no choice. Except for parts of northern Sweden, the wildlands of Europe were replaced centuries ago by the domesticated, managed landscape of agriculture and industry one sees today. In such an overpopulated and artificial terrain it was inevitable that people would come to appreciate the interdependence of social, economic, and environmental policy — a realization that proved more elusive for those in the New World, since they (for the moment at least) still retain enough wilderness to shield them from the more obvious and unpleasant consequences that ecological decline inevitably brings to every aspect of human welfare. With the looming threats of radiation, acid rain, and toxic waste in their own backyard, European environmentalists did not have the luxury of separating ecology from politics. Many environmentalists in America and elsewhere envy the Greens for their political clout, without realizing that to a great extent their success rests on the unfortunate fact that by the time environmentalism came on the scene in the Old World, the battle to defend the natural world had already been lost.

This should not depreciate the importance of the Green movement in Europe; on the contrary, as North America and Australia grow ever more populous and industrialized at the expense of wilderness, radical environmentalists may soon find themselves following the European model, which is more political, ideological, programmatic, and geared toward the direct interests people have in avoiding environmental collapse.

Moreover, there are places in Europe of great natural value still worth defending, such as France's Loire River, which thousands of Green activists are now trying to save from a government hydroelectric project. But the humanized landscape of Europe has understandably led to a radical ecology movement with its own unique concerns and an ideological turn of mind that sometimes seems to stray from the tangible, earthy questions of ecology.

In what now should seem like a familiar pattern, thirty Greenpeace activists in northern Germany found themselves more and more dissatisfied with their organization during the early 1980s because of its increasingly bureaucratic style of leadership. They broke off from Greenpeace, as Watson had, in 1982 and founded their own direct-action environmental group, Robin Wood — a not very good pun on the name of the legendary English outlaw. To dramatize the problem of acid rain and its lethal effects on German forests, Robin Wood members began a series of protests involving climbing and occupying the smokestacks of coal power plants, which are major contributors to acid rain. This kind of high-profile activism attracted attention, and Robin Wood was soon able to set up chapters in a number of German cities. On October 3, 1986, members of the Munich chapter blocked the Alpenpasse, a major route through the Bavarian Alps, with a mock landslide to demonstrate the kinds of ill effects deforestation causes.

Robin Wood was merely one of a number of small groups across Western Europe that sprang up during the 1980s to take part in civil disobedience and guerrilla theater on behalf of the environment. Individuals also took up the standard of environmental resistance. The Frenchman Pierre Kung has registered his opposition to electrical lines from a nuclear power plant passing over his farm in southwestern France by occupying the transmission tower, publicly sawing a piece of metal off of it, and chaining himself in front of the local prefecture. In Norway, Arne Naess put his Deep Ecology philosophy and his mountaineering skills to work by tying himself to the cliffs of a fjord and refusing to descend until the authorities promised not to go through with their plans to dam the fjord. The philosopher–rock climber got his way.

But actions such as these are mild in comparison with the

contemporaneous outbreak of ecotage the Continent experienced, mostly related to nuclear power plants or other large public works. Hundreds of electrical transmission towers leading to the Gorleben nuclear waste disposal facility in Bavaria have been sabotaged by antinuclear activists, and the practice continues to spread, despite tough new laws against it. In the Basque region of Spain, where the antinuclear struggle is closely associated with the Basque separatist movement, violent, commandolike attacks have been carried out against the nuclear industry. In the late 1970s the nuclear plant under construction at Bilbao was twice bombed, killing several workers and causing damage in the amount of $70 million. A factory involved in the repair of the reactor was also bombed, causing $6 million in damage. France, which has a strong nuclear establishment, has also experienced transmission tower sabotage and worse. When its Superphénix breeder reactor was under construction it was attacked by a bazooka, while ecoteurs in southern France also blew up two transformer stations. Ecoteurs in Scandinavia have damaged transmission towers as well as drilling equipment at prospective nuclear waste disposal sites. According to Mary Davis, who has researched ecotage in Europe and is completing a book about the French nuclear establishment, Norwegian organizers say *Ecodefense* "is very popular" among the opponents of nuclear power there, whose sole complaint about the book is that heavy machinery in Scandinavia differs from the American bulldozers and skidders the manual targets for destruction.[26]

Not all the ecotage in Europe is the act of anonymous raiders; it is often the very public response of whole communities that are up in arms against the policies of the central government. Thus the French journal *Revue Générale Nucléaire* reported that in August 1986, a group of 200 winegrowers near the village of Beaufort went en masse in broad daylight to where Cogema, the government-owned uranium mining company (whose American subsidiary operates a controversial uranium mine near the Grand Canyon), had set up a drilling rig and destroyed it along with seismic equipment and a Cogema truck.[27] There was a similar incident in Portugal some years before in which 1,500 people from the village of Ferrel marched to the site of an uncompleted nuclear power plant and destroyed all the construction equipment. In cases like these, people obviously are acting directly in defense of their own health or economic interests rather than out of the distinct ecological commitment Earth First! or the Sea Shepherds proclaim. Nevertheless, this direct interest in environmental policies, especially regarding nuclear power, contributed to the political ascent of the Green movement, which in many European countries overshadows the use of localized, hit-and-run ecotage as an expression of ecological discontent. Some European environmentalists, however, consider the Green movement the ecotaging of the entire system, an "anti-party party."[28]

The Green movement embraced a number of social movements and countercultural sentiments that blossomed throughout Western Europe during the late 1970s, including antiindustrialism, decentralization of power, feminism, leftist-libertarianism, and grass-roots democracy. However, Green politics has fared well or ill according to local, not to say idiosyncratic, conditions and concerns. Europe's first Green party, the Ecology party of Britain (later renamed the Green party), was founded in 1973, but except for winning a few local council seats it has languished in obscurity under labor and conservative governments alike. In contrast, Belgium has given birth to two relatively successful Green parties. The Flemish ecology party Agalev (an acronym for *Anders Gaan Leven* — "Live Differently") grew out of a Catholic revival movement founded by the Jesuit priest Luc Versteylen and his often colorful protests on behalf of the environment and the poor. After modest electoral showings in the early 1980s, Agalev received 7.1 percent of the vote in the 1984 European elections and 7.3 percent in the national parliamentary election of 1987. Belgium's Francophone ecology party, Ecolo, was started by activists in Brower's far-flung Friends of the Earth. It received 9.9 percent of the vote in the 1984 European elections and 6.5 percent in the 1987 parliamentary elections. In France, the 1977 killing by police of an antinuclear protester at the Superphénix reactor is widely held to have dampened direct, mass opposition to the nuclear industry, but not the development of Green politics. In 1981 Brice Lalonde of Les Amis de la Terre ("Friends of the Earth") garnered more than one million votes in the presidential election. Nationwide, Les Verts–Parti Ecologiste won 9 percent of the vote in the municipalities where they competed in 1989. The Green party of Italy had thirteen deputies and one senator in the government by 1987.

In Sweden, Finland, Switzerland, Austria, Ireland, Luxembourg, and the Netherlands, ecologically oriented parties have been able to field candidates and win between 2 and 7 percent of the vote in general elections.[29] More recently, the Green movement has played an important part in the prodemocratic efforts in the Soviet Union and the Eastern bloc countries. "In a serious sense," writes Michael Redclift of London University, "the new Green movements of Eastern Europe are the political opposition."[30] In the Baltic state of Lithuania, where anti-Russian and antinuclear sentiments go hand in hand, the environmental movement has been the first entrée of many people into the democratic opposition. Activists in the main opposition group, Sajudis ("Movement"), have made environmentalism the rallying point of reform. The same is true for the states of Georgia, Armenia, and Azerbaijan, where the antinuclear movement, although little reported on, is very much at the core of the nationalist movements. In Bulgaria the first stirrings of reform have been brought about by a group called Ecoglasnost. In November 1989 it organized the first public display of opposition to the government in forty-five years by presenting the government with a petition, signed by eleven thousand citizens, against a river-diversion project. Significantly or not, it was in another East bloc nation, Romania, at Bucharest's World Future Research Conference in 1972, that Arne Naess first delivered his paper mentioning the political implications of the emerging Deep Ecology movement, which seems suddenly to have arrived.

But the Greens have attracted the most attention in West Germany, not only for the degree of public support they have won (more than 8 percent of the national vote in 1987, and higher percentages at municipal and state levels), but also for the vigor and breadth of their ideas about reshaping industrial society and Western culture along more humane and ecological lines. When the Green party contingent first walked into the Bundestag, the German Parliament, in 1983, bearing a tree limb withered by acid rain, its gesture seemed to ensure that concern over the ecology had entered the field of German politics for good.

The West German Green movement was, like the radical environmental movements in the United States and Australia, both grass roots and ideologically diverse. It germinated in the mass protests against nuclear power during the mid-seventies, which brought together an unlikely coalition of conservative farmers, environmentalists, communists, and the new left activists, leftists-libertarians who had rejected traditional ideological formulations of Marxism. Perhaps equally unlikely, this coalition building began with a demonstration of 150 people near the small southern village of Wyle in a wine-growing region of Baden-Württemberg.

Near Wyle, the Bonn government had decided to build a nuclear power plant against the wishes of the local residents, who feared radiation would ruin their economy and change their way of life irrevocably. The people of Wyle sought to reverse the government's decision through legal and administrative channels but failed, no doubt because the minister-president of Baden-Württemberg, Hans Filbinger, was chairman of the supervisory board of the company that was to carry out the project — a fact not lost on the local community. In February 1975, therefore, their political channels exhausted, they staged a peaceful protest at the proposed site, which the police unceremoniously and forcefully broke up.

The drama of this small rural community being overpowered by distant and unfeeling technocrats galvanized support from all around the region. Students, clergy, socialists, and anarchists from nearby Freiburg joined the villagers in massive, nonviolent demonstrations involving tens of thousands of people. The police reacted with more force, and the government's plans ground to a halt.

The incident at Wyle was repeated with increasing intensity at other proposed nuclear sites, again bringing together a curious alliance of conservatives and revolutionaries, urbanites and rural folk, old and young. After futile attempts at petitions and lawsuits, protesters climbed over fences to occupy a proposed nuclear power plant site near Brockdorf in Schleswig-Holstein in 1976. Again the police response seemed unnecessarily harsh; officers on horseback charged into the crowds, burning the demonstrators' tents and belongings and allegedly mistreating those arrested. Two weeks later the activists were back, 40,000 strong, only to find the site ringed with barbed wire, a moat, and a contingent of police armed with water cannon and tear gas launchers. One participant, who later emigrated to America and became an Earth First! activist, describes the scene: "Most of the people were peaceful, but bands of radicals, what exactly was their thing I don't know, would come running up with cables and grappling hooks to attach to the fences. Then they would pull the fences down and enter the enclosure. The police were setting off tear gas grenades and counterattacking. A lot of people were hurt."[31]

Equally violent incidents followed in the next several years at Grohnde, Kalkar, and Gorleben, with the crescendo coming in October 1979, when 150,000 demonstrators rallied in Bonn, the largest protest in the history of the Federal Republic.

And yet the Bundestag continued with its nuclear policies, backing them up with increasingly aggressive law enforcement. It seemed to many politically aware West Germans that the dystopian vision of German author Robert Jungk's bestselling book, *The Nuclear State,* was coming true, that the massive and dangerous technologies of nuclear power were giving rise to a police state with the single-minded mission of protecting the complex infrastructure of industrial economy.

While some West Germans rallied in the tens of thousands against nuclear power, others began to make use of local political channels by fielding citizen initiatives (*Bürgerinitiativen*), grass-roots efforts to institute specific political action at a community level that bypassed traditional party politics (a process similar to California's ballot initiatives). By the late 1970s citizen initiatives concerning the environment began to coalesce into state parties, the first being the Green List for the Protection of the Environment, organized in 1977 in Lower Saxony. Many of these parties found that despite disparate backgrounds they shared an overriding commonality of interest when it came to keeping West Germany's ailing environment livable in the face of industrial development. Because many of these groups prospered, their leaders were able to meet in Karlsruhe in January 1980 to create formally a national Green party. After much wrangling among conservative, reformist, and radical socialist contingents, the conference was able to agree on a program for the new party, whose preamble read: "The aim of the Green Alternative is to overcome social conditions, in which the short-term emphasis on economic growth, which only benefits part of the entire population, takes precedence over the ecological, social and democratic needs for the life of humanity."[32]

The resulting organization encompassed much of the kaleidoscopic diversity that marked the antinuclear campaigns — a diversity that it pleased the Greens' critics to label "amorphous."[33] The divergent viewpoints in the party would later crystallize into two (to be simplistic) major factions: the realists ("Realos") and the fundamentalists ("Fundis"). The Realos emphasized a reformist approach and were willing to build coalitions to reach their largely leftist goals, while the Fundis called for a dramatic overturn of Germany's industrial consumer society and saw themselves as a pure opposition group that would not compromise its position by cooperating with other parties. A third faction within the party, the "authentic" environmentalists, who came predominantly from a conservative background and wanted to place ecological considerations above all else, was destined to leave the party fold.

The eventual departure of this faction marked a watershed in the development of the Greens. The chief spokesman for the authentic environmentalists was Herbert Gruhl, a former conservative member of Parliament and author of the influential book *The Plundering of the Planet*. Gruhl argued that the Green party should downplay ideological niceties and base its actions solely on what was good for the environment. Social programs that involved economic growth, even if they had the meritorious purpose of helping the disadvantaged and promoted justice, had to be avoided or the uniqueness of the Green message would be watered down. This vision of an ecology party was at odds with the outlook of the Greens from a leftist, alternative-movement background. These activists had definite ideological and constituent-oriented programs they wanted to institute, which were tangential to ecological questions or, according to Gruhl and his faction, even antithetical. The ideological Greens predominated and were able to get their agenda adopted by the party, prompting Baldur Springman, an "ecological" farmer who was an associate of Gruhl's, to make the somewhat exaggerated complaint that the Greens were becoming a party that was "mainly concerned with the rights of women and of sexual minorities."[34] A year after the founding of the Green party, Gruhl and his followers left to form their own organization, the Democratic Ecology party, which fell into the black hole of fractional electoral support.

It is interesting to speculate, however, what would have happened had Gruhl and the authentic environmentalists been able to forge a coalition based on the primacy of ecological issues — assuming that is what they really wanted and that they were not using ecology to mask a right-wing agenda, as some have charged. Commentators on the origin of the Greens usually contrast the conservative environmentalists with the utopian and revolutionary factions in the party. But a truly ecological party would be revolutionary in its own, perhaps more profound, way. Ecological concerns demand an end to industrial growth and consumer values on which a modern state relies. The concerns of the new left for a more just and humane society may involve the same demands on a general level, but at a specific level the new left has a constituency of the poor and powerless, whose very real present needs sometimes demand policies incompatible with ending industrial growth. A Green party based solely on ecological concerns would have avoided the temptation to rationalize some industrial growth policies as environmentally sound "qualitative growth," as some Greens have.[35] Of course, the fact that Gruhl has sunk into obscurity while the Greens have prospered indicates that this kind of ecological revolution has little attraction at present, at least within the context of political parties.

It might be noted that Earth First!, as a movement, was founded on just this idea of ecological primacy and has become influential in the sphere in which it operates. According to Howie Wolke, Earth First! was founded to "fight for actions and programs that are necessary in order to preserve the health and diversity of our biosphere. We need not worry about how to restructure society in order to accommodate our proposals. . . . We're not in the business of trying to save civilization."[36]

This attitude is similar to that of many Greens at a stage

when they were part of a movement involved in direct action. As they evolved into a political party, however, most Green members wanted to address exactly the question of reconstructing society, though a substantial minority have tried to avoid being enticed by the traditional political process. Thus Petra Kelly, a Green member of Parliament who has acquired an international reputation, has asserted that "as Greens, it is no part of our understanding of politics to find a place in the sun alongside the established parties, nor to help maintain power and privilege in concert with them. Nor will we accept any alliances or coalitions."[37]

In practice, many Greens at the state level have followed a course of moderation after rebukes by their constituency. When, for instance, intransigent Greens in the Hesse state legislature voted *against* a resolution to fight acid rain because the Social Democrat majority refused to include an amendment to shut down all nuclear power facilities, grass-roots Greens were outraged and the Green legislators adopted a more accommodating stance.

The disagreements between pragmatists and hard-liners have predominated in the literature written by and about the Greens. But there is a more interesting matter from a radical environmental perspective. The advent of Green politics raises a question about how far an ecologically oriented political philosophy can be carried out in conjunction with traditional concerns for social justice, such as better working conditions, the equalization of power, and care for the poor and underprivileged. The Marxist background of many West German Greens, especially the so-called ecosocialists in the Realo camp, produced a robust critique of the consumer fetishism of industrial society and its pernicious effects on the working class. But classic Marxism, with its disregard for nature and its nineteenth-century belief in technological progress, offered little aid in understanding the environmental crisis, which was a direct result of technological progress. Marxism had no qualms about the social mastery of nature; it merely disagreed with the oppressive social results of capitalist mastery. Many Greens agreed with the latter view, but as Rudolf Bahro says, "We can no longer *share the spirit*" of Marxism's belief in the Promethean overcoming of nature through industrial growth.[38] Post-

Marxists like Bahro, who played a part in the early development of the Green party, were happy to mine Marxist ideology
for insights into a critique of capitalism, but ultimately it was
a sense of ecological limitations that shaped the contours of a
Green social philosophy.

The tension between Marxism's hyperhumanist critique and
the humbling conclusions of ecology lingers in Green politics,
with some Greens still believing in qualitative growth made
possible by a radical reform of industrialism and others reject-
ing industrial economy altogether. A Green party candidate
from Hamburg, for example, suggested that "if there was really
intensive research" into alternative energy sources, it would
only be a few years before the energy crisis would begin to be
solved.[39] The Hamburg Greens also proposed that "the introduction of the most modern technology" could alleviate many
of the problems of industrial pollution and environmental degradation.[40] It was in part the perception that some of the social
welfare reforms of the Greens would require more technological growth that hastened the authentic environmentalists' departure from the party.

The Greens attempted to reconcile the two perspectives in a
remarkable document, the Federal Programme, published before the general election of March 1983, in which they were first
elected to Parliament. The program attempted to harmonize
the "four pillars" of the Green movement: ecology, social responsibility, grass-roots democracy, and nonviolence. Describing the ecological pillar, it stated: "Proceeding from the laws
of nature, and especially from the knowledge that unlimited
growth is impossible in a limited system, an ecological policy
means understanding ourselves and our environment as part
of nature. Human life, too, is enmeshed in the circuits of the
ecosystem: we intervene in it by our actions and this reacts
back on us. We must not destroy the stability of the ecosystem."[41]

The program went on to call for strict environmental protection, the creation of extensive nature reserves "free from human settlement in which economic activity is carried out only
for the purpose of preservation," legal status for animals, and
the promotion of ecologically sustainable agriculture. It related
these environmental concerns with women's equality, the de-

centralization of industry, a shorter work week, and democratization of society at every level.

Because the Greens are a minority party, they have not been tested to see if indeed their social and ecological agendas are compatible, and, if they are not, which will give way. The validity of Green politics may ultimately turn on this point. In his study of ecology parties, Herbert Kitschelt notes the "ambiguity" of the Green movement insofar as traditional leftist and liberal values,

> appended with a concomitant to ecological compatibility, do not lead to principles that would help ecologists identify specific social institutions necessary to achieve these goals. Private property, contractual relations, and the marketplace were the bedrock of liberalism; socialism called for replacing them by political planning and collective decision making; and anarchism sought to bypass them entirely with informal primary groups.[42]

The Greens, he claims, are unwilling to commit to any of these social institutions.

There are without a doubt inconsistencies and ambiguities in Green politics throughout the world, as the critics of the Greens never tire of mentioning. But that is hardly the issue. The real question is whether the Greens have, in a groping, tentative way, created a politics that can mobilize people to make the kinds of changes necessary to avoid environmental collapse. Perhaps they have melded together the necessary political energy and ideas, perhaps not. It is, however, obvious that the political parties from the right and left now in power in Europe have failed to do so. The dying forests, dead rivers, and nightmarish industrial landscapes stand as proof to their political failure. Ideological consistency in light of this is less important than results.

The spectral existence of the American Green party, in contrast with the thriving European Green movement, proves this point. Under the looming presence of Murray Bookchin, American Greens have worked out a massive and abstruse ideological stance on creating a society without hierarchy. But unlike the European Greens or the radical environmental movement in America, they have not been able to capture the imagination of the public to any degree and have remained in the no-man's-land of third-party politics, no doubt because of their ideological punctiliousness, which has caused them to spend a great deal of energy criticizing Earth First! and Deep Ecology on philosophical grounds. As Foreman sees it, the Greens "seem content to sit around and hammer out detailed agendas and statements of principles and they never do anything about it. Earth First! is the only activist Green group around if you want to look at it that way. The others are only debating societies."[43]

Many radical environmentalists also feel that the Green movement worldwide is too preoccupied with ideology, too remote from the tangible, nonhuman world of nature — characteristics some have attributed to its heritage of European political thought, and others to the already domesticated and humanized landscape in which the Green movement sprang up. For radical environmentalists like the Sea Shepherds and Earth First!ers, who still have a natural landscape to defend, actions in defense of nature have spoken louder than words.

But there are words also, the diverse body of ideas called Deep Ecology, which taken as a whole express the vision behind the activism. Unlike the Greens, radical environmentalists may have let their actions set the finer points of their philosophy, but they have also shaped an ecological sensibility that fundamentally challenges the traditional ethics on which industrial civilization depends. That sensibility deserves closer attention if we are to understand what kind of relationship between nature and culture the radical environmental movement is attempting to fashion.

PART 2

GREEN THOUGHTS

CHAPTER 7

DEEP ECOLOGY

Annihilating all that's made
To a green thought in a green shade.

— *Andrew Marvell,*
"The Garden"

ARNE NAESS, the Norwegian philosopher who coined the term "Deep Ecology," tells the story of a Laplander herdsman who refused to leave the banks of a river about to be dammed. When the police arrested him, they asked why he was willing to break the law for the sake of a river. His answer: "It is part of myself."[1] This prephilosophical sense of identification with the natural world has existed in all cultures in every epoch, and to a greater or lesser degree (mostly lesser) it affects all of us today, even within the confines of our technological culture. Humans respond to sunsets, birdsong, cloud patterns, spiderwebs, moss, the trickle of brooks, without necessarily having any particular environmental ethics in mind and often in spite of the very antienvironmental values their culture imposes on them. In the twentieth century, however, with nature reeling under the calamitous rush of industrial society, this inexplicit affinity with the natural world, not surprisingly, was brought into focus, thematized, articulated, and reevaluated in terms of the social context of industrial humanity. One result was the mainstream, bureaucratic environmental movement, which never got beyond seeing our relationship with nature in anything but utilitarian terms. The other was Deep Ecology.

Although it certainly advocates some standards for social practices and life-styles, Deep Ecology is not so much an attempt to fabricate a relationship between humanity and nature based on philosophical principles it holds dear, as it is a response that flows from a relationship that already exists and that has moved increasing numbers of people to resist in thought and deed what is happening to our environment. When, in 1972, Naess presented his paper "The Shallow and the Deep, Long-Range Ecology Movement" to the World Future Research Conference in Bucharest, he was not claiming to have invented a new philosophy or to have discovered the ideal relationship between nature and humanity. He was only identifying a sensibility that, as the incident of the Laplander herdsman suggests, was becoming more acute and more relevant to social action as hypertechnology surged confidently onward into biological meltdown. Bill Devall, a sociology professor and prominent voice in the Deep Ecology movement, has taken pains to mention that his own involvement with Deep Ecology did not begin with philosophical speculation, but with a personal commitment he felt to prevent the cutting of redwood trees near his community.[2]

Determining what thoughts and actions are best suited to the concerns people have already expressed about their role in ecology is the starting point of Deep Ecology's task — "the search for a viable consciousness," John Seed calls it[3] — while many of Deep Ecology's critics have remained in an academic wasteland still debating whether nature is a meaningful concept. Of necessity, then, Deep Ecology brings together people of diverse traditions and intellectual horizons, all of whom are attempting to come to grips with the reassessment of our relationship with nature that the times require. In the words of Devall, "We are arguing that you can start from Buddhism, you can start from Darwinism, you can start from Native American traditions and work your way to a Deep Ecology position . . . that some kind of environmental humility is in order."[4] Because Deep Ecology begins with a crisis that has deeply touched people of every condition, it is not and has never attempted to be that type of ideology, like Marxism or capitalism, that makes itself sharp by being narrow. "The values that supporters of the Deep Ecology movement share in common," writes Naess, ". . . are the product of a dynamic social movement and cannot therefore be pinned down as if they belonged to a painstakingly formulated philosophy of the relationship between man and nature."[5] Intellectual pluralism is clearly a virtue and without a doubt a necessity if people from different economic systems and cultural backgrounds are going to combat the global threat the environmental crisis represents.

But to say that Deep Ecology is not meticulously formulated is not to say it lacks substance. It encompasses a number of explicit themes, described by Naess as a platform, which when taken together address the issue of our role in nature and how it can be transformed into something less destructive to nature and human nature.

In the book *International Environmental Policy*, sociologist Lynton Caldwell suggests that the breakdown of the world's ecology is causing a shift in environmental sensibilities tantamount to a second Copernican revolution. In the first Copernican revolution, humanity was forced to abandon the erroneous but gratifying view that we and the planet we walked upon were the center of the universe — geocentrism. In the second Copernican revolution, we may be forced to abandon the even more self-aggrandizing belief that we are the center of the moral universe and have a special, privileged status in the biosphere — anthropocentrism. For Deep Ecology, the ethics of anthropocentrism are the key to understanding the environmental crisis.

According to Devall and George Sessions, coauthors of the influential book *Deep Ecology*, the "majority tradition" that dominates modern technological society is characterized by a narrow definition of community, along with centralization of power, the perception of nature as an accumulation of natural resources, and the reign of monolithic ideologies.[6] This is the civilization complex, the combination of institutions and ideologies that drives human societies to exploit nature on a grand scale. As the doomed parade of lost civilizations from Sumeria to Rome indicates, the majority tradition has proved to be adept at building monuments but rather unsuccessful at sustaining the ecology on which it depends. For in Deep Ecology, the critical factor in this lemminglike march into environmental oblivion is the narrowness of the moral community the civilization complex recognizes. Because the majority tradition views the world in utilitarian terms and refuses to include as part of its ethical community the plant and animal communities that sustain it, there is no restraint, at least in the short term, on its destruction of the natural world. In the long run, of course, this myopic utilitarianism turns on itself by depleting the environment to the point that it can no longer be exploited as a storehouse of resources. John Maynard Keynes said that in the long run we are all dead; and cultures, like our own, that are based on an anthropocentric view of the world seem intent on proving him right. The paradox of anthropocentrism is that a world conceived of only with human ends in mind seems destined to become inhospitable to any human ends in the long run.

By identifying anthropocentrism as the root of our troubled relationship with nature, Deep Ecology was taking on more than just a dubious moral precept. It was attacking a cherished principle of the Enlightenment, the raison d'être of capitalism and socialism, the pretensions of the major religions of Judaism, Christianity, Islam, Hinduism, and institutional Buddhism, the central myth of civilization. But Deep Ecology was not alone in this endeavor. Charles Darwin's *Origin of Species* had already undercut the metaphysical underpinnings of anthropocentrism by displacing the notion of the *scala naturae*, the Great Chain of Being, which situated mankind in a privileged station above the "lower" life-forms of a divinely instituted world. Evolutionary theory denies the existence of a hierarchy of beings, declaring that there is only genealogy, similarities and differences arising out of a three-and-a-half-billion-year saga of organic inheritance in which we are only minor players. Taken seriously, evolution means that there is no basis for seeing humans as more advanced or developed than any other species. Homo sapiens is not the goal of evolution, for as near as we can tell evolution has no telos — it simply unfolds, life-form after life-form. Elephants are no more developed than toadstools, fish are no less advanced than birds, cabbages have as much ecological status as kings. Darwin invited humanity to face the fact that the observation of nature has revealed not one scrap of evidence that humankind is superior or special, or even particularly more interesting than, say, lichen.

Along with biological science, the cutting edge of philosophy also turned its back on anthropocentrism. Martin Heidegger, perhaps the most influential figure in philosophy during the first half of this century, argues in *The Question Concerning Technology* and "Letter on Humanism," among other works, that modern societies' preoccupation with human values and human ends since the Enlightenment is but another episode in the "forgetting" of Being in all its limitless possibilities. By trying to fix beings in a utilitarian mode, technological society is converting the world into a "standing reserve" of fungible goods. Things are no longer allowed to present themselves even as objects but are reduced to interchangeable parts in a network of use. This "unworld," as Heidegger calls it, eventually diminishes the humanity it purports to serve as humans themselves are converted into "human resources," with significance only to the degree they are useful to the imperatives of technology.

Michel Foucault, who is the dominant figure in philosophy during the second half of the twentieth century, also rejects the notion that humankind has a privileged status among the things of the world. He attributes this idea to the interplay between institutional power and the human sciences of anthropology, psychology, and philosophy. The knowledge that the human sciences generate is from the start destined to augment, consolidate, and disperse institutional power. It is "true" only in the sense that for Foucault truth is a strategy institutional power uses to manage the behavior of populations. The Enlightenment, with its rational humanism, was not the flowering of the human spirit, according to Foucault's radical critique of the concept of man. Rather, it was merely another totalized value that institutions could apply to everyone at all times for whatever purpose they wanted.

Foucault's grim assessment of anthropocentrism is given support, on separate grounds, by David Ehrenfeld in *The Arrogance of Humanism*. Ehrenfeld indicts anthropocentrism for the sensible reason that it does not work. The naive faith in human reason and innovation has created a technological society that continually promises progress but succeeds only in creating new problems, or, as Ehrenfeld calls them, "unintended consequences." The promise of humanism is never fulfilled but leads to constant, futile innovation; "humanity is on

the march; earth itself is left behind."[7] In *Minding the Earth,*
Joseph Meeker argues for a more tempered evaluation of humanism, claiming that it is time for us to declare the Enlightenment and its humanistic values a moderate success and
move on to a more appropriate way of fitting into the scheme
of things. Many Deep Ecologists agree with this conclusion,
though they would probably prefer to get there by declaring
the Enlightenment a failure.

The pertinence of Deep Ecology to this debate lies in the fact
that it did not stop with a critique of anthropocentrism but
applied that critique to the environmental crisis. In contrast to
anthropocentrism, Deep Ecology proposed that there was another way to experience the world and to order human affairs:
biocentrism. The term "biocentrism" is a misnomer that stuck,
since Deep Ecologists were placing not life, *bios,* at the center
of this new ethic, but the entire community of living and non-
living entities that make up an ecosystem (for this reason some
Deep Ecologists, like Warwick Fox, prefer to use the word "eco-
centrism").

Devall and Sessions place biocentrism in a tradition of opposition to the majority tradition. This minority tradition is
exemplified somewhat in modern times by the thinking of
Thomas Jefferson and Henry David Thoreau, but in the larger
context of human evolution before the rise of civilization, it is
the predominant attitude our species cultivated toward the
natural world, sustained through millennia in the form of primal, tribal societies. The minority tradition embraces a
broader definition of community, which includes plants and
animals, those in the next generation, and the dead. This is the
Penan notion of *Adat,* or "law," on which Mike Roselle has focused his hopes for restoring a balance between nature and
culture. In the minority tradition, under *Adat,* plants and animals and the ecosystem as a whole have rights and therefore
are not to be wantonly destroyed for the short-term gain of a
few individuals, or even an entire generation.

The preferred starting point for the formulation of biocentrism into an environmental ethic is Aldo Leopold. In his *Sand
County Almanac* Leopold expressed the biological equivalent of
the minority tradition in terms of right and wrong — an implied ethical "ought" — in his famous land ethic. Leopold's

land ethic has been parsed mercilessly by critics of environmentalism to discover contradictions and hidden appeals to the utilitarianism Leopold abhorred.[8] Such contradictions may indeed exist, but the sense of Leopold's thinking is clear: we can approach the natural world as a storehouse of resources for our use, or we can give it a degree of ethical standing that permits it to exist for its own sake and in its own way. Although Leopold never denied that humans would not benefit from the latter approach, his emphasis was not on what humans value but on the assertion that nature had value in and of itself, an intrinsic, or inherent, value. As he said, the land ethic would change "the role of Homo sapiens from conqueror of the land-community to plain member and citizen of it."[9]

The biocentric ethics of Deep Ecology distinguishes it from the mainstream environmental movement, which followed the Gifford Pinchot school of thought that the natural world was merely a collection of resources available for human use. Mainstream environmentalism expanded the definition of those resources to include the benefits nature confers on people in the forms of recreation and wilderness experiences. And it also brought some common sense into resource management by preventing the resource industry from determining for itself who would derive the benefits of natural resources and how they would be exploited. Nevertheless, mainstream environmentalism remained within the anthropocentric camp, even if it attempted to pitch its tent on slightly higher moral ground.

Biocentrism also distinguishes Deep Ecology from the New Age and animal rights movements. Although there are some superficial affinities among these movements, they are essentially distinct. As Sessions points out in "Deep Ecology and the New Age," the New Age movement often characterizes the world as sacred and criticizes the approach of industrial society for its materialism and lack of humaneness.[10] But to New Age thinkers humans occupy a special place in the world because we possess consciousness, reason, morality, and any number of privileged traits that make us fit to be stewards over the natural processes of the planet. "The coming age is to be seen as the age of stewardship," says Henryk Skolimowski, all agog: "We are here . . . to maintain, to creatively transform, and to carry on the torch of evolution."[11] In pursuit of this transformation, New Age thinkers laud the use of genetic engineering and the domestication of the landscape to suit human desires. Essentially, then, New Age thinking is anthropocentrism in priestly garb. It disagrees fundamentally with Deep Ecology's call for greater environmental humility, and it spells the end for free nature if realized.

The animal rights movement has a closer relationship with Deep Ecology, since it also disowns the centricity of humanity. It situates its ethics, however, not in the natural world but in a moral world where the imperative to avoid suffering is all. Thus, for animal liberationists, humans have no right to use animals for their own purposes if that use causes suffering. But the animal rights movement is willing to extend the circle of ethical and moral standing only to animals; indeed, it has in mind only those animals that are sentient and hence can suffer. It does not include nonsentient beings such as plants or rivers or mountains, which have to seek protection from some source other than the animal rights movement.

Dave Foreman makes the following comparison between the two positions:

> Deep Ecology is based on a respect or a reverence for the life community which consists of innumerable individuals interacting in a variety of ways; Animal Rights is based on a concern for the well-being of individual creatures foremost. Deep Ecology is ecological, recognizing that life depends on life, that some suffering and pain is inherent in nature, that death is not evil; Animal Rights is compassionate, desiring to eliminate suffering and pain, and is, if taken to its logical extreme, anti-death. Deep Ecology is naturalistic, believing that nature knows best, going beyond good and evil to simply letting being be; Animal Rights in its more extreme forms is anti-nature, arguing that although "primitive" peoples may have eaten meat, we as civilized humans have advanced to a point where we can change our animal natures and operate on an ethical basis, to even claiming that nature is not perfect, that windstorms, forest fires, and predation are bad because they cause suffering.[12]

Animal rights thinkers argue that an ethic against suffering also implies the protection of habitat, since habitat destruction would injure sentient beings; but this ethic does not preclude the exploitation of habitat short of total destruction, nor does it preclude destroying areas, like central Iceland, that support no sentient life.[13]

The use of ethics and appeals to values has created various intellectual problems for Deep Ecology. How the essentially human concepts of rights, values, and ethical standing were to be worked out in application to the nonhuman world became an important topic in the literature of environmental ethics, often resting on such quibbles as whether a biocentric ethic taken seriously would imply that swatting a fly was as morally reprehensible as murdering a person.[14] Some charge that applying the language of rights, ethics, and values to nature in itself is a diminution of the otherness of nature in relation to culture. As John Livingstone says in *The Fallacy of Wildlife Conservation,* "In all ethics there must be the fundamental assumption that the underlying values, beliefs, duties and obligations are fully mutually understood, accepted and shared. In speaking of ethics in the non-human context, we are jabbering into a void. Nature does not need ethics; there is no one to hear."[15]

Some Deep Ecologists might take exception to the contention that nature is not capable of listening, but the basic point is problematical. One response to Livingstone's objection is that nature of course does not need ethics, but we do, and the ethics that allows us to live in a satisfactory relationship with nature (and hence with ourselves) requires that we extend values and rights to the natural world.[16] It is still *our* system of ethics, and in some ultimate epistemological sense they are *our* values, but their effect is to cultivate the kind of environmental modesty that enables the natural world to fulfill its own way of being. This, after all, is the issue in the environmental crisis, not epistemological purity. In this approach, the application of rights and values is a positive expression of what Warwick Fox calls the negative task of Deep Ecology — the decentering of humankind.

Employing ethics and values, which are cultural objects, may appear to contradict the content of biocentrism, and it is undoubtedly incongruous to talk about the rights of nature when the concept of legal rights is traditionally associated with the triumph of culture over nature, or, in Kantian terms, duty over instinct. Perhaps because of this, Deep Ecologists have also attempted to frame the issue of our relationship to nature in ways that are not based on traditional ethics. In a lecture delivered at Murdoch University, Australia, Naess ventured to introduce the concept of the Ecological Self. As with the concept of Deep Ecology, the idea was not new; it was latent in Paul Shepard's eloquent statement that "ecological thinking . . . requires a kind of vision across boundaries. The epidermis of the skin is ecologically like a pond surface or a forest soil, not a shell so much as a delicate interpenetration. It reveals the self ennobled and extended rather than threatened as part of the landscape and ecosystem because the beauty and complexity of nature are continuous with ourselves."[17] Naess, however, was able to articulate the concept in terms that were directly applicable to the environmental crisis. He argued that our self includes not only our ego and our social self, on which the imperatives of ethics play, but also a broader identification with the ecology itself: "Society and human relations are important, but our self is richer in its constitutive relations. These relations are not only relations we have with humans and the human community, but with the larger community of all living beings."[18]

This notion of a preethical participation in the existence of nature had important implications for how the issue of environmental protection might be framed. As Devall sees it, "If we experience the world as an extension of ourselves, if we have a broader and deeper identification, then we feel hurt when other beings, including nonhuman beings, are hurt."[19] In the concept of the Ecological Self, human interests and natural interests become fused and there is no need to appeal to the traditional discourse of rights and values. The integrity of the biosphere is seen as the integrity of our own persons; the rights of the natural world are implied in our right to be human and humane.

Among the second generation of Deep Ecologists who are just entering the debate, there seems to be a desire to push even further beyond the framework of ethics and value theory toward what David Abram calls "a radical theory of nature." Using the phenomenology of French philosopher Maurice

Merleau-Ponty as a point of departure, Abram argues that the reevaluation of our place in nature requires regaining our depth perception, the recognition that our own embodiment as humans is "entirely internal to, and thus wholly dependent upon, the vaster body of the Earth."[20] In this radical theory of nature, nature is not merely an extension of the human self, linked by empathy and the physical principles of ecology; it is its *element*, the realm from which all culture, thinking, and language take shape:

> The region of thought and ideality . . . is always inspired by invisibles that are there from the first perception — the hidden presence of the distances, the secret life of the Wind which we can feel and breathe but cannot see, the interior depths of things, and, in general, all the invisible lines of force that constantly influence our perceptions. The invisible shape of smells, rhythms of cricketsong, or the movement of shadows all, in a sense, provide the subtle body of our thoughts.[21]

From this perspective, reevaluating humanity's role in nature means attending to the primacy of perception, the sense of things, over intermediary cultural systems. The assault on nature becomes not just an assault on value but on meaning.

Devall has said reevaluating our place in nature will require a "new language."[22] Deep Ecology is an ongoing attempt to find the voice to articulate the language appropriate for a time of environmental crisis. Its vigor has come not from trying to evince ultimate truths but in providing a forum in which people can express their deep personal concerns about the death of nature — a forum not found in the mainstream environmental movement or the ideologies of the right and left. As Langdon Winner says, "For a society that has gotten used to all things as potential commodities to be mined, developed, processed, packaged, marketed, used, and discarded, clearly more would be needed to turn things around than just a new set of clever arguments. . . . That is why the ideas of deep ecology, whatever their philosophical merit may be, are basically appeals to the heart."[23] Because Deep Ecology appeals to more than just the logic of technology and responds to the profound spiritual attachment people have to nature, it has attracted a large following of activists among militant environmental groups like Earth First!. Even in the mainstream groups it has made inroads, so that one poll suggested 19 percent of Sierra Club members adhere to beliefs that might be characterized as part of the Deep Ecology movement.[24] In its commitment to addressing the problem of our place in the biosphere, Deep Ecology stole the environmental show and made itself "the most influential new way of interpreting the environmental crisis," according to the editor of the *Amicus Journal,* Peter Borrelli.[25] And those on the left and the right who were trying in vain to capture or defuse the ecology issue were not amused.

CHAPTER 8

THE CRITICS

Nothing is natural.

— *Allan Savory*

THE CRITICS of Deep Ecology and radical environmentalism have been anything but restrained. They have accused radical ecologists of being fascists and Marxists, terrorists and mystics, people with axes to grind and hucksters in pursuit of wine, women, and song, destroyers of local economies, purveyors of distrust, obscurantists, atheists, misogynists and misanthropes. To paraphrase Edward Abbey, if any insult has been left out of the list, apologies are in order.

It is probably best to distinguish between critics who are avowedly pro-environmental and those who see any kind of environmentalism, radical or not, as an impediment to free markets, scientific progress, and other resplendent values behind the plundering and domination of nature.

"This juggernaut," economist Julian Simon writes of the environmental movement, "fueled by false information and special interest values, must be stopped before the world is led too far along the road to disaster."[1] Although the world seems to have already gone a long way toward disaster without any help from environmentalists, this logic typifies one strain of criticism of radical ecology. Its premise is that there is no environmental crisis and that warnings to the contrary are therefore being used as a pretext for carrying out a hidden agenda of apparently sinister special interests — the "dark side of environmentalism," as William Pendley, director of the conservative Mountain States Legal Foundation, ominously puts it.[2]

Roland Barthes has remarked that the mythologies of the right have always been richer, more garrulous, and expansive than those of the left.[3] The antienvironmental critics of radical ecology bear this out. They draw on a dense literature of quasi-scientific texts attempting to disprove the existence of any grave environmental consequences resulting from the activities of industrial society. Most of these works appeared in the wake of Donella and Dennis Meadows's *Limits to Growth*, published in 1972, which articulated the not unreasonable proposition that industrial expansion cannot continue forever in a finite world.[4] Defenders of the industrial society, however, were anxious to prove otherwise. Within a year Cy Adler's *Ecological Fantasies*, H.S.D. Cole's *Models of Doom*, and Petr Beckmann's *Eco-Hysterics and the Technophobes* appeared, preaching an eerie faith in technological innovation and insisting that there never was and never would be an environmental crisis.[5] The chorus was soon joined by Peter Vajk's *Doomsday Has Been Cancelled* and Simon's own *Ultimate Resource*, which emphasized the "replaceability" of nonrenewable resources and the wondrous capacity of the human mind to solve all problems. "The only limits that put restrictions on what we can do with what is available to us," said Simon in a Promethean speech before a resource learning session of James Watt's Interior Department, "are the limits of our own imagination. That is why we have nothing to fear and everything to hope for from technological progress."[6]

The two themes in this literature — that no environmental crisis exists and that technology will be the salvation of humankind — form the basis of a conservative critique of radical ecology. The first assertion contradicts everything people are experiencing about the state of the world's environment and need not be taken too seriously, except as an example of the uncanny ability of self-interest to override common sense. The second claim does set out a real issue, however. Radical environmentalists are necessarily opposed to technological progress, as it has been defined up to the present, because technology is the proximate cause of the destruction of the natural world. To talk about the environmental crisis in its modern context is to talk about the role of technology in human affairs. At least part of the problem has to do with the fact that the "we" Simon used in his speech does not correspond to all of society, but only that part of it powerful and affluent enough to hold the reins of technological innovation. According to Lewis Mumford, throughout history there have been two technological traditions: "one authoritarian, the other democratic, the first system-centered, immensely powerful, but inherently unstable, the second man-centered, relatively weak but resourceful and durable."[7] It is unpleasantly obvious that in today's corporate society the monolithic, authoritarian form of technology predominates. Nobody asked society at large if it wanted nuclear power or DDT or asbestos insulation. Government agencies and multinational corporations make most of the decisions about what technologies are introduced into society, and it is a bold person indeed who would argue that they do so not out of greed and self-aggrandizement, but to benefit the rest of us. As Gregory Davis says in *Technology — Humanism or Nihilism*, "Never before have so few been able to bring about so much damage to so many" as under the authoritarian regime of modern technology.[8]

But even if we lived in Simon's perfect world, where decisions about technological innovation are made democratically and therefore presumably serve all members of society, Deep Ecology would still have to oppose such progress, if, as seems inevitable, the larger *ecological* community were done a disservice. Almost by definition technological progress is directed at converting the natural world into domesticated forms useful to humans: forests into board feet, iron into automobiles, plains into cornfields, wildlands into recreation areas. Deep Ecology, in contrast, stands for the proposition that the natural world should be allowed to remain wild both for its sake and, if we accept the notion of an Ecological Self, our own. Therefore, our attitude toward technology is at the heart of the question the environmental crisis raises: is our species going to step back, reevaluate our role in the ecology, and cultivate some degree of environmental humility, or are we going to continue the practice of environmental imperialism that threatens the existence of millions of life-forms, including our own?

Perhaps a technology that includes the interests of both

the human and ecological communities is possible, but one suspects it would look very much like the crafts that primal peoples pursue and not the high-tech dreams of the antienvironmentalists.

The literature of antienvironmentalism is an interesting case study in sociological denial, but it has its own logic. If there is no environmental crisis, if there is nothing problematic about technology, then radical ecologists must have a hidden agenda for spreading these fables of impending doom. In the book *In Defense of People: Ecology and the Seduction of Radicalism*, for instance, Richard Neuhaus argues that ecological activists are using nature in the same way Hitler did, that is, to legitimize a desire for political power.[9] William Tucker, on the other hand, presents an interpretation of environmentalism in which the desire to protect the natural world is really an attempt by the affluent to retain privileges over the poor. Others see the taint of anti-Americanism within the radical environmentalist's soul. "These people aren't motivated to save more wilderness. . . . They're more a Marxist organization," says Sue Joerger of the Southern Oregon Timber Industries Association about Earth First! and its cofounder Dave Foreman, a former Goldwater supporter.[10] The radical environmental movement, however, could not be more straightforward about its motives. "Our goal," Foreman says, "is to save as much of the natural world as possible,"[11] while industrial society works out its contradictions, one way or another, through transformation or some less congenial occurrence.

The avowedly environmental critics of Deep Ecology have, curiously, been more vituperative than the antienvironmentalists. Emeritus director of the Institute for Social Ecology in Vermont, Murray Bookchin began the attack with an unexpectedly ferocious diatribe in a paper he distributed at the first national conference of American Green activists, in July 1987 (up until then Bookchin's works often received high praise in Deep Ecology literature). The paper castigated Deep Ecology as a "black hole of half digested, ill-formed, and half baked ideas," filled with "utterly vicious notions."[12] Playing to a basically East Coast audience, Bookchin seemed especially eager to associate the movement with California and the New Age sensation: "Deep Ecology has parachuted into our midst quite recently from the Sunbelt's bizarre mix of Hollywood and Disneyland, spiced with homilies from Taoism, Buddhism, spiritualism, reborn Christianity, and in some cases, ecofascism."[13] Brian Tokar, author of *Green Alternative* and admirer of Bookchin, labeled Deep Ecology "outrightly hostile to the human race."[14] Miffed over the fact that *Earth First!* did not publish one of his letters, George Bradford of *Fifth Estate* dedicated an entire issue of his anarchist-oriented journal to denigrating Deep Ecology, linking it to fascism, genocide, corporate power, and, worst of all, bad epistemology.[15] On the other side of the political spectrum, Alston Chase, like Bookchin, got confused, and spent a chapter in his book, *Playing God in Yellowstone*, attempting to show that Deep Ecology was a New Age phenomenon from California caught in a "swirl of chaotic, primeval theorizing."[16]

As has already been noted, there is a fundamental antipathy between Deep Ecology and New Age thinking — so much so that, as will be seen, Bookchin and Chase ironically show a closer affinity to the latter than do any of the Deep Ecology thinkers. And of course Deep Ecology has proponents all over the world, not just in California, with Naess, a Norwegian, and John Seed, an Australian, in the forefront. To the charge of being eclectic, Deep Ecology pleads guilty for reasons discussed in the last chapter. In response to this frequent criticism, Naess turns the tables and asks: "Why monolithic ideologies? We have had enough of those in both European and world history."[17]

It has been suggested that the virulence of the criticism of Deep Ecology is a product of envy.[18] Murray Bookchin has labored for decades in the vineyards of his complex ideology, known as social ecology, with very little — one might say no — result. In contrast, the message of Deep Ecology has been able to touch people's lives and attract a following of young activists, especially among the ranks of Earth First!, who have changed the complexion of the environmental movement in a few short years. As with Marxism, the Hegelian pretensions of social ecology promised a new synthesis, of rationalism and ecology, that would inevitably sweep the world. But for Bookchin the unpleasant reality was that social ecology succeeded only in sweeping the halls of the Institute for Social Ecology. Similar tales of frustration, woe, and excess cerebration can be told about Bradford, Henryk Skolimowski, and other critics of Deep Ecology.

Invective aside, however, the criticism of these and other humanist environmentalists does at one point crystallize into a pivotal issue in the project of redefining humanity's place in nature. "Every contention . . . of Deep Ecology is a human contention," writes Skolimowski in an ongoing debate with George Sessions and Australian philosopher Warwick Fox.[19] Skolimowski's point is that we are destined to be anthropocentric, because our discourse about nature is always a product of human understanding. In his view, everything we say about nature is ultimately only about ourselves and our own society. This position was the tip of a vast epistemological iceberg that humanist environmentalists were eager to plumb.

George Lukacs observes that "nature is a societal category."[20] For humanist environmentalists discomfited by the decentering of humankind Deep Ecology proposed, this singular notion became a saving grace, allowing humanity to be in harmony with nature and yet still occupy the center stage of evolution. With nature-as-societal-category as a premise, it was possible when convenient to claim everything that humanity did — industry, farming, genetic engineering, hypertechnology — was natural. And when it was not convenient, when certain social practices caused obvious disruptions in the biosphere (like continued economic and population growth), it was possible to claim that nothing was natural and that humans therefore had a right to manipulate the physical world in any way they wanted for their own ends. The elastic proposition that nature is a social construct binds together the diverse creeds of humanist environmentalism, whether in the form of Bookchin's social ecology, Bradford's anarchism, Chase's neo-Aristotelianism, or Skolimowski's New Age millennialism.

Perhaps the fullest expression of the societal-category theme as a critique of Deep Ecology and biocentrism appears in Bradford's relentlessly epistemological "How Deep Is Deep Ecology?":

Positing itself as a critique of "humanism" . . . deep ecology claims to be a perspective taken from outside human discourse and politics, from the point of view of nature as a whole. Of course, it is a problematic claim, to say the least, since deep ecologists have developed a viewpoint based on human, socially-generated and historically-evolved insights into nature, in order to design an orientation toward human society. At any rate, any vision of nature and humanity's place in it that is the product of human discourse is by definition going to be to some degree "anthropocentric," imposing as it does a human, symbolic discourse on the non-human.[21]

To what degree it is anthropocentric Bradford is not willing to say. But this is precisely the question to be answered if we are serious about facing the environmental crisis as a real human problem and not a philosophical abstraction. In response to Skolimowski's comments on anthropocentrism, Warwick Fox notes that critics of Deep Ecology often confuse the "weak" sense of anthropocentrism (the inescapable fact that anything a human thinks about nature is indeed a human thought) with the "strong" sense (the belief, which has set in motion the biological meltdown, that humans have a right to dominate nature). The weak sense, the sense Bradford latches on to, is trivial and not really pertinent to the debate about our role in the natural world. The strong sense, however, is exactly the problem that confronts us when we consider the environmental crisis. In Fox's words, "The tautological fact that everything I think and do will be thought and done by a human . . . does not mean that my thoughts and actions need be anthropocentric in the strong, informative, substantive sense, which, again, is the sense that really matters, i.e., unwarranted, differential treatment of other beings on the basis of the fact that they are not human."[22]

Obviously, radical ecologists' views of nature are human views, derived from particular societies — Deep Ecologists have never claimed otherwise, despite Bradford's assertion. And precisely *because* those particular societies are in the throes of an environmental crisis, the role of humanity in nature has become a theme to be explored by Deep Ecologists as well as others. Whether Deep Ecology has done a good job has to be determined by how well it addresses the environmental crisis, how well it changes people's attitudes and fosters activism, not by the inevitable and prosaic fact that the understanding which radical environmentalists bring to the problem is always an understanding of particular people in a social context. Bradford and Skolimowski may very well be right that we can never know nature in itself without the mediation of culture. This epistemological conundrum may be of great interest to traditional philosophy in search of ultimate grounds for knowledge, but it is irrelevant to dealing with the environmental crisis as a social reality, which is Deep Ecology's goal.

To Bradford the philosopher, nothing is natural, and all of nature is merely a bundle of concepts; but that metaphysical conclusion is simply not relevant to how people in the everyday world are experiencing the environmental crisis, where the distinction between nature and culture, rain forests and cattle ranches, old-growth forests and urban sprawl, is all. One does not have to solve the mysteries of how we know what we know to feel outrage at the ecological devastation going on around us. For this reason, perhaps, Bradford's own prodigious intellectual efforts have borne meager fruit in the real world of social activism.

Lukacs's dictum has sent some critics of Deep Ecology in the opposite direction, to the proposition that *everything* is natural, since through the evolution of the human mind (inevitably characterized as "wondrous" or "miraculous") nature was destined to become a social construct (in a literal sense). Bookchin sets the tone:

> This marvel we call "Nature" has produced a marvel we call homo sapiens — "thinking man" and, more significantly for the development of society, "thinking woman." . . . [N]atural evolution has conferred on human beings the capacity to form a "second" or cultural nature out of "first" or primeval nature. Natural evolution has not only provided humans with the *ability* but also the *necessity* to be purposive interveners into "first nature," to consciously *change* "first nature" by means of a highly institutionalized form of community we call "society." . . . Taken together, all of these human traits — intellectual, communicative, and social —

have not only emerged from natural evolution and are inherently human; they can also be placed at the *service* of natural evolution to consciously increase biotic diversity, diminish suffering, foster the further evolution of new and ecologically valuable life-forms, reduce the impact of disastrous accidents or the harsh effects of mere change.[23]

This high-sounding declaration — that humanity occupies a special place in nature through consciousness or reason or culture, and that therefore we have the right, if not the duty, to "change" the natural world (i.e., manage it) — is shared by virtually all the humanist critics of Deep Ecology. Chase, for instance, argues in less operatic fashion that we must play God in nature because nature as we know it is infused with human culture and therefore would deteriorate without our enlightened management. Chase realizes that our control of nature has up to now been unenlightened, but he expresses confidence that humanity possesses the potential reason and ecological knowledge to make nature a better place.

Ironically, this is also the basic position of the New Age thinkers whom Bookchin and Chase use to such unflattering effect in their denunciations of Deep Ecology. Pierre Teilhard de Chardin, one of the New Age's patriarchs, states that humankind's purpose on Earth is to be the "steward" over evolution, creating a humanized landscape without the imperfections of free nature brought about by the Fall, a melding of human mind and biosphere into a new synthesis called the noosphere. As Teilhardian scholar Conrad Bonazi puts it: "In response to the question, What is the earth? [Teilhard] would say, the earth is man. . . . In us, evolution may come to a halt, because we are evolution."[24] James Lovelock also emphasizes the destiny of humanity through hypertechnology, saying, "Our species with its technology is simply an inevitable part of the natural scene."[25] Walter Truett Anderson concludes, along the lines of Bookchin and Chase, that humankind must take up the top of the food chain's burden and become "managing director of the biggest business of all, the business of evolution."[26] In *Out of Weakness*, Andrew Bard Schmookler proposes that human consciousness is leading to a new evolutionary order that is similar to Teilhard's noosphere but that he calls the bio-civisphere, in which enlightened human rationality will manage the world to new heights of peace, plenty, and biological diversity. The unsettling environmental implications of this view of nature are expressed by Peter Vajk: "Should we find it desirable, we will be able to turn the Sahara desert into farms and forests, or remake the landscape of New England. . . . We are the legitimate children of Gaia; we need not be ashamed that we are altering the landscapes and ecosystems of Earth."[27] "We" may not be ashamed of it, but the history of authoritarian technology suggests most of us will regret it. Without a doubt, the animal and plant communities of the Sahara and New England will.

Demonstrating that extremes eventually meet, the Faustian ambition to seize control of evolution that characterizes Bookchin, Chase, and the New Age thinkers is also the vision of antienvironmental theoreticians such as Ron Arnold. In *Ecology Wars* Arnold propounds a new interpretation of humanity's role in nature, called the econosystem, which bears an uncanny resemblance to Bookchin's social ecology views:

> In brief, an econosystem is human ecology. "The" econosystem is the entirety of interrelations between human beings and the physical universe, including all other organisms. A basic premise of econosystemic thought is that humans and our disequilibria are as much a part of the biological construction we call the biosphere as the birds and the whales. While we cause havoc in some places we serve as a potent survival force in others. . . . An econosystem is different from an ecosystem in that human beings, which create econosystems, *characteristically think rationally and make purposeful choices* about their interrelationships with existence. . . . The scientific implications of this definition are profound: the econosystem — human ecology — is not just another example of natural ecology, it is a qualitatively and quantitatively *different kind* of ecology, yet still embedded in the biological construction called the biosphere.[28]

Despite the similarity of this concept to Bookchin's, Arnold reaches an entirely different conclusion about the type of society it entails. According to Arnold, sociologists (not identified by him) have "discovered that the gigantic multinational corporations so hated by environmentalists were perfect models of the new coalitional network style of organization," necessary to face human-caused "disequilibria" in the environment.[29] Humanist environmentalists argue that Deep Ecology's view of nature can be used to justify anything; but as Arnold's unearthly worldview demonstrates, this is all the more true for those who accept nature as a societal category.

Thus Chase, in the name of creating a better natural world, can support the Holistic Range Management technique developed by the highly paid ranching consultant Allan Savory. Savory's basic argument is that we need to graze more cattle on the already overgrazed public lands of the Desert Southwest in order to prevent plant communities from becoming "decadent" and the whole ecosystem from collapsing. Among other problems, Savory's premise that cows play the same ecological role that bison used to is contradicted by the fact that bison never grazed the arid Southwest, but his solutions are exactly what the cattle industry wants to hear. It seems inevitable that the policies of those like Chase, who want to improve on nature, will actually accomplish improvements only for those with enough power and influence to remake the world to their liking.

The desire to redeem nature from a fallen state, or "mere change," as Bookchin puts it, is an ancient theme in Western civilization and, as both Roderick Nash and Lynn White argue, one of the main causes of ecological destruction.[30] This soteriological desire has nothing to do with evolution as a scientific theory. The claim that there is a first nature and a second nature in evolution harks back to the quaint *scala naturae* view of the natural world and its hierarchy of beings (an ironic conclusion for Bookchin, who has spent his philosophical career critiquing social hierarchies). But in the vast web of life there is no first or second, higher or lower, superior and inferior. All life has made the same journey of organic evolution, over billions of years, and those that survive, whether worm or human, are equally, if differently, evolved. Survival is the only index of development in evolutionary theory, not brain size or consciousness, so that every one of the millions of species that dwell on this planet is as evolved as Homo sapiens.

The unwarranted teleology that humanist environmentalists

project onto evolutionary theory is reason enough to dismiss their criticism of biocentrism. But worse is the analysis of the environmental crisis this vision produces. Bookchin, Chase, Schmookler, and the rest certainly deplore the environmental destruction wreaked by industrial society (though it is not clear on what grounds, since industrial society is also the product of the "marvel" of humankind and its institutions), but their answer is to impose yet another regime of cultural control of nature, enlightened by reason and science, which will improve upon nature through domestication and through interventions to reduce both suffering (stop predation?) and the impacts of "mere change" (natural evolution?). But the domination of nature is precisely the problem that has inspired the reappraisal of our role in nature. Antinature is hardly an auspicious stance to take in purporting to address the environmental crisis.

On what grounds humans have the right, much less the obligation, to control the planet remains a question largely unexamined by these thinkers. They usually place great emphasis on the uniqueness of human consciousness and reason, but why the possession of consciousness as opposed to the possession of feathers or poison fangs or the ability to photosynthesize bestows planetary hegemony as a matter of right is a consideration left to dangle. Our ancestors in tribal societies (and tribal peoples still extant) presumably had the same degree of reason and consciousness as Bookchin and Chase have, but they certainly did not come to the conclusion that the human way of being is accompanied by the right to govern evolution, dominate the planet, and improve on nature. And, of course, it is not at all clear that consciousness and reason are unique to humans.

In a sense, humanist environmentalism can be seen as one of the last sputtering candles of the Enlightenment. In laying the theoretical foundations for human rights that have dominated ethics for two centuries, Kant argued that rational beings (humans) are "ends in themselves," meaning that they are worthy of moral consideration and ought not to be used merely as means. Reason and self-consciousness are the critical factors in Kant's ethical system, because only these qualities impart a sense of duty, an "ought," that makes morality possible. Kant's contribution to legal protection of individual rights is undeniable, but it came at a price. By using reason and consciousness as the bases for ethics, he denied moral worth to the entirety of creation outside humanity: "So far as animals are concerned, we have no direct duties. Animals are not self-conscious and are there merely as a means to an end. That end is man. . . . If a man shoots his dog because the animal is no longer capable of service, he does not fail in his duty to the dog, for the dog cannot judge."[31]

This moral demarcation was an invitation to great mischief. By shifting the definition of who had reason, it became a justification for exactly the kinds of indignities to individuals it was intended to prevent. In its wake, the Nazis could fabricate an "ethical system" that condoned persecutions and murders of Jews and other minorities by defining them as *Untermenschen*, subhumans, half animals, bereft of the glorious rationality of the master race. In fact, the Holocaust brought down the curtain on the Enlightenment for many intellectuals. But the ethical justification for the worldwide destruction of nonhuman life because it lacks reason and self-consciousness — that other holocaust of the Enlightenment — continues. Civilization has of course always assaulted nature, but the Enlightenment gave this destruction the highest moral sanction possible. When Bookchin claims his philosophy is "avowedly humanistic," he must also take responsibility for its ethical exclusion of the natural world.[32] As philosopher Christina Hoff points out, "One who accepts this view will believe that all the pleasures and miseries of billions upon billions of sentient creatures had no meaning — no value — until the arrival of rational humanity."[33] This is not a very convivial position on which to build a better world.

At the beginnings of Western thought, the philosopher Heracleitus said that if donkeys had gods, the gods would have long ears. The same applies to humanist environmentalists and their attempts to privilege human qualities over those of other species. If we privilege longevity instead of the particular traits of modern human thought, bristlecone pines would be the superior beings toward which all evolution was tending. If we privilege speed, cheetahs are the pinnacle of the *scala naturae*. And so on. But of course, nature privileges nothing; only particular human societies do. Humanist environmentalists cannot come to grips with the fact that they, their species and its cultural achievements may not be the center of the biosphere after all, may in fact be no more important from the perspective of evolution than the simplest bacteria in a mud puddle. It is particularly unfortunate that the American Green movement, by falling under Bookchin's ideological shadow, where it seems destined to wither, has taken up this burden of saving the sovereignty of humankind.

We find ourselves as men and women in a world declining toward ecological impoverishment and domestication. This is not a philosophical abstraction but a genuine experience that people are undergoing as they see the natural world vanishing into the cultural, wildlands becoming resource parks, rivers turning into industrial sewers, and the incredible abundance of life shrinking into a few favored domestic species such as cattle and sheep. Humanist environmentalists have produced an intellectual bind for themselves in which they cannot articulate the difference between the cultural and the natural worlds, the very distinction that turns the destruction of the environment into an issue. They simply reiterate the problem in a special, quasitheological language of enlightened domination by right.

In contrast, Deep Ecology has tried to keep to the perception that makes the environmental crisis a subject of discourse: the deep feeling people have that nature is under siege by the artificial, destructive cultures of modern humanity. The grief and outrage many people feel at the extirpation of nature is directly addressed by Deep Ecology's message that we must unlearn anthropocentrism and develop a less imperial culture that allows for the continued existence of the natural world. While humanist environmentalism remains in its academic setting, Deep Ecology has inspired people to begin educating the culture of extinction about the necessity of environmental humility. Some have likened the theory and practice of this activism to the civil rights movement of the 1960s, a new civil rights movement seeking moral recognition for that vast part of the biosphere — the nonhuman — that the Enlightenment spurned.

CHAPTER 9

CIVIL DISOBEDIENCE

It is not desirable to cultivate a respect for the law, so much as for the right. The only obligation which I have a right to assume, is to do at any time what I think is right.

— *Henry David Thoreau*

When people are caught up in what is right and are willing to suffer for it . . . non-violence, effectively organized, is an unstoppable force.

— *Martin Luther King, Jr.*

Even if I have to suffer personally, . . . I don't really care about man-made law.

— *Jeffrey Hoffman,*
Earth First! activist

IN *THE RIGHTS OF NATURE* and various articles, Roderick Nash argues that, throughout its history, American democracy has progressively, if begrudgingly, expanded the boundaries of its legal and ethical community to include formerly disenfranchised groups — from slaves to unpropertied workers to women to blacks in the segregated South.[1] This principle, sometimes called the evolving concept of liberty, finds its constitutional expression in the Ninth Amendment, which states: "The enumeration in the Constitution of certain rights shall not be construed to deny or disparage others retained by the people." The conviction that people possess an array of natural rights, whether or not they are enumerated in statutory law, is at the heart of the political theory of Rousseau, Locke, and Jefferson, which substantially shaped the American form of government. It has also legitimized the struggle for equal rights by those against whom the written law discriminates.

For Nash, radical environmentalism is best understood as an attempt to enlarge the circle of legal and ethical standing to include other species and even entire ecosystems. In this interpretation, radical environmentalism is anything but revolutionary and extremist; it borders on patriotic. "If conservation is defined ethically," he writes, "it fits quite squarely into the most traditional of all American ideals: the defense of minority rights and the liberation of exploited groups."[2]

This argument appears in the literature of radical environmentalism. George Wuerthner, forest ecologist and frequent contributor to *Earth First!*, writes:

> At the time of the American Revolution, not all men were as equal as others. It took a civil war to extend certain inalienable rights to all people in our society. Next rights were conferred upon women and other minorities. This recognition of rights has even been extended beyond the human species. Family pets are now protected from inhumane treatment. The next major extension of rights is to the land.[3]

The protests of radical environmentalists also often stress this theme of expanding civil rights. On November 3, 1987, two Earth First! activists, Valeri Wade and Barbara Dugleby, were arrested for unfurling at the foot of the Lincoln Memorial, in Washington, D.C., a banner that read "EQUAL RIGHTS FOR ALL SPECIES." Both the place and the phraseology were chosen for their historical resonance. Commenting on the action in an article entitled "Deep Ecology and the New Civil Rights Movement," Mike Roselle writes: "This new civil rights movement is our only hope. . . . We must shift the focus from land management to civil rights for all people. The tree people, rock people, deer people, grass-hopper people and beyond."[4]

Making an even more direct connection between the civil rights movement of the 1960s and the new biocentric civil rights movement, in 1989 a group of Earth First!ers in Montana demonstrated on January 16, the holiday in honor of

Martin Luther King, Jr., in front of the state's Department of Fish, Wildlife and Parks using a banner that also called for equal rights for all species, with the significant preface: "WE HAVE A DREAM." In a statement to the press, a spokesman declared: "Earth First! shares Dr. King's commitment to individual rights. Today . . . we publicly extend his vision to include oppressed members of our planetary society."[5] The spokesman went on to explain that those members included the large number of species that are forced into extinction every day by destructive human activities.

The American people, not to mention humankind in general, are not accustomed to thinking of such nonhuman entities as mountain lions, forests, and rivers as exploited groups whose rights can be violated. From the perspective of the biocentric civil rights movement, this state of affairs is exactly the problem. In the antebellum South, people were not accustomed to thinking of slaves as human beings who had any claim to the protection of the law. We now find this position both repugnant and ridiculous. In the future, so goes the biocentric argument, we will feel the same toward contemporary society's refusal to extend legal and ethical standing to the "deer people" and "tree people."

The parallel with the civil rights movement is not exact, of course, since radical environmentalism urges society to extend status to entities *even though* they are nonhuman, rather than *because* they are humans deprived of recognized human rights. But, in any case, like their predecessors in the 1960s, many radical environmentalists resort to civil disobedience with the belief in the evolving concept of liberty in mind.

From its origins in Thoreau's famous night in jail, the use of civil disobedience has always involved a complex interplay between questions of conscience and questions of political strategy. Thoreau expresses it succinctly in "Civil Disobedience": "Let your life be a counter friction to stop the machine. What I have to do is to see, at any rate, that I do not lend myself to the wrong which I condemn."[6] The new civil rights movement reflects both these imperatives: on the one hand, to try to stop the machine, to affect the public, to influence legislation; and on the other, to express personal moral opposition to environmental destruction. The two may be complementary, even dependent upon one another, but they have not always existed in harmony in the radical environmental movement.

Appropriately, the first act of ecological civil disobedience was apparently as much a matter of conscience as of politics. On May 21, 1979, Mark Dubois, a leader in the fight to prevent the damming of California's Stanislaus River, chained himself to a boulder on the riverbank just as the floodgates of the dam were about to be closed and the gorge flooded. He had left word of his protest with the agency in charge of the project, the Army Corps of Engineers. In order to avoid drowning Dubois, the corps had to postpone stopping the river's flow until he could be located and taken out of the area. He was, and the floodgates closed. Dubois said later that he did what he did because he felt he "had to make a personal statement." At the same time he had the hope, admittedly somewhat forlorn, that his action might delay the completion of the dam long enough to "give time for long term protection."[7]

For radical environmentalists in the Dubois tradition, civil disobedience is a form of bearing witness to injustice, a way of highlighting the violence of environmental exploitation by standing up peaceably in opposition to it. One Earth First!er who in October 1988 was convicted of disorderly conduct for blockading a timber road in the Kalmiopsis made the following statement to the court upon sentencing:

> It's plain to see that the Earth is dying, our species is committing suicide. But there is still some room for optimism. My friends and I, who work to save the North Kalmiopsis wilderness from roads and clear-cuts, are living proof that there is an alternative to rape, consumption and death; we are living proof that there is still hope for the long-term survival of humanity. For this I feel joy and thanks and not the slightest twinge of guilt.[8]

In this use of civil disobedience as testimony against the despoiling of the environment, a credo of nonviolence is all-important. It is embodied in the Peaceful Direct Action Code many environmental protesters affirm before taking part in a road blockade or tree-sit:

1. Our attitude is one of openness, friendliness, and respect toward all beings we encounter.
2. We will use no violence, verbal or physical, toward any being.
3. We will not damage any property and will discourage others from doing so.
4. We will not run.
5. We will carry no weapons.

The code's emphasis on a personal ethic of pacifism has not always been easy to uphold in the tense conflict between environmentalists and the timber industry over old-growth logging. In the summer of 1987 this became apparent to Randy Prince, a tree sitter who awoke on the fifth morning of his protest in the Kalmiopsis forest to the sounds of a chain saw and angry curses eighty feet below. Prince had conceived of his vigil in religious, ethical terms similar to those characterizing Dubois's protest. He did not even consider himself an Earth First!er, since he had reservations about "people doing anything they want."[9] Unbeknown to him, however, a logger working in the area had struck a spike driven into a tree. The chain had broken and flown off the saw, though without injuring him. The logger decided to take out his dislike of radical environmentalists on Prince. He had cut a third of the way through Prince's tree before the pleas of the tree sitter brought him to his senses. Unlike Ron Huber, who found himself in the same situation a few years earlier, Prince never considered the option of bombing the logger with some heavy object.

The use of civil disobedience as an expression of pacifist values does not always sit well with those radical environmentalists who are more interested in being the Thoreauvian "counter friction" that actually stops the machine and affects the politics of ecology in the nation. This conflict came to a boil in an editorial by Dave Foreman, who chided those who put "excessive emphasis on the personal growth element and forget that it is protecting ecology that counts."[10] Although Foreman later apologized, the division persists. Many radical environmentalists see civil disobedience not as a matter of conscience but as a tactic to make the public aware of the plight of the ecosystem.

If a better tactic becomes available (and for many that means ecotage), then it should be pursued. The point is to harass the resource industry until change is brought about. "In every campaign, there comes a time when you have to escalate the tactics to get results," Roselle explains. "You saw that in the anti-war movement."[11]

Nonetheless, radical environmentalists recognize the difference between the political strategy of the biocentric civil rights movement and that of its predecessors. The most obvious is simply a matter of numbers. Civil disobedience worked for women seeking the vote and blacks seeking to end discriminatory laws because their efforts involved enough people to send a clear message to national political leaders that their demands could not be ignored without disrupting society. In some instances, environmental coalitions have been able to reach this level of influence, as the massive antinuclear protests in Germany proved. While the German protesters may have been motivated less by biocentrism than by the threat that nuclear power poses to human health, Australian radical environmentalists have been able to generate mass protests involving biocentric rights. In a successful blockade to halt construction of a dam in Tasmania, fifteen hundred protesters were arrested and an incumbent prime minister was voted out of office partly because of the controversy.

In general, however, radical environmentalism has no pretensions of being a mass movement and does not expect the huge demonstrations the civil rights and antiwar movements produced. It aims to harass more than obstruct, with the hope that the public awareness it generates will do the rest. Given these circumstances, Bill Devall suggests, direct action "is aimed at a larger audience, and the action should always be interpreted by the activists. Smart and creative communication of the message is as important as the action itself."[12]

A more important difference in strategy stems from the extreme urgency of the environmental crisis. The expansion of civil rights is a laborious process, excruciatingly so for those deprived of their rights. But at least the participants can see the light at the end of the tunnel. For the "constituency" of the biocentric civil rights movement, however, there is often no tomorrow. Once an old-growth forest is cut, it will not grow back for hundreds of years, if ever. Once a species becomes extinct the battle is lost. This sense of urgency often motivates the use of ecological civil disobedience, not to make far-reaching changes in society's views of the environment, but merely to buy time for legal redress or for the emergence of public pressure. The Little Granite Creek blockade was one such rearguard action.

One activist, asking himself what he expected to accomplish by sitting atop a pile of dynamite about to be detonated to build a road into an old-growth stand, considered both the motivations of conscience and politics and reached a Solomon-like conclusion that neither was sufficient in itself to drive the biocentric civil rights movement: "I do not have the energy to stay up all night, sit half a day in a freezing rain, and spend months fighting through a court system just for a matter of conscience. But neither do I have the courage to trip around two acres of wired dynamite charges and go to jail just for publicity."[13]

Whether or not environmental civil disobedience is founded on conscience or political strategy, Nash is probably correct that it is related to a view of law influential at the birth of this country, which held that people possessed natural rights, independent of and more compendious than statutory law, that could thus be invoked in opposition to the mandates of government. The idea was fundamental to early American jurisprudence and political theory, finding its most prominent advocate in Thomas Jefferson. Natural rights theory was still being invoked in Supreme Court opinions as late as 1875,[14] and it continues to lurk in the background of our jurisprudence, for example, in the now largely unsuccessful necessity defense, which allows a person who breaks the law to be considered innocent if his or her actions were carried out with the reasonable expectation of preventing harm to others. The theory of natural rights was incorporated into the traditional civil rights movement, though purged of its Augustinian origins in the belief that reason was the key to discerning natural law.

Environmental civil disobedience can be seen as a descendant of this impeccably patriotic lineage, and it is perhaps with this tradition in mind that both Foreman and Roselle have said they consider their views "conservative."[15] It also prompted Nash to write that the "alleged subversion of environmental ethics should be tempered with the recognition that its goal is the implementation of liberal values as old as the republic."[16] The notion of natural law emerges from time to time in the discourse of radical environmentalism, though it is not particularly important in the writings of Deep Ecology. Thus Earth First!er Jeffrey Hoffman says about his arrest for dressing up as a bear and chaining himself to the restaurant in Yellowstone built on grizzly bear habitat that "the only law I recognize and consider important is natural law."[17] Without invoking natural law specifically, Devall states that direct action in defense of the environment is often taken "because of a sense that there is a higher purpose than the existing laws."[18]

The concept of natural law fell on hard times very early in the history of the United States, for a compelling reason, or at least a reason compelling enough for a nation undergoing the strains of industrialization: it can lead one down many divergent paths. In *The True Law of Free Monarchy* King James I of England could argue that natural law required absolute obedience to monarchy, while Jefferson used it to legitimize the overthrow of kings. Appeals to natural law generate conflict, something Jefferson was willing to live with, but not his more mercantile successors.

It is precisely here that Nash's analogy between the traditional civil rights movement and radical environmentalism seems to break down and the more interesting and unique implications of environmental resistance emerge. In "Deep Ecology and the New Civil Rights Movement," Roselle argues that rather than trying to discover the elusive tenets of natural law, which he suggests humans are probably too "stupid to ever learn . . . or codify or conform to," the biocentric civil rights movement should pursue the more modest goal of espousing a system of human-made laws that will allow us to avoid environmental collapse. Obviously this excludes the system of laws that has developed in the environmentally reckless "civilized" nations, but Roselle points out that such a system existed (and still exists) among tribal peoples, a system he calls Pleistocene law (a term he later abandoned for the Penan word for "law": *Adat*[19]). *Adat* is not some vague predecessor of modern law; it is, according to Roselle, a full-blown jurisprudence in itself, tested over millennia for its ability to support ecologically sustainable societies. Although tribal peoples may have widely different forms of *Adat*, they apparently all share the affirmation that humans are part of a larger ecological community toward which they have certain responsibilities. *Adat* recognizes the rights of all the life-forms in a place, as well as those yet to arrive in the next generation and those that have passed from the scene through death. Elements of *Adat* survive in Devall and Sessions's minority tradition, previously discussed, which they also construe as a positive legal basis for ecological resistance.[20]

In this understanding of environmental resistance, the biocentric civil rights movement is not just an expansion of rights, but also an appeal to a different body of law. It is thus quite subversive, Nash's caveat notwithstanding, in a way the traditional civil rights movement could never be. The evolving concept of liberty has indeed enlarged the ethical and legal community to include those who had once been excluded, but it never before required the community's code of law itself to cease to exist (although Thoreau had no qualms on that score[21]). Civil rights demonstrators were not asking for the demise of American jurisprudence, only for the recognition that minorities had standing in it. The biological egalitarianism of *Adat*, however, is a different matter. It fundamentally opposes the way industrial society goes about its business. It presents itself as an alternative, not an augmentation.

If industrial society is not merely wrong for excluding non-human entities from its ethical and legal community, but also doomed by the ecological havoc this stance has produced, the biocentric civil rights movement is significant precisely because it offers such an alternative. Whether it is succeeding in this project is another matter. The use of civil disobedience by radical environmentalists has focused national attention on ecological issues like old-growth cutting and the biological meltdown, which only a few years ago received little public notice. When dozens of people blockaded a timber road into Oregon's Middle Santiam forest in April 1989, using rocks and logs and even burying themselves in mounds of stone, the media coverage included reports by CBS Evening News, *Good Morning America, Today, Life* magazine, and the *New Yorker* — a level of interest that suggests the biocentric civil rights movement has at least managed to capture the attention of many Americans disturbed over the fate of the environment. In his book on old growth, *Fragile Majesty*, Keith Ervin acknowledges the contribution Earth First! and the radical environmental movement have made to preserving the last great forests by presenting the media with the compelling drama of "brave young men and women risking their freedom, even their lives, to save the forest from rape at the hands of the Forest Service."[22]

At the same time, however, the resource industry and the Forest Service have developed new ways to try to limit the impact of civil disobedience, including the use of intimidation lawsuits, the deployment of the special wilderness police force called pot commandos, and the legally dubious closure of large parts of forests to protesters and the media. The stakes of civil disobedience have gone up, with stiffer sentences being imposed and the use of violence by law enforcement officers, security guards, and timber industry employees on the rise.

Some radical environmentalists have become disenchanted with nonviolent civil disobedience, especially if it emphasizes nonviolence and not disobedience. In an interesting article in *Earth First!*, one activist who participated in the 1989 Middle Santiam blockade suggests that nonviolence is unnatural and has become a dogma to some people, undermining the effectiveness of radical environmentalism. The article begins with a quote from Martin Luther King: "I am only effective as long as there is a shadow on white America of the black man standing behind me with a Molotov cocktail."[23] Many radical environmentalists have always felt that civil disobedience is not enough, that the environmental crisis calls for more drastic action, that it is necessary to pursue the environmental movement's equivalent of King's Molotov cocktail — ecotage.

CHAPTER 10

ECOTAGE

I think we're morally justified to resort to whatever means are
necessary in order to defend our land from destruction, from
invasion.

— *Edward Abbey*

HOW FAR should a person go in defending the natural world?
This is likely to become an increasingly pressing question as
the pernicious consequences of deforestation, the greenhouse
effect, and atmospheric ozone depletion merge into an endless
hot summer of environmental discontent affecting everyone.
All but the most retrograde critics of radical environmentalism
allow for the use of civil disobedience as a legitimate means of
environmental protest (perhaps because the protesters usually
end up in jail). The attitude changes, however, when ecotage
is at issue. The practice of damaging property to prevent
ecological damage is unanimously condemned by government
agencies, industry, and the mainstream environmental organizations. It has become a litmus test of sorts, separating the
radical from the mainstream environmental movement, the
socially acceptable defense of nature from the intolerable.
"Monkeywrenching," Foreman contends, "symbolizes our fundamental strategy for dealing with the mad machine."[1] And in
many ways the opposition it evokes says as much about our
culture as it does about radical environmentalism.

Commenting on the monkeywrenching of a uranium mining
operation on the south rim of the Grand Canyon, one newspaper editorial asked, "Does a road across public land or a mine
on public land do more damage than spikes in trees, or tires

ruined, or a life marred by injury or taken?"[2] The question
concisely states the ethical issue that ecotage raises for radical
environmentalists. Excluding the alternatives of injury and
death, which have to be discussed separately, radical environmentalists have no difficulty answering in the affirmative:
property damage in defense of the environment is a justifiable,
even potentially heroic action. As Peter Steinhart says, this is
the heart of monkeywrenching, "the reminder that we need
more than profits, that we need meaning, wit, vision, dreams.
. . . When forests are cut because a financier has ingested too
many junk bonds, someone deserves at least a pie in the face."[3]
The ethics of satire has real utility to a society when some of
its more powerful members pursue self-interest at the expense
of the whole community, as many feel the resource industry is
doing. Resisting those "alien forces from Houston, Tokyo,
Washington DC, and the Pentagon" is, according to Foreman,
not only ethical, but also "fun."[4]

In Roderick Nash's view, radical environmentalism attempts
to claim a more elevated station for ecotage as part of the liberal tradition of the defense of minority rights, with the com-
plication that the minority in this case is the unprotected
animal and plant communities being destroyed. Like the abo-
litionists of pre–Civil War America, radical environmentalists
break the law out of opposition to a moral wrong. "Many tree-
spikers would argue," writes George Wuerthner, "that the U.S.
Forest Service does not and can not 'own' the old growth trees
any more than a southern plantation owner could own
slaves."[5] In this same spirit, Bill Devall makes the comparison
between ecoteurs and resistance to Nazism: "I don't think anyone would have any qualms about committing sabotage
against concentration camps, and yet everything done at
Auschwitz was 'legal' under Nazi law. Ecotage also responds
to principles higher than secular law in the defense of place."[6]

Those higher principles may be part of the liberal tradition,
but they also flow out of the particular ethical implications of
Deep Ecology itself. In defining ecotage, Foreman remarks,
"It's basically a means of self-defense. It's becoming part of the
wilderness, and saying don't go any further, don't go into this
place [to destroy it]."[7] This position follows from the idea of
the Ecological Self articulated by Arne Naess, Devall, and other

Deep Ecologists. If our selves belong to a larger self that encompasses the whole biological community in which we dwell,
then an attack on the trees, the wolves, the rivers, is an attack
upon all of us. Defense of place becomes a form of self-defense,
which in most ethical and legal systems would be ample
grounds for spiking a tree or ruining a tire.

Self-defense as an argument for ecotage becomes less compelling to radical environmentalists, however, when defense of
place involves injury to other persons. The subject arose in
1987 when a worker in Louisiana-Pacific's Cloverdale mill was
lacerated by fragments from a saw that shattered on a tree
spike. Although the incident almost certainly had nothing to
do with radical environmentalism, it produced a firestorm of
criticism from all sides, and even some Earth First!ers felt
obliged to distance themselves from monkeywrenching. Mainstream environmentalists like Harold Gilliam saw it as the evil
fruit of Deep Ecology, whose biological egalitarianism led to
the "implication" that "although spiking could kill mill workers, it would serve them right for killing trees."[8] Industry reaction has been less subtle. The editor of *Forest Industries*,
David Pease, advises his readers that "as for the spikers, if I
could warp logic and law to my own notions like they do, I
would shoot them down (apologies to Hunter Thompson) like
the yellow curs they are."[9] President of Louisiana-Pacific Harry
Merlo remarks, "Terrorism is the name of the game for radical
environmental goals."[10]

Because tree spikers are trying to prevent logging, not hurt
people, the issue is the risk of *unintentional* harm, rather than
the willful attack on innocent parties that defines terrorism.
"To use the word 'terrorism' for monkeywrenching is to totally
cheapen the real meaning of what terrorism is all about," Roselle says, "and what people do when they are really desperate."[11] Real terrorists would not be spiking trees, he adds, but
spiking Merlo. Some radical environmentalists find that any
risk of harm to humans is unacceptable, while others do not,
so long as every reasonable precaution is taken to make sure
no one is hurt. "Risk to humans hasn't stopped the timber industry from cutting old growth," Roselle points out, referring
to the fact that the forest-products industry has the worst
safety record of any enterprise in the United States, which fre-

quently leads to disputes between management and workers over safety conditions. "It's strange they should use that as an argument against responsible monkeywrenching."[12]

Nevertheless, if ecotage raises ethical questions for radical environmentalism, questions its critics are eager to explore and its advocates explain, it also raises questions about the environmental ethics — or lack thereof — held by society at large. With growing numbers of people willing to break the law to protect the environment, our culture is forced to confront the fact that its own ethical choices concerning ecotage sometimes seem strangely out of place in the context of an environmental crisis unparalleled in history. In the long run this illumination may be a much more important consequence than any amount of dollar damages done to bulldozers.

Under present law a timber company can purchase the trees in an old-growth forest, cut them down (often at taxpayers' expense), and leave the forest biome so disrupted that the animal and plant communities it previously supported perish or migrate. Erosion may make local streams unsuitable for the spawning of salmon and therefore affect the ocean food chain hundreds of miles away. Pursued on a large scale, as is certainly happening today, the fragmentation of forests will increase global warming and inevitably lead to a higher rate of extinction, as the findings of island biogeography demonstrate. All this is totally legal. In contrast, those who try to preserve the forest by spiking the trees are guilty of vandalism under present law. If there is something slightly absurd about a scenario in which those who want to destroy a forest can accuse those trying to preserve it of property damage, it is an absurdity we may no longer be able to afford. The notion that the world is an assemblage of interchangeable resources to be sold to the highest bidder may satisfy the nostalgia for 1950s-style endless growth, but it is belied by the gravity of the environmental crisis we face. The world is a web of interdependent living communities, not a department store.

And yet, when faced with a choice between ecotage and environmental havoc, between spiking trees and losing an old-growth forest, our society — or at least those who speak for it in government, industry, and mainstream environmental organizations — continues to condone the latter and condemn the former. This conclusion is usually reached by an appeal to two principles: the rule of law and property rights.

In a very thoughtful discussion of ecotage, Peter Steinhart explores its affinity with the American values of independence and fairness but concludes that it must not be condoned, since "one form of lawlessness tends to invite the other."[13] This is the most common argument mainstream environmentalists use to criticize ecotage, and it may indeed be true. But the charge of indiscriminate lawbreaking can also be made against many critics of monkeywrenching. Ecotage itself has arisen against a vast backdrop of illegal practices on the part of the resource industry and government agencies:

November 1973 — U.S. District Court rules that excessive clear-cutting in West Virginia's Monongahela National Forest is illegal under the Organic Act of 1897.

August 1976 — U.S. District Court orders a halt to further clear-cutting in the national forests of East Texas, citing violations of the Multiple Use–Sustained Yield Act and the National Environmental Policy Act of 1969.

March 1977 — U.S. District Court prohibits Forest Service use of the herbicides 2,4,5-T and Silvex until an adequate environmental impact statement is prepared for Oregon's Siuslaw National Forest.

October 1982 — U.S. Ninth Circuit Court prohibits development in roadless areas in California due to inadequate environmental impact statement (*California* v. *Block*).

May 1983 — U.S. District Court finds the Forest Service in violation of Native American religious freedom, prohibits logging in the 67,000-acre Blue Creek roadless area of California on the grounds that it would violate NEPA, the Wilderness Act, and the Administrative Procedure Act.

May 1983 — U.S. District Court finds that herbicide use in six watersheds of the Siuslaw National Forest and the Bureau of Land Management's Medford district in Oregon is illegal due to lack of an adequate environmental impact statement.

July 1983 — U.S. District Court declares the Bald Mountain road in the Kalmiopsis illegal (*Earth First!* v. *Block*).

October 1983 — U.S. District Court issues an injunction against timber sales in the Kettle Planning Unit, Colville National Forest, Washington, due to inadequate environmental impact statement.

January 1984 — U.S. District Court in Wyoming closes a fifteen-mile Forest Service snowmobile trail through grizzly bear habitat due to an inadequate environmental impact statement.

The list can be extended forward and backward in time with alarming continuity. In violation of the Multiple Use–Sustained Yield Act and the National Forest Management Act, one third of the forests in the Pacific Northwest (private and public) were understocked (either inadequately or never replanted) in 1982. Steinhart himself cites the fact that when the California Water Resources Control Board reviewed one hundred timber-harvest plans, it concluded that more than half violated forestry rules and in many cases had been approved without a forester's even having visited the site. While Harry Merlo complains of the lawlessness of radical environmentalists, his own Louisiana-Pacific Corporation has been convicted of antitrust violations and forced to pay $1.5 million in damages. In this context of rampant disrespect for environmental law, the refrain that lawlessness begets lawlessness seems to be an argument *for* ecotage, not against it. Taking the point to an extreme, Devall even suggests that "there are already existing laws on the books to protect the environment, and in a certain sense, strongly supporting those laws means that you *have* to engage in sabotage because the government is not supporting them at the present time."[14]

Of course, radical environmentalists feel obliged to commit ecotage even where environmental laws are being obeyed if in their estimation the statutes are inadequate to preserve natural diversity. This position has led a number of critics to compare radical environmentalists with such an interesting array of characters as Lenin, Oliver North, radical antiabortionists, and others perceived to hold the Machiavellian position that the ends justify the means. As the last chapter showed, however, statutory law has always had an ambiguous status in America. Most everyone agrees we would be a poorer people indeed if we had allowed appeals to the rule of law to quell the civil rights movement or the antiwar protests, where in retrospect the ends did indeed seem to justify the means. As a general proposition, Americans have never had an obsequious attitude toward the law per se, but rather a respect for the many good laws the democratic process tends to produce. The rule-of-law argument against ecotage really comes down to an assertion that a defense of the natural world is not of the same caliber as ending discrimination or stopping a senseless war. Whether that contention will continue to be intelligible as the consequences of environmental degradation begin to be felt in people's everyday lives remains to be seen. But it tells us something about how industrial society values property over the natural world and its efflorescence of life.

In 1983 Eugene Hargrove, the editor of *Environmental Ethics*, condemned the use of monkeywrenching as a tool for environmental protection, noting that even if breaking the civil law was defensible under some natural rights theory, Locke himself had included property as among the most precious natural rights. Needless to say, industry has consistently made even stronger arguments that ecotage is an assault on that most American of values, property. In fact, the sanctity of property in the extreme forms Locke and industrialists have maintained has never been accepted by American jurisprudence. It was intentionally left out of the Declaration of Independence's list of inalienable rights — "Life, Liberty and the pursuit of Happiness" — since Jefferson had a genuine distrust of the mercantile tenor behind property law. It failed to appear in the Preamble to the Constitution, alongside justice, tranquillity, general welfare, and liberty, as one of the purposes of the document. It emerges as a right for the first time in the Fourteenth Amendment's due-process clause. Even here, however, American jurisprudence never recognized property as an inalienable right, but rather as a "bundle of rights" (to use the Supreme Court's words) and responsibilities.[15] The most unregenerate industrialist would have to admit that if everyone used their property as they wanted, by polluting the air and water, for instance, everyone's rights would be impaired in the long run. Congress and state legislatures have already spoken, no doubt not forcefully enough, on the right of the public to regulate private property to prevent pollution and other forms of environmental degradation. The harvesting of trees on the private forests of timber companies is likewise subject to state regulation, inadequate though it may be.

The right to property in its abstract, metaphysical form is not at issue in the ecotage debate, but instead what kinds of property rights society should recognize in relation to environmental protection. Ecotage compels our culture to face the fact that it currently considers a bulldozer of higher value than a living, intact ecosystem that supports a diverse community of plants and animals. In the future, as more and more species become extinct and forests are recognized for their role in maintaining a livable biosphere, this value system may be judged equal to such historic extravagances as the burning of women suspected of witchcraft or the internment of loyal Asian-Americans during World War II.

As the Cloverdale incident demonstrates, ecotage also seems inescapably to invite some examination of the morality of violence in the defense of nature. Sue Joerger of the Southern Oregon Timber Industries Association raises the issue in its starkest terms, claiming that "until these people start saying 'We don't think it's worth human life to save these areas,' they're in a sense condoning murder for saving a roadless area."[16] As already mentioned, Roselle has pointed out the equivocation in this position: the timber industry is quite willing to risk human lives in order to develop a roadless area, and can actually predict fairly accurately how many workers are going to get hurt or die during the course of an operation (an ability not unique to timber companies but possessed by all industries). This does not make timber executives murderers, in the usual sense of the word, any more than ecotage makes radical environmentalists terrorists. But it does define a curious ethical stance: our society — or at least that portion of it in control of industry — is willing to risk injury to humans for economic reasons, but not to preserve the natural world.

Even this almost sacrosanct position that human and non-human life are not on the same par is undergoing change, however, in some parts of the world as the biological meltdown raises troublesome questions about the value of the wild and wildlife. Faced with the imminent extinction of Africa's black rhino population at the hands of poachers who sell the horns for their supposed aphrodisiac properties, the government of Zimbabwe instituted a shoot-to-kill policy against the poachers in 1988. More than sixty poachers have been killed. In response to the criticism the policy has generated, the head of the anti-poaching patrol said, "When a group of Arabs makes an assault on the British crown jewels there is a skirmish and lots are killed — to protect rocks — and nobody minds. Here we're protecting a world heritage, but it happens to be animals and that hangs people up."[17] The moral choice here is complicated by the fact that the government has a considerable economic stake in ensuring the survival of the rhinos, since wildlife tourism is big business in Zimbabwe. It should be remembered that medieval feudal lords also executed poachers, for reasons somewhat less magnanimous than the love of nature. Still, this new "lesser of two evils" problem, with its choice between watching a species become extinct or using violence to prevent it, is likely to confront society in different forms again and again in years to come, and there is no guarantee events will deal kindly with Joerger's moral certitude. A century from now the children of ecological scarcity may look back and consider the powerful interests that run the resource industry the real terrorists.

Ultimately, like baroque music, the ethical arguments that swirl around the practice of ecotage are fascinating and seemingly endless. But the main point remains: even in our technological society, people feel an attachment to the natural world, and some of them are willing to destroy the offending implements of technology to defend the environment on the basis of a number of ethical and practical grounds. Green protesters trying to stop the expansion of the Frankfurt Airport attacked police barricades, because, as one observer puts it, "they loved their little bit of green even though the trees were no thicker than your arm."[18] Similar feelings of commitment motivate Earth First!ers to spike two-hundred-foot-tall Douglas firs in the mighty forests of the Pacific Northwest. Radical environmentalists consider these actions ethical, even "the

most moral of all actions," to quote Dave Foreman.[19] Those in
control of our ecology do not. The two positions are not destined to be reconciled in our lifetime, and from the radical
environmental position, they do not have to be. Since the ethical question has already been settled for most radical environmentalists, the more important issue is what effect ecotage is
actually having on the environmental movement and the culture in general.

"Ecotage will only further corrupt and brutalize a society
which is already sufficiently corrupt and brutal," writes Ed
Marston of *High Country News.* "The environmental movement
must decide whether it is a reform effort, working within society to improve society, or an apocalyptic movement not subject to ordinary rules."[20] This was not a new criticism, nor did
it always fall on deaf ears within the ranks of radical environmentalists. One of the first editors of *Earth First!*, Peter Dunstad, resigned over the journal's sympathetic coverage of
monkeywrenching, and the debate has flared up intermittently
ever since. But by presenting the terms "reform" and "apocalyptic" as opposites, Marston suggests that ecotage is a product
of the specific worldview of radical environmentalism, whose
detrimental result is lawlessness.

Even if radical environmentalism did not exist, however, industrial society would probably still have to contend with ecological sabotage in some form or other as its dangerous and
intrusive technologies infringe on other values besides productivity and efficiency. In the mid-1970s, for instance, the decidedly unrevolutionary farmers of northern Minnesota carried
out a wave of sabotage against high-voltage electrical transmission towers the government forced through their rural community as part of an energy project involving several coal-fired
power plants. Among other things, the farmers cut bolts on the
legs of the towers, earning them the name bolt weevils. Over a
year and a half, thousands of farmers protested, and 140 were
arrested for various acts of sabotage and civil disobedience. In
what was the largest mobilization of law officers in Minnesota
history, 215 state troopers were called in, eventually joined by
FBI and private security agents. There were a number of violent confrontations in which the police beat farmers, even per-
manently paralyzing one. Arrests were made on the flimsiest of

evidence; people were taken from their homes, detained long enough for the towers to be constructed on their property un-opposed, and then released. Nonetheless, the farmers contin-ued their resistance to the end out of concern over the health hazards that the high-voltage wires represented.[21]

Similarly, in the early 1970s the forerunner of today's mon-keywrenchers, a man known only as the Fox, undertook a one-man crusade against Chicago-area polluters by plugging fac-tory smokestacks, closing off industrial drains in rivers, and, in his most famous activity, dumping jars of fetid industrial effluent on the plush carpets of executive suites of corporations like U.S. Steel. The response of the companies was not unlike the present reaction of the timber industry to ecotage. A vice president of U.S. Steel was reported as saying of the Fox, "He should be called the hyena because that's what he is."[22] The Fox was not appealing to any special environmental ethic, just the commonsense notion that pollution is a threat to life. When asked over the phone by a member of the Advisory Committee on the United Nations Conference on the Human Environment if his tactics were not illegal, the Fox answered, "No more so than if I stopped a man from beating a dog or strangling a woman."[23]

The rise of radical environmental ecotage in the 1980s was yet another response to the seemingly boundless expansion of technology and its destruction of values that do not fit into the scheme of resource utilization. (In the dedication to *Ecodefense*, Foreman includes both the bolt weevils and the Fox.) That the ecotage of radical environmentalism has become so wide-spread suggests that the values it upholds — wilderness, bio-centrism, *Adat*, Deep Ecology — are touching the lives of a growing number of people confronted with the grievous results of technological culture.

Undoubtedly there is an apocalyptic strain in all this, if by that we mean the belief that industrial society is so harmful to the ecology that it is unsustainable. Many mainstream envi-ronmentalists also share this belief, which is supported not only by common sense but also by the findings of respected scientists. Marston, however, uses the term to suggest more than just the conviction that the biosphere is in trouble. He intends it to describe a recklessly emotional and revolutionary attitude on the part of radical environmentalists: "Rage is understandable, it is natural. . . . But if we simply act out our rage, we add to the problem. The rage must be used to stop the destruction — not to destroy in a different way."[24]

Marston is right to use the word "rage" in describing the reaction radical environmentalists feel toward the destruction of the natural world. But radical environmentalists are not simply acting out their rage; on the contrary, the theory and practice of ecotage are as well thought out as the politics of reform. In *Ecodefense,* Foreman develops the notion of strategic monkeywrenching, based on the belief that if profit brings the resource industry into the wilderness, loss of profit due to continuing equipment damage, production delays, and increased security will drive it out. "The cost of repairs, the hassle, the delay, the down-time may just be too much for the bureaucrats and exploiters to accept if there is a widely-dispersed, unorganized, *strategic* movement of resistance across the land," he concludes.[25] Such a movement has developed, though not on the scale radical environmentalists would wish. Ecotage probably costs the resource industry and government agencies between $20 million and $25 million annually.[26] De facto wilderness is still being developed by the resource industry and the Forest Service, especially old-growth forests, but as radical environmentalists point out, they have $20 million or so less every year to do it with. One can only speculate as to the effect that has had on the decisions made in corporate boardrooms.

Most radical environmentalists do not believe ecotage is a substitute for major social changes; rather, it is a stopgap measure — "damage control," Foreman calls it — to protect as much of the natural world as possible until such change is brought about, one way or another. "Tree-spiking is only a last minute measure," according to Wuerthner, in his more modest assessment of strategic monkeywrenching, "a stalling tactic used to preserve options in the hope that an enlightened citizenry will one day appreciate more fully the need for the conservation of natural ecosystems. Tree-spiking . . . may not be a rational response, but it may be the right thing to do."[27] In Devall's estimation, "ecotage is like working in the emergency room of a hospital."[28]

While Wuerthner and Devall demonstrate a certain amount

of faith that industrial society will somehow deviate into sense, other radical environmentalists are not as sanguine. "Quite honestly," writes Howie Wolke,

> I doubt anything, including thoughtful radicalism, will bridge the gap between saving some wilderness today and creating a society that lives within its ecological means. . . . It's my guess, though, that thoughtful radicalism will save some biotic diversity in the short term, and allow more to be saved and restored for the longer run. Then when [industrial society] finally, mercifully chokes on its own dung pile, there'll at least be *some* wilderness remaining as a seedbed for planet-wide recovery.[29]

Ironically, perhaps, the most tangible impact of ecotage may be its assistance to the cause of reform. The pseudonymous Earth First!er T. O. Hellenbach writes in a chapter in *Ecodefense* entitled "The Future of Monkeywrenching" that "the actions of monkeywrenchers invariably enhance the status and bargaining position of more 'reasonable' opponents. Industry considers mainline environmentalists to be radical until they get a taste of real radical activism."[30] Devall also points out that the disruption ecotage causes is often needed to force those engaged in environmentally destructive activities to reconsider their actions and entertain the kinds of compromises reform environmentalism seeks. "Ecotage upsets, disturbs, and distresses ordinary attitudes and policies of officials of giant corporations or government agencies," he writes, "because it is predicated on emotional responses to the situation."[31] At the very least it may bring public attention to an issue in a way bureaucratic environmentalism has not been able to rival. The very limited reforms that mainstream environmentalism was able to bring about in the 1980s were possible only because of the publicity monkeywrenching brought to a movement that had become mired in an unintelligible world of environmental impact statements and flowcharts. Some of the lawyers that participated in the spotted owl case admit off the record that it was Earth First!'s confrontational tactics that created the political climate necessary for bringing the complex case to court. As Hellenbach explains it: "Press coverage of monkey-wrenching can . . . alert the public in a manner that hurts the corporate image. . . . Scientific studies of propaganda and the press show that the vast majority of the public remembers the news only in vaguest outline. Details rapidly fade from memory. Basic concepts like 'opposition to logging' are all that are retained."[32]

Whether or not ecotage actually brings people to the negotiating table, Devall's observation about the disturbing effect ecotage has on industry and government is thought provoking. Why do the actions of the Fox, the bolt weevils, and radical environmentalists all arouse such fierce reactions from those in control of our ecology, reactions that often seem wildly out of proportion to the actual damage done? If the rhetoric of government and industry was attributable to a concern for human life and limb, it would be understandable, perhaps. But humanitarian impulses scarcely seem a credible explanation for the behavior of U.S. Steel, Louisiana-Pacific, or state troopers willing to beat farmers. Respect for the law is also often given as the reason, but, as we have seen, the history of corporate America in general hardly inspires confidence in management's unflagging dedication to legality. If different values are at stake in the practice of ecotage, they may be the real source of discomfort for those in control of the ecology when, through ecotage, people show they feel enough passion to put their values into practice. This is what ecotage does, after all — realize on a small scale the kinds of values technological rationality denies. The Fox's preference for clean air and water triumphed momentarily whenever he plugged a drain or smokestack. The bolt weevils kept their farms free from health hazards every time a power line fell. And the values of biocentrism that the modern ecoteurs espouse can claim a moment's victory when a bulldozer is decommissioned or a tree spiked. For all its monolithic power, the rationality of technological society suffers a loss, even if only temporarily, whenever ecoteurs strike.

Marston argues that these temporary victories are deceiving, because in the long run they will weaken reformist efforts, the only real hope for salvation. But a good argument can be made, based on the gravity of the biological meltdown, that reform environmentalism has already failed, both on its own political terms and on the more exacting terms required to maintain

ecological stability, big wilderness, and the continued existence of countless threatened species. Reform environmentalism had a chance in the early 1970s to embrace the kinds of
comprehensive changes that might have averted the present
crisis, but it squandered that opportunity. The ecological militancy of the 1980s was a consequence, not merely an antago-
nist, of the mainstream's moral timidity.

The rising tide of ecotage may come to nothing, but, rather
than being apocalyptic, it seems to be an attempt to walk the
fine line between an already failed reform movement and a
futile revolutionary response. Monkeywrenching "does not aim
to overthrow any social, political or economic system," writes
Foreman in *Ecodefense*, adding that "even Republicans can
monkeywrench."[33] Similarly, Roselle states, "I think in this
country there is a softer technique [than revolutionary resis-
tance]. Monkeywrenching isn't guerrilla warfare but monkey
warfare and people can support it because it's not threatening."[34] At the same time, radical environmentalism is based on
the premise that reform efforts will never be enough: "Our political approach is one of monkeywrenching," says Foreman.
"We file appeals and lawsuits, write letters and make wilderness proposals, but we aren't fooled for a minute that we are
engaged in liberal reform. We're sticking a wrench in the system, we're slowing it down, we're thwarting it, we're kicking
it in the face!"[35]

This curious tightrope walk between reform and revolt, hope
for change and the realization that change will probably fail,
is the political territory radical environmentalism has staked
out for itself in confronting the dynamics of industrial society.
It may be the only principled way to approach the challenge
of industrial ecocide at this point in history. The experience of
Europe suggests that societies are virtually incapable of responding to the environmental crisis until the environment is
so degraded that human health and prosperity are directly
threatened. By then much of what the environmental movement wants to preserve is gone. As Robert Paehlke notes in
Environmentalism and the Future of Progressive Politics, because
environmentalism "is not an ideology of self-interest, and because self-interest is deeply ingrained in our society, economy,
and polity, environmentalism does not easily attract an in-

tensely committed mass following."[36] This is all the more true
for the radical environmental movement, which does not support even the marginally self-interested values of recreation
and resource efficiency.

Peg Millett, an Earth First!er arrested in 1989 for allegedly
trying to knock down an electrical tower in bolt weevil fashion,
defined monkeywrenching as "the dismantling of the present
industrial system, but I would define it as dismantling the machinery *very carefully*."[37] This last condition, the idea of cir-
cumspect subversion, is an evocative idea. The aspiration of
carefully disarming the danger to the natural world as best as
one can while the reformers reform and the conservatives resist
suggests a unique response to a technological society whose
institutions are probably too powerful and remote to respond
to the environmental crisis before it is too late. Herbert Marcuse's hope in *One Dimensional Man* that students and workers
would someday develop an effective resistance to technological
culture has proved an academic's pipe dream. But radical environmentalism, through ecotage, seems to have taken a wav-
ering step in that direction. In the estimation of Howie Wolke,
who spent six months in jail for pulling up the survey stakes
of a road being constructed into a pristine forest, "the future
of monkeywrenching is that it is going to continue to be more
and more widespread, more and more people are going to en-
gage in it, some people are going to be caught, and some people
are going to go to jail. But I want the Forest Service and [the
Bureau of Land Management] and Exxon and Louisiana-Pacific
to know that their tools of destruction are not safe and no
longer will be safe. We will continue, we will expand, and monkeywrenching will become an effective tool for protecting the
wild portions of the Earth."[38]

The reaction of the resource industry and government agencies over the past several years suggests they have taken
Wolke's words to heart.

PART 3

REACTION

CHAPTER 11

THE TRIALS OF
RADICAL ENVIRONMENTALISM

I'm proud to be here facing harassment by the FBI. I think I'm here because I've been effective in bringing attention to the crisis on this planet.

— *Dave Foreman*

ON JUNE 1, 1989, Dave Foreman awoke to tangible proof that the radical environmental movement he had helped shape over the past decade was beginning to attract the attention of people in high places. Obliged to sleep with earplugs because his neighbor's Doberman pinscher barked, he did not hear the knock on the door of his suburban Tucson home, or the scream of his wife, Nancy, or the click of guns being cocked. What he saw, however, was three FBI agents wearing flak jackets and brandishing .357 Magnums in the stance made all too familiar by bad television cop shows.

They rousted him from bed and placed him under arrest. The charge: participation in a conspiracy to cut electrical transmission lines leading from three nuclear power plants in the western United States. The flamboyant history of radical environmentalism was about to take a new, unpleasantly serious twist.

At about 8:15 on the night before Foreman was arrested, the moonless desert sky near Wenden, Arizona, had suddenly taken on an unnatural orange glow. A brilliant flare, the type the military used in Vietnam, had been fired into the air, signaling some fifty agents of an FBI swat team hidden in the brush to close in on the figures crouched under an electrical tower. Acting on information from an undercover agent, the team arrested two men in their late thirties who were allegedly using a propane torch to cut down an electrical tower near a pumping station along the Central Arizona Project, a colossal water supply system opposed by environmentalists. Marc Baker, a Ph.D. biologist, and Mark Davis, an antinuclear activist, tried to get away, but the boards they had taped to their feet to hide their footprints tripped them up. To the FBI's chagrin, a third person somehow evaded the small army of law officers, despite pursuit by agents with bloodhounds, on horseback, and in two helicopters, which were known menacingly as Black Hawk and Night Stalker and were equipped with infrared and night-vision devices. Peg Millett, a longtime Earth First! activist from Prescott, Arizona, was arrested the next day at the Planned Parenthood Center where she worked and charged along with the two men. For those who knew the exuberant, well-liked Millett, a self-described "redneck woman for wilderness," it was not surprising that she would give the FBI a run for its money.

As they were leading Foreman, dressed only in his shorts, off to prison, the FBI agents gave his wife some unsolicited marital advice to the effect that she should save her own neck by divorcing the controversial environmental activist. Coincidentally or not, that day, June 1, was the couple's wedding anniversary.

According to the FBI, the incident in the Arizona desert was merely a dry run for a grander conspiracy involving Foreman, Baker, Davis, and Millett. The FBI charged the four with plotting to damage electrical transmission lines leading to the Rocky Flats nuclear weapons facility in Colorado, from the Diablo Canyon nuclear power plant in California, and from the Palo Verde nuclear power plant in Arizona, acting under the whimsical acronym EMETIC — the Evan Mecham Eco-Terrorist International Conspiracy. When Arizona's conservative former governor Evan Mecham, who was impeached in 1988 for financial misconduct, was contacted by reporters, his bemused response was "I haven't the foggiest idea what they're up to."[1] The FBI presumably believed him.

Ironically, at the time of the arrests, the FBI was also investigating the Rocky Flats installation for hazardous radioactive waste violations serious enough to be a threat to people's health, prompting Mike Roselle to observe that the bureau "would have discharged its duty better by *assisting* in a conspiracy to cut power to Rocky Flats, instead of trying to stop one."[2] Even with the FBI making accusations of terrorism, no one could accuse the radical environmentalists of losing their sense of humor.

In anticipation of just such a law enforcement crackdown, some Earth First!ers a few years earlier had contacted Gerry Spence, an attorney from Jackson, Wyoming, considered by many one of the best trial lawyers in the nation and known for representing ordinary people against large corporations. Spence's reputation sprang from his success in the highly publicized lawsuit brought against the Kerr-McGee Corporation by the family of Karen Silkwood. Silkwood had died mysteriously after criticizing the company for environmental hazards at its nuclear fuels facility, and many people believe she was murdered by the corporation. News of the four arrests was barely out before Spence was flying down to Arizona in his private jet to take on Foreman's defense pro bono. Wearing his Stetson cowboy hat and fringed buckskin jacket, he seemed willing to make his defense of Foreman a spirited, populist vindication of the radical environmental cause.

"Picture a little guy out there hacking at a dead steel pole, an inanimate object, with a blowtorch," he told a staff member of the journal *Earth First!*, suggesting the way he would frame the issue to the jury. "He's considered a criminal. Now see the image of a beautiful, living, 400-year-old tree, with an inanimate object hacking away at it. This non-living thing is corporate America, but the corporate executives are not considered criminals at all."[3]

The merits of the case against the activists — which amounted to the charge, denied by Foreman, that he gave Davis $580 to carry out the alleged conspiracy — were much less interesting than the facts surrounding the investigation of the defendants. According to Stephen McNamee, the U.S. attorney handling the case, the $2 million surveillance operation, which began back in 1986, represented "a significant development in law enforcement."[4] He was referring to the first known use of wiretaps and infiltrators against an environmental group, an investigation dubbed Thermcon by the bureau. One of the infiltrators was Michael A. Fain, a special agent of the Phoenix office of the FBI. Going under the name Mike Tait, he posed as a marginally literate renovator, a recovering alcoholic, and a Vietnam vet to befriend Millett and gain entrée into Earth First! circles. Wearing a body wire, Fain attempted to involve staff members of *Earth First!* in acts of ecotage, but they refused. The other infiltrators were Ron Frazier, a Prescott metal sculptor and artist, and Katherine Clark of Tucson. Frazier had a personal grudge against Davis and also secretly recorded conversations with Earth First!ers for the FBI. While in the employ of the agency he even held a seminar at Earth First!'s 1988 national gathering in Washington, during which he described how to decommission a diesel engine.[5] Several other agents apparently were assigned to investigate particularly prominent activists, as Jesse Hardin, a well-known advocate of ecotage, learned when he was approached by a man who claimed to be the agent appointed to keep an eye on him.[6] All in all the FBI collected thirteen hundred hours of secret recordings of Earth First!ers, a job that occupied some fifty agents for more than two years in surveillance, paperwork, and weekly progress reports to the U.S. attorney. The estimated damage to the electrical tower was under $16,000.

The scope of these operations prompted Spence to say that the FBI's actions in the case were "very similar to the procedures the FBI used during the 1960s against dissident groups." He argued that the agency was acting "as if [it was] dealing with the most dangerous, violent terrorists that the country's ever known. And what we're really dealing with is ordinary, decent human beings who are trying to call the attention of America to the fact that the Earth is dying."[7] Most Earth First!ers agreed that the case was politically motivated and that Foreman had been targeted because he was a prominent spokesman in the radical environmental movement. The FBI claimed its probe was not directed specifically at Earth First! or Foreman but was a response to the sabotaging of power lines to the Palo Verde nuclear power plant in 1986. However, at the bail hearing the government went out of its way to characterize Foreman as the mastermind of a radical environmental reign of ecotage vaster than the Central Arizona Project incident. "Mr. Foreman is the worst of the group," Assistant U.S. Attorney Roger Dokken told the court. "He sneaks around in the background. . . . I don't like to use the analogy of a Mafia boss, but they never do anything either. They just send their munchkins out to do it."[8] It was difficult not to come to the conclusions that the seeds of suspicion James Watt had sown against environmentalists during the Reagan years seemed to be bearing fruit and that law enforcement perceived environmentalism as the enemy.

This was further suggested when it was discovered that the wiretaps of Earth First!ers' homes had been authorized by the nation's chief law enforcement officer, Attorney General Edwin Meese. Such paperwork is often left to a subordinate unless the attorney general is particularly interested in an investigation. More evidence that Meese personally targeted Earth First! emerged when it was learned that FBI agents paid a visit to the Jameses, conservative Republican friends of Meese's in San Diego whose daughter was involved in Earth First!, shortly before the Arizona arrests. The agents allegedly warned the couple that it might be wise to keep their daughter away from the group for the time being.

If there was ever any doubt that the FBI targeted Foreman for political reasons, it was eventually dispelled when the defense team was allowed to listen to the tapes during the pretrial evidence-discovery process. Foreman and attorney Daniel Conner came upon a tape of a conversation between agent Fain and Foreman. Unfortunately, from the prosecution's point of view, Fain forgot to turn the recorder off after the conversation and inadvertently bugged the discussion he and two other agents, Robin Andrews and Paul Szczepaniak, later had about the case at a local Burger King. In that interchange Fain admitted he had no incriminating evidence against Foreman and went on to suggest the real purpose of the investigation: "[Foreman] isn't really the guy we need to pop — I mean in terms of actual perpetrator. This is the guy we need to pop to send a message. And that's all we're really doing, and if we don't nail this guy and we only get Davis, we're not sending any message he hasn't predicted." The "message" the FBI wanted to send by "popping" Foreman is apparent. The FBI hoped the arrest

of a prominent Earth First!er would intimidate radical environmentalists and unnerve their growing movement.

To the delight of Earth First!, the tape also contained a number of Fain's comments praising the radical environmentalists
for their dedication. Earth First! used the quotes in an adver-
tisement in *Mother Jones,* joking that the group's commitment
to the environment was endorsed by no less an authority than
the FBI.

In light of Fain's bungle, the case against Foreman may be
dismissed. However, if it does go to trial, it will probably begin
sometime in late 1990.

As if the attentions of the FBI were not bad enough, the plot
thickened when it was discovered that Earth First! had also
been infiltrated by a private security firm hired by a corporation involved in vivisection. The firm, with the thought-
provoking name Perceptions International, sent an agent
named Mary Lou Sapone to several Earth First! events (including one where Foreman was a speaker), and she eventually got
herself listed as the group's representative in Connecticut.[9]

Sapone was well versed in carrying out undercover operations for Perceptions against animal rights organizations, including the Animal Agenda, Friends of Animals, and the
Animal Rights Alliance; she even became president of the last
group for a short while. Perceptions was investigating these
groups for the U.S. Surgical Corporation, whose president,
Leon Hirsh, was anxious to thwart any possible actions by animal rights advocates against his company for its use of dogs
in testing surgical instruments. Sapone and another Perceptions employee blew their cover when they assisted animal
rights militant Fran Trutt in an alleged bombing attempt
against Hirsh. Trutt was arrested and Sapone became a witness against her.

Earth First! is not particularly involved in the animal rights
movement, and it has never acted against vivisectionists,
though most Earth First!ers would applaud the efforts of animal liberation activists to prevent abuse of animals. It appears,
therefore, that Hirsh was having Earth First! investigated on a
whim, merely to keep tabs on what the radical environmental
movement was up to. Perceptions has connections with the FBI
and government intelligence agencies and thus may have also

been supplementing the Arizona investigation.[10] This is further suggested by the fact that another Perceptions employee, Joel Karlinski, approached several animal rights advocates in an attempt to recruit them for a plot "to take out every nuclear reactor on the east coast," which sounds suspiciously similar to the alleged Arizona conspiracy.[11]

In a pathetic footnote to this strange tale of power lines and dead dogs, Millett had introduced Mike Fain to a widowed friend of hers not associated with Earth First!. The friend was attracted to Fain and over a period of time fell in love with him. When the arrests took place, he vanished. The woman called the FBI, asking Fain to please contact her. Of course he never did. "I guess I'm still waiting for him to come back," she told a reporter.[12]

All these complications might be entertaining were it not for their serious implications. The apparent political motivations behind the FBI's investigation are deplorable but not particularly surprising to those who have followed the agency's activities since the 1960s. But at least the FBI operates under recognizable legal constraints, even if it tends to ignore them. The corporate use of *private* investigators to spy on lawful environmental organizations, however, is a truly ominous development. Surveillance of groups that oppose a corporation's policies cannot help but have a chilling effect on public participation in the democratic process. It is a short step from this to the rise of the sort of private police forces that operate in Central and South American countries. Radical environmentalism seems to be forcing the hand of those who have grown accustomed to having their way on environmental matters.

For many Earth First!ers this was the real issue behind the investigation and arrests. Through civil disobedience and ecotage, radical environmentalists were creating a national issue out of the environmental degradation caused by government agencies and the resource industry. At the same time the gravity of the situation was making ecological resistance appear to be an increasingly legitimate course of action. In cases like the Bald Mountain road blockade, radical environmentalists were winning victories while the normal political processes seemed incapable of dealing with the environmental crisis, either because they were too slow or, worse, because they were controlled by powerful interests in the resource industry. Very few people in the country agree with the destruction of old-growth forests, for instance, and yet the cutting continues. "I think we're offering some effective resistance to the efforts of large multi-national corporations who treat the world like a smorgasbord of resources that they can just gobble up," says Foreman, commenting on his arrest. "When you offer that type of resistance, whether it's the Kayapo Indians in Brazil, the Penan tribal people of Malaysia, Chico Mendes and the rubber tappers in Brazil, or Earth First!ers in the United States, you're setting yourself up for intimidation and repression by the bully boys of the industrial state."[13]

Foreman is referring to a number of disturbing incidents during the seventies and eighties in which the government agencies and corporations that have gained control of the world's ecology have lashed out at activist environmental groups, at times violently, as if the people who wanted to protect the Earth were a political opposition. In a real sense they were, and whether or not radical environmentalists recognized themselves as such a force, they suddenly seemed to find themselves at the forefront of an unintentional revolution.

The intensity of organized opposition to environmental activism became apparent in the response of the French government to the organization Greenpeace. Throughout the seventies and eighties Greenpeace had been sending ships to the nominally peaceful South Pacific to monitor and sometimes disrupt nuclear bomb tests carried out by France. In fact, opposition to nuclear testing was the original motivation behind Greenpeace. As a result of these activities, Greenpeace had for years faced harassment by the French government, involving surreptitious means to "neutralize" the organization, which, according to the magazine *L'Express*, included methods "too shameful to be avowed."[14] The dirty tricks escalated into an armed assault in August 1973, in which French commandos attacked Greenpeace members who had sailed into a test site. The bad publicity forced the government to restrain its more overt antagonism to the group and even contributed to a short moratorium on testing. Nevertheless, the Direction Générale de la Sécurité Extérieure, France's secret service agency, began regular surveillance of Greenpeace and sent infiltrators. To prevent the environmentalists from disrupting a test on the Muraro atoll, the French made plans to blow up the Greenpeace ship *Rainbow Warrior* at sea with all members aboard. However, they settled on a harbor sinking in Auckland, New Zealand, and on July 10, 1985, several secret service frogmen placed demolition charges on the hull of the ship. The blast killed Fernando Pereira, a Greenpeace photographer. For France, it also meant a serious rift in relations with New Zealand, which did not appreciate the French government's sending hired assassins to its shores.

France had never been particularly reluctant to use violence against opponents of its nuclear policy. When sixty thousand people gathered at Malville, the site of the Superphénix breeder reactor, on July 31, 1977, the police responded with force, killing one protester (who happened to be a pacifist) and injuring hundreds of others. The violence traumatized the nascent antinuclear movement in France, which withered away, while in the rest of Europe such opposition was intensifying and evolving into the Green movement. In that instance, since it was engaging in crowd control, the government could at least claim to be acting in accordance with the law; it could not make the same assertion in the bombing of the *Rainbow Warrior*. Apparently, environmental opposition was such a threat that it had to be stopped at any cost.

France was not destined to retain the distinction of being the world's sole eco-assassin. It was not long before private interests with a stake in environmental destruction also used assassination as a means to stamp out opposition to their policies. Half a world away, in the African nation of Rwanda, Dian Fossey had made the study and protection of the highland gorilla her life's work. High on the forested slopes of a four-hundred-thousand-year-old chain of volcanoes, Fossey did her best to rally international opinion against the encroachment of development on the last refuge of the gorillas, whose numbers had dwindled to fewer than 250 due to poaching and habitat loss. In December 1985 she was battling to prevent another thirty-six thousand acres of untilled parkland from being turned into farms and rangeland when someone murdered her in her hut. The murderers were apparently poachers tired of the attention Fossey was bringing to the gorillas' plight. Whether the commercial interests behind the poachers were also involved was never determined.

The vast and fragile rain forests of Brazil were the next scene of murder for the right to destroy the ecology. In the remote western state of Acre, nestled on the eastern side of the Andes, Chico Mendes was leading his union of rubber tappers to resist illegal land grabbing by ranchers. The rubber tappers made their meager living by extracting renewable products such as rubber and Brazil nuts from the rain forest. This Earth-harmonious economy came under threat in the 1960s with the influx of large numbers of ranchers, who burned the forests and grazed cattle — in response to incentives from the Brazilian government, which paid settlers for making "productive" use of the land, as well as with the assistance of international lending institutions, which financed the construction of roads into the area. Through the use of violence and intimidation, the ranchers soon gained control of the state, sending their hired guns, *pistoleiros*, to murder their political opposition and force the rubber tappers from their land. Mendes's predecessor as leader of the union had been murdered, as was the leader before him, and so on.

Nonetheless, Mendes organized the workers to carry out *empates*, blockades of the bulldozers the ranchers illegally used to clear and expropriate land that belonged to rubber tappers. The plight of the rubber tappers and the destruction of the rain forest illustrated the close connection between social justice and the preservation of the ecology — a theme Mendes brought to the attention of the international community. His most important proposal, subsequently acted upon by the World Bank, was for areas of the Amazon to be designated extractive reserves where only sustainable economic activity, such as rubber tapping, would be permitted. For his efforts in protecting the rain forest he was awarded the prestigious United Nations Environmental Program Global 500 award in 1987. He was also put on the blacklist of the Rural Democratic Union (UDR), a virulently right-wing confederation of ranchers that dominates the politics of Acre.

Mendes survived five assassination attempts instigated by the ranchers. On December 22, 1988, however, the sixth attempt succeeded when the union leader and environmentalist was hit in the chest and shoulder by a blast from a twenty-gauge shotgun. The man who pulled the trigger, Darci Alves, was the son of a wealthy rancher and member of the UDR. Alves turned himself in shortly after the murder and claimed, Oswald-like, to have acted alone. There is very little doubt, however, that the UDR was behind the killing.

It did not take long for the press to declare Mendes the first "eco-martyr."[15] Given the intensity of conflict over the environment, especially in developing countries like Brazil, it is difficult to believe there will not be more environmental martyrs in the future — perhaps many more, and perhaps in this country.

Up till now the United States has been spared the lethal violence resulting from environmental tensions that other parts of the world have experienced, though each day the battle over old growth seems to bring us a little closer to that grievous end. Much of the ecological conflict between the resource industry and environmentalists has been carried on vicariously in the courts, a system preferable to death squads but not without its own risks. Over the years the resource industry has unfortunately learned to use the court system in ways that may be just as destructive to democratic institutions in the long run as brute force.

In 1984 the Sierra Club and a number of private citizens began a campaign to prevent the Perini Land and Development Company, a $23-million-a-year subsidiary of the Massachusetts Perini Corporation, from building a large resort — complete with ski lifts, hotel, homes, and golf course — in the alpine town of Squaw Valley, California. The issuing of illegal permits by the board of supervisors brought the debate into court, and Perini was obliged to modify its plans several times. The Sierra Club came to an agreement with Perini, but one Squaw Valley resident, Rick Sylvester, continued his opposition by speaking out against the project at public hearings and writing letters to newspapers encouraging his neighbors to do the same. On July 2, 1987, Perini slapped Sylvester with a $75 million lawsuit, alleging he had conspired to overturn the agreement it had reached with the other environmentalists.

The lawsuit was so effective in curtailing public participation on the issue that even the stodgy Army Corp of Engineers, which was holding hearings on the project, decided to take public comments anonymously. It described the problem in its public statement: "Due to a lawsuit filed by the Perini Land and Development Company against a number of individuals . . . the Corps has determined that a number of individuals who planned to make statements at the public hearing did not do so for fear of being drawn into the lawsuit."[16]

This was exactly Perini's intent. The case was without merit and destined to fail, but the message was a success: any citizens who opposed Perini would have to bear the cost of defending themselves in court. As Sylvester pointed out, "To us, this is a big deal; to them, it is a cost of doing business."[17]

The cost of doing business for many development companies now includes lawsuits intended to frighten citizen groups that oppose them. In 1988, Professors Penelope Canan and George Pring of the University of Denver published the results of a three-year study of dozens of such cases, which they called SLAPPs — Strategic Lawsuits Against Public Participation. They concluded that "every year in the United States, hundreds, perhaps thousands, of civil lawsuits are filed that are aimed at preventing citizens from exercising their political rights or punishing those who have done so."[18]

About 83 percent of SLAPPs are dismissed before trial for their lack of merit, and not one of the cases Canan and Pring studied resulted in a money judgment. But to the powerful interests who file SLAPPs, winning is not the main objective. The damage is done as average citizens are forced to spend tens of thousands of dollars in lawyers' fees as well as face the traumatic possibility of losing their homes and assets. Many citizens agree to discontinue their public opposition on an issue in exchange for having the strategic lawsuit dropped. The success of a SLAPP therefore comes not from a favorable judgment in court, Pring explained, but "from fear, protraction and the high cost of defense."[19]

SLAPPs have been filed by landlords, employers, developers, and even government agencies, with perhaps the most vicious example being a lawsuit brought by the crew members of a munitions train that ran over Brian Willson, a Vietnam vet who in 1987 lay on the tracks to protest U.S. arms shipments to Central America. Willson expected the train to stop; it did not, and he lost both his legs. The crew then sued the man they crippled for "mental anguish."

Not coincidentally, a large percentage of SLAPPs revolve around environmental issues. As the pace of environmental destruction has quickened in America, the resource industry and developers have faced mounting opposition to their plans and have responded with the kind of industrial activism Ron Arnold advocated. In 1987, for instance, the Alaskan timber company Shee Atika brought a $40 million damage suit against the Sierra Club for its attempts to prevent logging on the traditional hunting grounds of Alaskan natives. The case never had a chance, but the environmental group had to spend time and money defending itself. In one Colorado action, activist Betty Johnson petitioned the town board of Louisville to declare a moratorium on development in the small town. When she succeeded, a developer sued her for unlimited damages allegedly caused by her petition. If the Colorado Civil Liberties Union had not taken up her $10,000 defense, Johnson would have had to withdraw from her public activism.

These cases and hundreds more like them are a clear violation of the spirit if not the letter of First Amendment guarantees of free speech and the right to petition the government. But the present remedy, filing a counterclaim, is too expensive and time-consuming to be of any use to most citizens. Therefore, a number of states are considering legislation to make it more difficult for strategic lawsuits to be filed. The reactions of the resource industry to environmental militancy of the Earth First! type, however, raise more difficult questions about the extent of First Amendment protection.

In the fight to prevent the opening of California's Diablo Canyon nuclear plant (which has the dubious honor of being the only nuclear reactor built on an earthquake fault), members of the environmental group Abalone Alliance staged a number of nonviolent blockades, which delayed construction. Workers at the site, under the tutelage of the conservative Pacific Legal Foundation, then sued the protesters for $3 million; Professor Pring filed a friend-of-the-court brief in the case on the side of the demonstrators. Strictly speaking, this was not an example of a SLAPP, since the antinuclear protesters had broken the law by trespassing. But in this case, as it is in many environmental campaigns, it was necessary to engage in civil disobedience to get the issue before the public and thus to generate a free and open discussion in the spirit of the First Amendment. "We learned a long time ago," says Roselle, "that unless you had a *campaign*, which might involve a little civil disobedience and a little monkeywrenching, issues like old growth do not get into the press."[20]

Realizing this, a number of companies have brought civil suits against radical environmentalists involved in blockades and other disruptive protests in order to dampen their enthusiasm for activism. In 1988, for example, the southern Oregon timber company involved in old-growth logging in the Kalmiopsis sued six Earth First!ers who had occupied a logging site, chaining themselves to equipment and even using rock-climbing gear to scale a yarder, a large machine that gathers felled trees with cables. The occupation lasted only a day. Nonetheless, in addition to pressing criminal charges, the company asked for and won $58,000 in civil damages, including several thousand in punitive damages, which are ordinarily very difficult to obtain even against large corporations that recklessly injure people. The trial took place in the heart of timber country, with all the built-in biases that implies. It is being appealed.

In any event, the company probably will never be able to collect the damages, since, like most radical environmentalists, the six defendants have no property or assets to speak of (although their financial status was investigated by one Robert Drinen, a former Oregon state police officer turned private investigator and apparently retained by the company). But the daunting proposition of having a financial liability for the rest of one's life may cause potential activists to shy away from civil disobedience.

A similar but more raucous sequence of events has taken place in the battle to stop Maxxam and its subsidiary Pacific Lumber from cutting the last of the old-growth redwoods in California. During a protest in 1987 involving a hundred people at Pacific Lumber's Carlotta mill, six Earth First!ers climbed over the fence and began dancing on a pile of redwood logs. On the same day, several tree sitters also occupied a stand of redwoods belonging to Pacific Lumber. The company sued for

$42,000, claiming that the protesters had trespassed "maliciously and to oppress" the timber colossus.[21] In typical Earth First! fashion, one of the defendants, Darryl Cherney, attempted to make a virtue of necessity and turn the purpose of the suit against the company: "I'm very pleased that PL is suing us and enabling us to bring this matter into a public forum. I'm a bit surprised that three men climbing a tree and six women dancing on a log should cause them so much dismay and financial damage."[22] It would be ironic indeed if the publicity attending intimidation lawsuits backfired on the resource industry and highlighted the environmental issues it is trying to obscure.

The increasing use of intimidation lawsuits, infiltrators, and law enforcement investigations against environmental activists forces society to consider how far it will permit people to go to defend the environment and how far it will permit others to defend their interest in destroying the environment. If the FBI had had its way during the sixties, the civil rights movement would have failed. It possibly would have failed if at the time corporations had developed the practice of strategic lawsuits. Virtually no one would disagree that the changes the civil rights movement brought about were both necessary and good. And thus this has to imply agreement with the nonviolent civil disobedience of the protesters, since these tactics were necessary to force the American conscience to confront the evils of racial discrimination. The same argument can be made for the radical environmental movement. If one agrees that environmental policy in this country has to change drastically, that the destruction of wilderness has to stop, and that the reins of the resource industry have to be pulled in, then it is necessary to consider the role of civil disobedience and ecotage in bringing about those changes. These illegal tactics have brought such issues before the public so that they can be decided upon democratically instead of by default. In other words, because of the nature of the environmental crisis, the kinds of activism radical environmentalists practice may be necessary for the democratic process even if they are illegal. As Earth First!er Tim Jackson puts it, "Does a tree make any noise if it's cut in a forest without an Earth First!er around? Hell, no!"

If that is so, then the arrest of Foreman, the use of infiltrators, the misuse of civil lawsuits, are not directed merely against the radical environmental movement, but also against the democratic process, which in the age of environmental crisis may have to recognize civil disobedience and ecotage as integral to its workings.

CHAPTER 12

THE NATURAL RESOURCES STATE

The American people should be told the Forest Service is turning the national forests into an armed camp.

— *Tim Jackson,*
Earth First! activist

IN 1986 Congress passed the National Forest Drug Enforcement Act, budgeting twenty million dollars to fund a force of
five hundred special agents generally known as pot commandos because of their legislatively mandated purpose of com-
bating marijuana cultivation on public lands. It did not take
long for Donald Hodel, Reagan's languid secretary of the interior, to realize that this newly acquired muscle could be directed at a more embarrassing kind of grass-roots problem:
grass-roots environmentalists so frustrated with Reagan's antienvironmental revolution that they embraced civil disobedience and ecotage to contest Interior's management of
America's wildlands. Couple this with the use of private security measures by the resource industry, and what some environmentalists have called the armed occupation of the
American wilderness was under way.

Since the passage of the 1986 drug act, the pot commandos
have done their job well, and the cultivation of marijuana in
national forests, which was causing a substantial amount of
environmental harm, has dwindled down to nothing (mostly
because it was moved indoors). But the pot commandos are as
busy as ever. The Forest Service has relied increasingly on
them to deal with environmental protests despite the fact that
the act creating the force has no provision for such a use and

arguably would not have passed if it had. It is not at all clear that the American public would support either the establishment of a paramilitary force to patrol our wildlands or, for that matter, any politician who voted for such an idea.

The introduction of the pot commandos into the old-growth controversy has exacerbated the conflict between radical environmentalists and the timber industry. Dressed in military-style camouflage fatigues and often armed with automatic weapons, the commandos are a presence seemingly calculated as much to intimidate protesters as to carry out legitimate law enforcement, especially since the kinds of protests they typically break up are small and scrupulously peaceful, unlike the massive, violent environmental demonstrations that have occurred in Europe. Thus in July 1988 several pot commandos trained high-powered rifles on a group of tree sitters in the Middle Santiam, in Oregon. One was Mary Beth Nearing, whose disagreement with any kind of aggression, even ecotage, led her to publicly denounce the Pyramid Creek tree spiking several years earlier. The sheriff instructed the commandos to shoot the tree sitters if they made any hostile moves against the officers attempting to climb the trees after them. The possibility of dead environmentalists dropping from the forest canopy stands as a sobering contrast to the Forest Service's Smokey the Bear public image.

As might be expected from members of an organization groomed for paramilitarism, the commandos employ law enforcement techniques that sometimes lack subtlety, if not legality. In July 1989 four Earth First!ers dug a ditch in a logging road in Oregon's Siskiyou National Forest, filled it with quick-drying cement, and placed their feet in it. When sheriff's deputies arrived, one of the protesters, Michael Fuerst, looked them in the eye and shouted, "Officers, will you please find the person who cemented me to this road and arrest him!" The deputies smiled, but the smiling soon stopped altogether when the four immobile environmentalists had their wrists handcuffed behind their backs, were deprived of water, and had their hats knocked off their head, exposing them to the hot sun. Then several pot commandos whacked away at the cement with sledgehammers, over the complaints of the Earth First!ers (one of whom was a seventeen-year-old girl), whose ankles were being mangled. "You shouldn't have put your feet in fucking concrete," responded one pot commando after hitting a protester's leg with a hammer.[1]

Sternness of this kind may be a virtue in the drug war, but it seems somewhat out of place when directed at peaceful protesters. The obvious question is, Why are pot commandos involved in the arrest of environmental protesters at all when they were funded to stop illegal marijuana growers? While there has been a sharp decline in marijuana cultivation on public lands, the number of pot commandos was doubled, to a thousand, in 1988, and some environmental activists have alleged that fully half of their budget is going to law enforcement pertaining to environmental demonstrations, a state of affairs that, if true, amounts to criminal misappropriation of funds.[2]

The most disturbing use of pot commandos, however, has less to do with their military esprit de corps, alleged subbrutality, and dubious funding than with their involvement in another aspect of the militarization of the American wilderness: the enforcement of special closures.

In a 1985 government document called *Ecotage from Our Perspective*, supervisor of the Willamette National Forest Michael Kerrick threatened to declare areas of the forest off-limits to the public so that timber companies could carry out their work undisturbed by radical environmentalists:

> If we know that Ecotage or demonstrations are planned in any area where public safety and the resources may be threatened, *we will close the entire area to unauthorized entry.* That will mean that no one but the Forest Service employees, any lawful contractor, and law enforcement personnel will be authorized to be in the area. Anyone caught in violation of the closure will be cited and subject to legal consequences. The area closed will be large enough to prevent unsafe harassment of authorized personnel.[3]

The notion that an unelected official would have the power to close large areas of public land to the American people, including the press and those citizens who are trying to bring an important policy issue to light, in order to allow corporations to carry on controversial activities in secret may have seemed like an idle, Orwellian threat in 1985. Today it is a reality. Kerrick and other Forest Service supervisors now routinely close areas of the national forests to the public where old-growth logging is taking place, often using pot commandos to enforce the closure. They base their authority to do so on a provision of the Code of Federal Regulations giving Forest Service "line officers" (forest supervisors, regional foresters, and district rangers) the power to declare a special closure for the protection of public health or safety.[4] Tim Jackson, an Earth First!er involved in the cement protest who has also been cited for violating a closure order, ascribes a somewhat less public-spirited motive to the agency's use of closures: "They don't want us to see the nasty things they're doing."[5]

Jackson's observation is borne out by a number of incidents. In July 1989, for example, Tom Thompson, supervisor of western Oregon's Siuslaw National Forest, issued a closure order after there had been protests over old-growth logging in his jurisdiction. The order stipulated that "closures will be moving, periodic and unscheduled. They will affect only a fraction of the above noted area and lands at any one time. They are effective only if the restriction is posted or you are so advised by a Forest Service Officer."[6] This floating restriction, as environmentalists called it, included a substantial part of the old-growth stands, for some people the most attractive areas of the forest, and taken as a whole covered about eighty square miles. Backpackers or campers who had sought these areas to find solitude were suddenly transformed into trespassers, subject to fine or imprisonment.

The real object of the closure was of course environmental activists, not backpackers. Two law enforcement officers immediately rooted out a group of four Earth First!ers camped in the area and told them they had to leave. One protester asked where the boundary of the closure was, so they could set up camp there, but the agents refused to tell them. "Just get out of the area," said one. "You know what we mean." What they meant, according to the environmentalists, was that the Forest Service was going to close any area in which there were Earth First!ers, even if they had to shut the whole forest down. Without any further warning, while the four environmentalists were leaving the area they were taken into custody, brought to a

Forest Service security trailer, and questioned, one by one, from 8:00 P.M. to midnight, before being cited for trespassing and released. They were then driven to a remote trailhead seven miles from a phone.[7]

One of the most disturbing aspects of the incident was that the investigators told the Earth First!ers they had learned of their whereabouts through motion detectors hidden in the forest.[8] This may have been a feint, but the frightening prospect of a forest under constant electronic surveillance would later prove true elsewhere.

Closures have not only been ordered without any public safety rationale, they have even at times actually threatened the safety of the public. In July 1989, a number of Earth First!ers shut down a logging operation in the Kalmiopsis by chaining themselves to timber equipment. When the loggers arrived at a demonstration of supporters on the nearby public road, they threatened to march down to where the equipment was and kill the environmentalists. The sheriff's deputies refused to follow the loggers, so a group of supporters did. The Forest Service agent then immediately declared a closure and informed the protesters that if they moved he would sic the police dogs on them. The loggers did in fact start up a yarder to which a protester had chained himself. "Hey, boy, want to go for a ride?" one taunted.[9]

Curiously, no mainstream environmental group or public interest organization has brought suit over these closure orders. And yet the issue should very much concern the public at large, since it goes to the heart of what the national forest system is meant to be. Is it literally a *public* domain, there for everyone to enjoy in an egalitarian spirit? Or is it the private stock of the resource corporations, watched over for their benefit by an agency with the arbitrary powers of a medieval forest *"Meister"*? Congress and the courts have already spoken on the matter. When the forest supervisor of Northern California's Shasta and Trinity national forests issued a closure order in 1972 to prevent members of the Pit River Indian tribe from disrupting timber operations on disputed land, the Indians appealed their trespass convictions and won. The federal judge noted that because only limited closure power is given to the Forest Service by Congress, the regulations "cannot be construed as a broad,

implicit grant of power to close large areas of a national forest.
. . . The Supervisor could have posted restrictions against interfering with lawful logging operations, thus creating a violation for interference, but not for mere entry into the logging
area."[10]

Under this ruling, it is clear that the Forest Service's closure
policy is illegal and will be struck down as soon as some
aggressive environmental attorney challenges it in court,
thus adding to a long string of cases in which the agency found
itself on the wrong side of the law for the benefit of the resource industry. In the same white paper that broached the
idea of enforcing closures to stop environmental dissent, Supervisor Kerrick suggested that this kind of action was for "the
greatest good for the greatest number"[11] — the talismanic
credo of Gifford Pinchot's Magna Carta letter. It seems difficult to avoid the perception, however, that the closures are
more than likely calculated to benefit the few at the expense
of the many, and those particular few who seem to be in least
need of assistance.

But the use of pot commandos and floating closures is only
part of the militarization of America's public lands. Faced with
an onslaught of ecotage, timber companies and other corporations that have gained access to forests and rangelands are
bringing along with them their own security regime, often involving armed guards, watchdogs, helicopters, and sophisticated electronic surveillance devices. During a wave of
environmentalist protests in 1989 over continued old-growth
logging in the Kalmiopsis, timber companies reacted with extraordinary security measures, which left parts of forest seemingly more like a war zone than a wilderness area. In one
incident, two people on an evening hike along a well-marked
trail were suddenly confronted with spotlights, guards, and
bullhorns and were asked to state their names and purpose in
being near a timber sale.[12] This was on public land, not a company timber yard back in town. Environmentalists also later
learned that the area was ringed with electronic motion detectors, allowing the company security team to monitor the movement of people in the forest. In the ultimate transformation of
public land to private security zone, on the south rim of the
Grand Canyon, where Energy Fuels Nuclear operates a controversial uranium mine, Earth First!ers were amazed to find that

the company had actually set up a No Trespassing sign — right on a public road into the area.

Along with security come weapons. The armed guards of the timber companies are becoming a problematical side effect of the logging in the national forests. Often as ill trained as they are ill paid, guards have more than once brought the conflict between timber companies and radicals to the brink of lethal violence. Ed Hascom, the owner of a timber company logging the Kalmiopsis, warned that protesters who "trespass" on his logging sites run a serious risk of an armed confrontation with his guards. "Potentially," he told a local newspaper, "they can expect to get shot." [13] Several almost have been. Hascom's own guard pointed his rifle at the head of Earth First! activist Lisa Brown, who had locked her neck to a timber loader with a bicycle lock. He fired it a few inches to the side of her head — out of sheer malice. [14]

Law enforcement officers have been less than zealous about discouraging this kind of behavior by timber companies. A group of California Earth First!ers learned that when they were assaulted on a public road by the shotgun-wielding David Lancaster, son of the owner of the Lancaster Timber Company in Mendocino County. According to the protesters, he broke the nose of one woman, and a Lancaster employee fired a gun into the air twice before the sheriff's deputies arrived en masse in eight police cars. They took the statement of the Lancaster family and refused to arrest the assailant. The company seemed to have a penchant for firing off shotguns; they had been doing so every night for a week around their logging site to ward off ecoteurs, presumably as if they were crows. [15]

Part of the problem is that sheriffs elected in small communities based on timber can build their political career on antienvironmental bravura. Jim Weed, a sheriff from Washington's Okanogan County, the site of the unruly 1988 protest that defaced the national forest supervisor's office, has toured the Pacific Northwest giving talks to timber industry groups on radical environmentalism and how to combat it. In a speech delivered to the Washington Contract Loggers' Association in September 1988, he stated, "Basically what [Earth First!ers] are doing is taking old protest symbols from throughout history and prostituting them for their own views. . . . The Forest Service wants this big 'Everybody loves Smokey' image out there. These people don't love Smokey and the Forest Service hasn't awakened to that fact yet."[16]

Environmentalists who do not love Smokey, it seems, cannot expect too much impartial justice at the hands of Sheriff Jim Weed. This attitude is not at all uncommon, and again, like the forest closures, it calls for some kind of evaluation of law enforcement's role in the national forests. Were Earth First! an antiabortion organization, some of whose members engaged in civil disobedience, we would still expect the police to do their duty impartially and without espousing one position or another. But ecotage is such a controversial and successful tactic that law enforcement appears to be taking sides, a development that has ominous implications for America's tradition of having a police force without ideological and political affiliations.

This overall sad state of affairs, like many lamentable tendencies connected with the environment, has its roots in the policies of the Reagan administration. When James Watt took office as secretary of the interior, one of his first undertakings was to enmesh public lands policy in Reagan's crusade against "the evil empire." Watt entered into his job with the perception, garnered from such organizations as the Federation of Materials Societies and the popular press, that America was facing a "strategic mineral gap." While the Soviet Union had reached "mineral sufficiency," the United States, argued Watt, was dangerously dependent on foreign sources of cobalt, niobium, manganese, chromium, and other exotic metals used in the sophisticated equipment that made up the military's nuclear force. Therefore Watt proposed to open up the national forests and other lands to mining as a national security necessity. Watt's strategic mineral gap proved to be as illusory as the missile gap of the Nixon-Kennedy debates, but it did introduce the notion that development of the nation's wildlands was not an issue to be left to the vagaries of the democratic process, which might be unwary of the enemies of freedom lurking abroad. Rather, it was an imperative of national security, which, as history has proved, can be used to override both constitutions and common sense.

Watt extended this argument to his energy policy. Suddenly it was necessary to drill for as much oil and mine as much coal as possible, lest the Soviet Union outdo us in a "resource war," to use the phrase of Congressman James Santini, chairman of the House Mines and Mining Subcommittee at the time and much admired by Watt. Watt therefore proposed oil, gas, and coal leases on public lands noted for their wilderness values, the Gros Ventre and Little Granite Creek among them. "This Administration," said Watt before the annual meeting of the National Coal Association in St. Louis, "believes that a healthy mining industry is essential to America's national security, to a strong economy and to our environment." If it was not immediately evident how coal mining was essential to the requirements of a sound environment, especially in light of coal companies' long and well-documented history of strip-mining and other forms of environmental abuse, that hardly mattered. Under the aegis of national security all contradictions were reconciled. In this way environmental policy shifted from being a method of preserving nature to a strategy for augmenting the political, economic, and military strength of America against its foreign adversaries. "In making environmental decisions, I view every issue from the basis of America," Watt said. "Will that decision create jobs in the private sector, will they enhance our environment, will they improve our national security so that we might have political liberty and spiritual freedom?"[17]

The political implications of this kind of thinking were easy to imagine. Those who proposed strict wilderness protection and expansion in opposition to Watt were perceived not only as wrongheaded, but also as a threat to the security of the country. For Watt, environmentalism was being used "as a tool to achieve a greater objective," which was somehow related to Nazism and the Bolshevik revolution.[18] Watt's assistant secretary of agriculture, John Crowell, was more explicit about this sinister side of the environmental movement: "I think the bulk of the people who belong to the Sierra Club and Audubon Society are people who have a genuine concern about the treatment of our natural resources. On the other hand, I'm sure the organizations are also infiltrated by people who have very strong ideas about socialism and even communism."[19] In a climate in which environmental activism was equated with military adversaries abroad, and the national security shibboleth became associated with the exploitation of natural resources, it was only a matter of time before our national forests and rangelands would feel the excesses of military mobilization.

Unfortunately, this was not a mere metaphor. The U.S. military, spurred on by huge budget increases, quite literally expanded its operations into public lands in the West, often not even under color of law. In April 1984, without soliciting public comment or writing an environmental impact statement, the air force used the national security rationale to seize 89,000 acres of wilderness study area under the Bureau of Land Management in the Groom Range of Nevada. The acreage was annexed to the gigantic Nellis Air Force Range and Nevada Test Site, already roughly the size of Delaware, and was immediately closed to the public. The air force also began the process of appropriating 181,000 acres of public land in Nevada's Stillwater Mountains, which included additional wilderness study areas. In November 1989 public hearings began on the biggest military land grab yet. The air force proposed the conversion of 1.5 million acres of public land near its Mountain Home base, in Idaho. The land, which includes a population of bald eagles, would be used as a live bombing range.

The military has also made its presence felt on public lands in ways other than expropriation. The navy began installing several dozen automated electronic sites to help guide aircraft in Nevada's wilderness study areas and national forests as part of its Tactical Aircrew Combat Training System. Military officials claimed the transponders would not affect use of the areas, but they brought with them the usual array of security precautions such as fences and periodic inspection.

While the Reagan administration was turning over large areas of national forests and rangeland to the military with its right hand, it was surrendering other areas to state and private control with its left. This movement went under the name Sagebrush Rebellion, because it was spearheaded by the livestock interests in western range country who wanted to expand their grazing operations onto federal lands without federal restrictions on pesticide use and predator control, such as the extermination of wolves and coyotes, something the American people through Congress had limited. As announced by the Public Lands Council, a resource group associated with the rebellion, the laws governing rangeland should prevent the "adverse impacts" of "wildlife refuges, wilderness, wild and scenic rivers, or other government activities which could reduce or materially interfere with livestock production."[20] To the Sagebrush Rebels, the national forests and wilderness system were the enemy. Under pressure from the rebellion, Watt transferred or sold about 20 million acres of federal land to the states, where the livestock industry could exert its political influence to the fullest.

Watt's dream of handing over control of national forests and rangeland to private commodity interests was never completely realized, because of congressional opposition. But, as Denzel and Nancy Ferguson point out in *Sacred Cows at the Public Trough*, "the cowboys didn't really want the public land. They only wanted to put federal employees back in line, to dominate the use of public land, and to keep milking the federal treasury."[21] Watt arranged that in part through his Good Neighbor policy. Announced in 1983, the policy gave ranchers who built fences and carried out other capital improvements on the Bureau of Land Management rangeland they leased greater freedom from BLM oversight, including supervision of the number of animals using an allotment and range conditions. It was, in short, an invitation to cheat.

The Reagan administration set the tone, and public land management accordingly began to encourage private profiteering. As James Duffus III of the General Accounting Office says, "Some permittees have come to view the use of these [public] lands as a property right for private benefit rather than a conditional privilege conferred by the public at large."[22] And with private property rights come police enforcement and fences and guards and guns.

Clearly, the growth of the security regime on wildlands, with timber companies intent on protecting their property and law enforcement unmotivated to curb their excesses, is threatening the wild, unfettered character of our national forests and other natural areas, the very character that attracts most people and makes them worth protecting. This is reason enough to call for a change in how law enforcement approaches public lands. But there are even more disturbing implications to this security mentality that have not been considered. In *The Nuclear State*

Robert Jungk argues that the security precautions that attend
the operations of nuclear power plants would undermine and
eventually destroy democratic institutions. The American public has successfully beaten back the rise of a nuclear elite, although the nuclear industry is now attempting a comeback
with arguments that nuclear power is a clean alternative to
coal-fired plants and the greenhouse gases they produce. But a
more general menace to democratic rule comes from what
might be called the natural resources state. It is not at all clear
that industrial society can do without an ever-expanding resource base, though it is clear that the ecological havoc caused
by oil, mineral, and timber exploitation will eventually lead to
the addition of our name to the list of lost civilizations, perhaps
as the benighted Deforestation Age. The resource industry is
obliged to protect its operations and property; radical environmentalists are obliged to disrupt this domestication of the ecology. The irreconcilability of these forces suggests that natural
areas will increasingly fall under a security regime, for the
same reasons Jungk puts forth in his book, though with less
fanfare, since the areas involved are remote. If this is true, our
national forests are on their way to becoming resource parks
rather than wildlands.

The distinction makes all the difference, not only from an
ecological point of view but also from a social one. In *Rational
Landscapes and Humanistic Geography,* Edward Relph writes
that the transformation of the landscape to promote efficiency
and material "improvements" for humans systematically denies other human values, like spontaneity, emotional freedom,
and independence from authority. Rational space is marked by
"aesthetic confusion, ethical poverty and a disturbing degree
of dependence on technical expertise," all of which diminish
important aspects of our existence.[23]

"When we create parks we bow to increased bureaucracy and
surveillance," said the nature writer Wayland Drew in 1972,
prophetically, as it turns out, "but when we speak for wilderness we recognize our right to fewer strictures and greater freedom."[24]

The radical environmental movement, in associating itself
with the latter, may indeed be a threat to security, but in the
same way a free, egalitarian citizenry is a threat to the security

of the privileged and the powerful. Indeed, radical environmentalism may be one of the last bastions of resistance to a
society based on the constant administration of nature and human nature, leading to Relph's diminished person. As Drew
pointed out, once wilderness is gone, once there is no longer a
reference point outside the manipulations of culture, the state,
corporations, or other powerful interests will be able to shape
and form citizens any way they want. The natural world stands
as a limit to the manipulative power of social control, an "outside" that allows people to see they are "inside" a particular
culture that need not be the way it is. As nature falls under the
surveillance of law enforcement and private security teams, so
do we all.

At this juncture radical environmentalism takes on a significance beyond its aggressive call for the protection of nature
and embraces a vision of human freedom unacceptable to civilization, with its urge to contain, repress, and inscribe all that
is wild.

PART 4

THE UNMAKING OF CIVILIZATION

CHAPTER 13

CIVILIZATION AND OTHER ERRATA

Visualize industrial collapse.

— *Michael Fuerst,
Earth First! activist*

DONALD WORSTER, author of *Nature's Economy*, asks an important question: "If ecology is a 'subversive science,' as Paul Sears suggests, what is it trying to subvert?"[1] Worster proposes several possibilities, including the reductionist views of traditional science, the antinature bias of Western religions, and the values and institutions of industrial capitalism. The radical environmental movement certainly recognizes these factors as obstacles to its task of preserving natural diversity from the expanding culture of extinction. The critical literature of Deep Ecology targets the science, religion, and political economy of modern times as driving forces behind the destruction of the natural world, which must be confronted if we are to deal with the environmental crisis. In contrast, reform environmentalism sees science and industry as inevitabilities, permanent features of our society that must be made more sensitive to environmental limitations but not rejected as a whole. (Moderate environmentalism's view toward religion is not as clear.) As Dave Foreman concisely explains it, "The worldview of the executive director of the Sierra Club is closer to that of James Watt or Ronald Reagan than Earth First!'s."[2]

With uncharacteristic insight, Ron Arnold writes in *At the Eye of the Storm* that "eco-terrorists are not preservers of the status quo, or even 'New Luddites' anxious about technology stealing their jobs, but rather deeply primitivist activists opposed to industrial civilization itself."[3] Except for the unflattering use of the ecoterrorist epithet, the statement is an essentially correct description of how most radical environmentalists feel toward industrialism. "Modern technological society," says Foreman, "is cut off from the natural world, it's alien, it's arrogant, and it's a failure to recognize that we're part of the Earth."[4]

According to George Sessions and Bill Devall, the Deep Ecology perspective inevitably leads to an uncompromising stand against the main thrust of modern, technocratic culture.[5] That thrust is the progressive conversion of the natural world into cultural artifacts measured by industrial output. The gross national product, which economists and politicians are constantly attempting to increase, is in reality the measure of how much of the natural world has been absorbed into the realm of culture.

In questioning the validity of the industrial state, radical environmentalists find themselves in good company. Martin Heidegger took up the theme of the technological domination of humanity and nature in the 1950s with the essay "The Question Concerning Technology." According to Heidegger, the threat of technology consists not of the proliferation of its ugly and dangerous instruments, although they are certainly deplorable enough. Rather, technology represents a relationship between humanity and the world, a portrayal of the entirety of existence as a standing reserve of raw material valuable only insofar as it augments human power. Technology totalizes existence along one axis, the axis of utility, and all the other rich, poetic, wild ways in which a human being is able to encounter the world are excluded. The spiritual aridity Heidegger explores takes on social form in Herbert Marcuse's *One Dimensional Man,* which argues that mass industrial societies, whether capitalist or socialist, are moving toward the total control of all aspects of human life, not through overtly oppressive or violent means (though there is plenty of that too) but through a closing of the "universe of discourse" through which we experience the world. In technology's universe of discourse, the world is represented only in terms of production and consumption, efficiency and profit, making the technological mode of existence seem inevitable, universal, absolute. Jacques Ellul developed the same theme of humanity's subjection to the dominion of techniques in *The Technological Society*. Lewis Mumford's *Myth of the Machine: The Pentagon of Power* continued this explication of the totalizing effect of monolithic technologies that destroy and debase human values in the name of progress.

To account for the rise of this authoritarian reign of technology, critics naturally looked to the origins of the Industrial Revolution in the Renaissance and the Enlightenment. For historian Morris Berman, something went awry with the West's view of nature in the seventeenth century.[6] What had been a living, organic, green world in the Middle Ages became abstract and mechanistic during the Renaissance under the influence of rising empiricism. In *The Turning Point*, Fritjof Capra discerned this shift from life to mechanism in the person of René Descartes, whose philosophy of an abstract self in a dead, objective world sanctioned the exploitation of nature. French philosopher Michel Foucault also traced the predicament of modernism to a change in worldviews, or *épistèmes*, as he called them. At the end of the eighteenth century Western culture ceased to look at a human being as something that existed alongside other living beings in a world of transcendental origin and invented "Man" as both the "difficult object and sovereign subject of all possible knowledge," as a subject observing not only the objective world, but also his own involvement in the objective world.[7] Theodore Roszak is another thinker who places the source of industrial totalization in the Enlightenment, saying "humanism is the finest flower of urban-industrial society; but the odor of alienation yet clings to it and to all culture and public policy that springs from it."[8]

Without a doubt, industrial society has alienated us from nature and from each other. Radical environmentalism shares in the condemnation of the detrimental effects on the human community and psyche enumerated by Marcuse and the rest. But industrial society has also progressively undermined the natural world and the diversity of nonhuman life. This is a separate ground on which radical environmentalism opposes technology — its incompatibility with biocentrism. As Mike Roselle says, "The only way you can have industrial society is

to trample on other nonhuman communities. If you really believe that we're just one of the five, ten or twenty million species that inhabit this beautiful planet, then I don't think you
could conceive of a system that could do so much to degrade
the whole system as industrialism."[9]

Industrial society may indeed be the most deleterious and
unsustainable economic system the world has ever seen, since
it constantly eats into the ecological systems on which it depends. It violates one of Barry Commoner's four ecological
laws — "There is no free lunch." To our grief, we are beginning
to realize just how costly a system it is as the health and
cleanup bills from years of environmental abuse come due. Not
surprisingly, those who benefited most from the extravagant
rise of the industrial economy have done their best to pass the
burden on to others: the poor, the unwary, or the next generation. Industrialism is perhaps the greatest pyramid scheme in
history.

But industrial society is only the crescendo to a long line of
environmentally destructive cultures that have clambered over
the Earth since the rise of civilization. More than a century ago
George Perkins Marsh noted the relationship between ancient
agrarian cultures, deforestation, and eventual cultural extinction. In *Topsoil and Civilization*, Vernon Carter and Tom Dale
recounted the remarkable consistency with which environmental stupidity appears in the course of history. The names of
history's grandest empires in fact compose a list of ecological
disasters: Sumeria, Egypt, Greece, Rome, India, Aztec Mexico — all deforested, desiccated, eroded.

From the perspective of biocentrism, therefore, the problem
goes deeper than the monolithic and destructive technologies
of industrialism. Civilization itself seems to be the problem. It
is this conviction that prompts Foreman to say that "we
haven't had any progress on this planet in sixteen thousand
years. The only good invention since the atlatl [a spear-
throwing device considered to be the first compound tool] is
the monkeywrench."[10]

In indicting civilization, radical environmentalism is again
not alone, though the field thins out at this point. To his credit,
Murray Bookchin has contributed greatly to understanding the
theme of domination and hierarchy throughout history, though

he has been remiss in applying his insights to his own humanistic views. In *The Ecology of Freedom* he deconstructs the contention that the domination of nature and human nature is natural:

> The notion that man is destined to dominate nature is by no means a universal feature of human culture. If anything, this notion is almost completely alien to the outlook of so called primitive or preliterate communities. I cannot emphasize too strongly that the concept emerged very gradually from a broader social development: the increasing domination of human by human. Perhaps only by examining the attitudes of certain preliterate peoples can we gauge the extent to which domination shapes the most intimate thoughts and the most minute actions of the individual today.[11]

This position is similar to Foucault's, although unfortunately Foucault never took up the theme of environmental imperialism explicitly. For Foucault the distinguishing trait of civilization is a particular set of power relations, a "circuitry of power," existing between institutions, fields of knowledge, and populations, which produces social practices. The actions of hierarchical states are validated in terms of value, so that the real effect of the actions — the accumulation and dispersion of power — disappears from view in the shimmer of ethics. In the example Foucault investigates in *The History of Sexuality*, human sexual behavior (as opposed to alimentation, for instance) became a locus of moral values after the rise of Christianity. A biological act was transformed into a social means of regulating human bodies — what Foucault calls bio-power — based on such imperatives as following biblical dicta, increasing population, and promoting the economic productivity of the nuclear family. The particular values are not of fundamental importance to Foucault; in fact, they often seem incoherent, even meaningless, to present society. What is important is that civilization seems to rely on a totalization of values, values represented as universal, applicable to everyone, at all times. Through totalized values, organized societies have at their command a medium through which to dictate the kind of human behavior that enhances the power of those in control. Whether those values result in people plowing a field, working in a factory, or dropping an atomic bomb on helpless civilians, the discourse of civilization can find a justification in God's commandments, progress, national security, or humanism. Bookchin is indeed correct that social power shapes the most intimate and quotidian acts of civilization's citizens.

We tend to think of power only in terms of its ability to repress behavior. The king's army puts down an insurrection, the police arrest a criminal, a principal expels a student — this is tangible power at work. But Foucault suggests in *Discipline and Punish* that the power of organized societies is also generative. It causes people to act in certain ways, not only by the limited means of coercion, but by creating a field in which various actions are privileged as *good, just, moral,* or *civilized.* Values envelop the members of civilized societies and act as rationalizations for social practices that benefit those powerful enough to influence what is considered moral.

In contrast, to pick up on Bookchin's theme, the power relations in primal societies tend to be discontinuous and negative, discouraging rather than producing certain behavior (the notion of taboo is an example). The shamans, priestesses, witch doctors, and sibyls of primal communities are invested with a certain amount of power, but it usually comes into play only in extreme circumstances, such as sickness or famine. They do not possess and enforce a continuous regime of power over an individual's every thought, as the totalized cultures of civilization tend to do. As a result, the values of primal cultures are usually local, communal, conceived not as universal truths but as practical guides for humans to get along in this contingent world of ours.

Foucault never links his analysis of power to the domination and destruction of nature, but it is not difficult to do so. In *The History of the Idea of Progress*, sociologist Robert Nisbet argues that the concept of progress has been a driving force in civilization at least since classical antiquity. Although Nisbet is clearly enamored by progress and writes in an antienvironmental tone, his point that there is a deep connection between civilization and constant development has merit. In fact, the myth of progress seems to be the central means by which civilization validates itself. The separation between the natural and cultural worlds, which civilization brought about, created two moral realms: one chaotic, anarchistic, and dangerous; the other ordered, regulated, human. Thus, even in as ancient a work as the Sumerian epic *Gilgamesh*, the walled city is represented as the bastion of human value while the forest is a place of monsters to be conquered and destroyed. At its very beginnings organized society set into motion a constellation of oppositions that enveloped its citizens and prodded them to overcome the natural world.

Why organized society arose in the first place, why some humans gave up the primal worldview for the alienation of civilization, is a question that has never been answered and probably never will be. In *Paleopathology at the Origin of Agriculture*, Mark Cohen suggests that population pressure forced hunter-gatherer communities to organize themselves into agrarian states, with all the institutions of control that implied. Andrew Bard Schmookler's *Parable of the Tribes* also attributes the rise of oppressive social institutions, such as the military, to overpopulation. All this makes sense, but it merely raises another question, which is why some communities became overpopulated and others, like the Penan of Malaysia, the Kayapo of the Amazon, and the aborigines of Australia, did not.

Although we will probably never know why the civilization complex arose, it is undeniable that its particular mode of social organization is unstable and destructive to the natural world. But identifying the civilization complex as the source of the environmental crisis is not the same as effectively resisting it. In the context of industrial culture, Heidegger, Marcuse, Ellul, Mumford, and Roszak all despair at the formidable task of undoing the reign of technology. For Foucault, however, within the circuitry of power that makes up our society, there are always "points of resistance," areas where the control of institutions fails. These points of resistance can be the springboard to deconstructing the values, like progress, to which civilization grants privilege. This notion seems to anticipate the strategy of direct action that radical environmentalism has developed.

"Direct action in the ecology movement," writes Bill Devall, "is one way to generate tension, to expose myths and assumptions of the dominant mindset, to create a situation in which corporations, developers and government agents are willing to negotiate."[12] In this interpretation of direct action, radical environmentalism is contributing to the deconstruction of civilization's views and policies toward nature. By being a point of resistance in the flow of power, radical environmentalism forces industrial society to explain itself, to justify its actions.

Devall and many other radical environmentalists have faith that through nonviolent resistance to the civilization complex our society can be transformed into the more Earth-harmonious aspect seen in the minority tradition of Jefferson, Thoreau, and primal communities. By exposing the myths of civilization, its unwarranted anthropocentrism, its privileging of technological progress, its claims of hegemony over the natural world, radical environmentalism may have begun the unmaking of the civilization complex and its institutional power. This became a possibility only because the environmental crisis has allowed people for the first time in history to see how unnatural and unnecessary the majority tradition is. For ten thousand years the institutions of the state, the military, and the priesthood have represented themselves as an inevitable consequence of human existence. With the Deep Ecology movement in the forefront, that claim to universality is breaking down.

Whether it will break down in an orderly fashion or simply collapse is a matter of dispute. For Foreman and many other radical environmentalists, industrial society is doomed to debacle because of the dislocations it has already wreaked: "There is no way to take five billion people in the world today, with the worldview they have, and the economic and industrial imperatives they live under, and turn it into a sustainable Earth-harmonious culture. That's just not going to happen. What is going to happen is that the system is going to collapse of its own corruption. The next several decades are not going to be a very pleasant time to be alive."[13] Foreman's pessimism identifies the central factor that will probably determine whether civilization will transform or collapse: population. In the hectic logic of technics, we require continual technological advancement to feed and care for the burgeoning billions of humans whose numbers continue to increase because of technological advances. Paul Ehrlich's *Population Bomb* has inspired almost universal condemnation from technocrats and humanists alike for predicting a disaster that has not yet happened. But with the population doubling every half century in a world already undergoing biological meltdown, it is difficult to conceive how human population can draw down in a sensible manner without the catastrophe Ehrlich foresaw.

Indeed, as sociologist William Catton brilliantly demonstrates in *Overshoot: The Ecological Basis of Revolutionary Change,* we should not be too comforted by Ehrlich's critics, since in Catton's view the present population levels are sustained only by a "phantom carrying capacity," the temporary availability of exhaustible fossil fuels. Like yeast in a wine vat, our numbers have exploded past the point our environment can eventually sustain once the fossil fuel feast finally comes to an end. "Our species bloomed," concludes Catton, "and now we can expect a crash (of some sort) as the natural sequel."[14]

Our culture finds it all but impossible to face up to the terrible fact that a large percentage of humanity in both the undeveloped and developed world may be subject to this kind of ecological redundancy. This is understandable: mass starvation is not a pleasant thought. But recognition that human populations are subject to the same ecological limitations as other living beings is necessary if there is to be even the possibility of adjusting to population drawdown with a minimum of suffering. "To understand the human predicament," Catton writes, "now requires a truly ecological perspective."[15]

The mainstream environmental movement, as already shown, has balked at pursuing such a perspective. In contrast, radical environmentalists have at least tried. Thus, some Earth First!ers have suggested in Malthusian fashion that the appearance of famine in Africa and of plague in the form of AIDS is the inevitable outcome of humanity's inability to conform its numbers to ecological limits.[16] This contention hit a nerve with the humanist critics of radical environmentalism, who contend that social problems are the cause behind world hunger and that suggesting plague is a solution to overpopulation is "misanthropic."[17] They have also produced a large body of literature attempting to show that Thomas Malthus was incorrect about the relationship between population and food production.[18] Malthus may have been incorrect, famine may be based on social inequalities, plagues may be an undesirable way to control population — but the point remains that unless something is done to slow and reverse human population growth these contentions will soon become moot. There are ecological limits to how many people can live in dignity on this planet; to quibble over whether that line has yet been crossed is to invite a game of ecological brinksmanship that there is no need to play. And even if, despite Catton's arguments, human population has not exceeded carrying capacity, the arguments of the humanist critics leave out the whole question of the effect present population levels have on the nonhuman world.

We may have already gone too far to dismantle industrial society and bring it down to a level compatible with the real world. Nevertheless, most radical environmentalists feel obliged to try. But after the dismantling, after we have defused the threat of ecological extinction, after the holocaust of the Enlightenment, what?

CHAPTER 14

BEYOND THE GREEN WALL

Back to the Pleistocene!

— *Earth First! slogan*

"OH, HOW GREAT and divinely limiting is the wisdom of
walls and bars!" expostulates the narrator of *We*, the dystopian
novel by the early twentieth-century Russian writer Yevgeny
Zamyatin. "This Green Wall is, I think, the greatest invention
ever conceived. Man ceased to be a wild animal the day he built
the first wall; man ceased to be a wild man only on the day
when the Green Wall was completed, when by this wall we
isolated our machine-like, perfect world from the irrational,
ugly world of trees, birds, and beasts."[1]

The Green Wall of Zamyatin's fiction surrounds a perfectly
managed, sanitary, domesticated society in which reason and
logic leave no room for passion, spontaneity, misery, love, pain,
or rapture. But metaphorically a similar barrier has, in a fragmentary way, surrounded the civilization complex from the
time the first wooden stakes were driven into the ground to
mark the boundaries of a barley field. The cultural world has
always feared the unruly, imponderable profuseness of nature,
its discursiveness and plurality, especially when these traits
manifest themselves in Homo sapiens.

As the environmental crisis suggests, however, the perfection
of the cultural world is deadly. The success of environmental
imperialism has left in its wake a history of one perished culture after another, victims of their own ability to manipulate
and exploit the natural world on which they depended. Our
society now finds itself blundering down the same well-worn

path, for the most part oblivious to the ruins along the way admonishing that ecological dominion simply does not work.

But some people, radical environmentalists among them, are beginning to look beyond the Green Wall civilization has built between nature and our society and to question the suppositions of technological culture. This is not an easy task, since our society invests a great deal of energy in trying to establish its own historic necessity. Ask people if electricity, public schools, and the police are among the necessities of life — or at least of the good life — and they will probably say yes, however absurd this is in historical perspective. Our culture disseminates a view that life without industrial economy is virtually impossible. Its historiography is an accumulation of fictions about the misery of existence before the invention of the steam engine. To claim there is another way, to claim that another way is *required*, assaults some of the core beliefs that define, for good or ill, who we are as a people.

It is not surprising, therefore, that even the critics of civilization have often seemed unable to break free from a fundamentally technocratic view of the world. Ernest Callenbach's vision of the postindustrial world in his influential novel, *Ecotopia*, inspired a reappraisal of hypertechnology on the part of many environmentalists.[2] But upon examination, Callenbach's utopia, with its elaborate recycling systems and elegantly efficient technologies, is not fundamentally different from our present society; it is merely run more rationally and less wastefully. Similarly, Theodore Roszak's *Where the Wasteland Ends* is a biting exposé of the spiritual hollowness of modern society, but his postindustrial vision still finds a place for machine technologies and industrial means of production, if on a small, decentralized, and hence less offensive scale.[3]

The problem with these views — and they are representative of much of the literature of antiindustrial social visions — is not that they are utopian; on the contrary, they are perfectly rational and achievable. But they fail to address technological society in its wholeness. Appropriate technology certainly makes more sense than the vastly inappropriate technologies that are now thrashing about on the planet. But even appropriate technology, as conceived by Callenbach and Roszak, has its price. To have recycling technologies, for instance, requires people to design and produce the machinery, roads to transport raw materials and finished products, institutions of learning to train people for this end, currency, government to print currency, police to protect government interests — in short, the entire structure of technological culture we now have. We tend to look at appropriate technology, such as a solar power panel, in isolation, without realizing that its appropriateness requires an entire social structure that is inextricably entwined in the domination of nature and human nature.

Of course, it is better to have less destructive forms of technology than the hypertechnology now destroying the planet at breakneck speed. As Mike Roselle says, "No one has made the kind of mistakes we're making now. I would be happy to go back to the earlier mistakes to give us time to figure out just how we're going to live with nature."[4] This is reason enough to work for the kind of decentralized, small-scale technologies Callenbach and Roszak propose. Nevertheless, such an approach does not satisfy most radical environmentalists, who are attempting to generate a more fundamental critique of civilization. "Many of us in the Earth First! movement," says John Davis, editor of *Earth First!*, "would like to see human beings live much more like the way they did fifteen thousand years ago as opposed to what we see now."[5] By this he means the kind of hunter-gatherer, shifting-agriculture economies of tribal peoples. Indeed, many radical environmentalists see themselves as part of a tribe rather than a political movement, as a resurgence of primal culture that has been quiescent since the Neolithic. Their vision of the world beyond the Green Wall does not come from the wondrous innovations of science and engineering, but from the simple ecological modesty of primal society.

Inevitably, such a total rejection of civilization and its institutions opens up radical environmentalism to the charge of primitivism, or arcadianism, appellations that depending on their meaning many radical environmentalists do not mind accepting. In *Primitivism and Related Ideas*, Arthur Lovejoy states that primitivism is "the discontent of the civilized with civilization, the belief of men living in a relatively complex cultural condition that a life far simpler is a more desirable life."[6] If this were all the word connoted, however, we would probably all be primitivists. But the terms "primitivism" and "arcadianism" are often used to suggest utopian, unrealistic longing for a mythic Golden Age, "a naive surrender to nostalgia," as Donald Worster puts it.[7] Thus Alston Chase thinks radical environmentalism, like prelapsarian movements before it, is trying to recapture the mythical paradise of Eden.[8] Walter Truett Anderson claims that Deep Ecology has adopted a stance of "innocence" by deploring technological innovation, a stance he claims has become unrealistic for humanity on the verge of a biotechnology revolution.[9]

The problem with this kind of criticism is that it assumes people lived in balance with nature only in the distant past, if at all, and that therefore primitivism seeks to regain some lost pastoral vision of the world that has fallen by the wayside, probably for some good reason. Although it is easy enough to prove that at one time all peoples lived in tribal hunter-gatherer societies, which were quite compatible with wild nature, the more pertinent fact is that at present there are still communities that follow the life of environmental modesty. The Penan, the Mbuti, the !Kung, have for tens of thousands of years woven their rich cultural patterns of life without destroying the ecosystems in which they dwell. They stand as an alternative to the civilization complex — an alternative that works ecologically and hence is pertinent to our situation, not a wistful afterglow from the mythic past. Whether we can transform our lumbering society using the knowledge of primal peoples is impossible to say. But the path of environmental modesty is not utopian; it is being lived this minute by millions of tribal peoples around the world. And up until a few centuries ago it was the predominant way humans related to the natural world. On the contrary, *our* way of life is utopian, in the sense that it is unrealistic and naive and cannot realize its fantasy of unlimited affluence and power free from all ecological restraints.

In *In Search of the Primitive*, Stanley Diamond distinguishes between the balance of primal cultures and the disquiet, the continual dis-ease, of civilization, which suggests to him that primitivism is far from being a nostalgic weakness:

Primitive society may be regarded as a system in equilibrium, spinning kaleidoscopically on its axis but at a relatively fixed point. Civilization may be regarded as a system in internal disequilibrium; technology or ideology or social organization are always out of joint with each other — that is what propels the system along a given track. Our sense of movement, of incompleteness, contributes to the idea of progress. Hence, the idea of progress is generic to civilization. And our idea of primitive society as existing in a state of dynamic equilibrium and as expressive of human and natural rhythms is a logical projection of civilized societies and is in opposition to civilization's actual state. . . . The longing for a primitive mode of existence is no mere fantasy or sentimental whim, it is consonant with fundamental human needs.[10]

The balance and equipoise of primal culture can be seen in the Penan, a tribal people who occupy the dwindling rain forests of the Malaysian state of Sarawak. Deep in the interior of the forest, the Penan still practice a hunter-gatherer life-style, much as their ancestors did during the last Ice Age. They supplement their diet with the products of shifting agriculture, but because their customary law, *Adat,* holds that the living things around them, the next generation, and even the generation that has passed away are worthy of respect, they use the harvest of their forest carefully, not disrupting the soil or destroying the large trees, some of which are considered sacred. The forest belongs to all members of the tribe under a system of usufruct — everyone can take what he or she needs, so there is no need to take more. Living this life of ecological modesty, the Penan have been able to pass on to their children an intact cultural and natural world for uncounted generations. The Penan live with nature, not above it. They feel no moral necessity to seize control of evolution or redeem the natural world from its so-called irrationality. Nature and culture for the Penan are in harmony, although this delicate, thirty-thousand-year-old culture of balance, under pressure from multinational logging companies, may be destroyed within a decade.

A future primitive society based on hunting-gathering and shifting agriculture may sound unrealistic, and given the present population of the planet it is. But the concept does provide a sense of direction, of context, for an environmental sensibility beyond technocracy, a look beyond the limitations of the Green Wall. It is a starting place for learning to reinhabit the world. George Sessions and Bill Devall write, "As deep ecologists re-evaluate primal peoples, including the diverse nations and tribes of Native Americans, they seek not a revival of the Romantic version of primal peoples as 'noble savages,' but a basis for philosophy, religion, cosmology, and conservation practices that can be applied to our own society."[11]

Learning to reinhabit the world, to restore a culture in balance with nature, will not be easy. It may in fact already be impossible because of the overpopulation industrial society has created. Yet there is no alternative but to pursue it. Calls for a more rational regime of technology have a superficial appeal, since they require only a slight readjustment rather than a rethinking of our place in the natural world. But such a rethinking is not only required by the environmental crisis, it is something worth pursuing for its own sake. The task of rediscovering and relearning the elegance and simplicity of primal cultures offers its own strange beauty, at least for radical environmentalists, who have gotten over the need to place the cultural world above the natural. "Our goal," Foreman states, "is the day when there is no word in any language on Earth for the concept of wilderness. Because that concept is no longer needed. Because everything is wilderness. And it just is."[12]

A world in which everyplace is wilderness — this ecotopian vision seems remote from the environmental politics of our day, mystical, atavistic, even threatening. And yet the human race was born into just such a world. It was our home for uncounted millennia. It is still the world of dwindling populations of primal people. It is where we learned the values of community, art, creativity, curiosity. That we should be more comfortable now with the artificial industrial landscape of modern times, with its imperatives of competition, exploitation, and selfish consumption, suggests how successful civilization has been in demonizing nature.

There is good reason to believe that, like it or not, the Earth is destined again to become the wild world radical environmentalists envision. Founded on the idea of human dominion, the cultures of the civilization complex observe no limits and thus seem driven to commit suicide through ecocide. "I predict," wrote Edward Abbey,

> that the military-industrial state will disappear from the surface of the Earth within fifty years. That belief is the basis of my inherent optimism, the source of my hope for the coming restoration of a higher civilization: scattered human populations modest in number that live by fishing, hunting, food-gathering, small-scale farming and ranching, that assemble once a year in the ruins of abandoned cities for great festivals of moral, spiritual, artistic and intellectual renewal — a people for whom the wilderness is not a playground but their natural and native home.[13]

If Abbey is right and the regime of technology is ending, the question we need to face is what kind of world will come in its wake: the world Abbey envisions, in which there is enough hospitable habitat to support a modest but ecologically rich way of life; or a barren world ravaged by modern industry and warfare, devoid of otters and redwoods, orchids and elephants, blue whales and salamanders.

Nature is indifferent to the outcome. The life-forms that will predominate in the future may be grizzly bears and bison or scorpions and roaches, as far as evolution is concerned. For our children's sake, however, we do not have the luxury of indifference. Perhaps the most important and lasting legacy of radical environmentalism is that it has raised the possibility that there is another path for humanity besides the ecological imperialism of civilization and the destruction that it brings. We do not have to be the masters of the Earth, the paragons of animals, the demigods of evolution. We can, if we are smart, simply dwell here, along with all the other beautiful, terrible, and fascinating forms of life that fill the world with their constant evolving. We can for the first time in ten thousand years at least try to make ourselves feel at home.

EPILOGUE

_____

Life is the only game in town.

— *John Seed*

WE ARE ALL AWARE of the path taken. The history of ecological decline on this continent is nasty, brutish, and short; the more striking images are all too familiar. In 1810 the ornithologist Alexander Wilson observed a flock of passenger pigeons so numerous that their wings blotted out the sun for three full days. A century later, billions of the birds had been slaughtered as meat for the pot, and in 1914 the last passenger pigeon, patriotically named Martha, perished in the Cincinnati Zoo. At the time of the Declaration of Independence the world's largest terrestrial predator, the grizzly bear, roamed from the Pacific to the Mississippi in numbers approaching 100,000. The great bear's existence south of Canada is now restricted to two mismanaged and precarious populations, in Montana and Wyoming, and is secure only as the emblem on the California state flag — a dubious distinction at best. And, of course, there were the bison. At 60 million strong they were perhaps the largest congregation of ungulates ever to grace and graze the planet. "From the top of Pawnee Rock [in Arkansas]," wrote Colonel R. I. Dodge in 1882, "I could see from six to ten miles in almost every direction. This whole vast space was covered with Buffalo, looking at a distance like a compact mass."[1] A few decades later, Theodore Roosevelt recounted the eerie experience of an acquaintance who had just traveled a thousand miles across the northern part of Montana: "During the whole distance he was never out of sight of a dead buffalo, and never in sight of a live one."[2]

There were a thousand other, less dramatic but no less important ecological confusions brought about by the introduction of Western culture to this continent: the replacement of the West's native bunchgrass and grama with a poisonous combination of exotic species like cheatgrass and Russian thistle; the displacement of native elk and pronghorn by cows; the damming of rivers; the building of roads; the poisoning of the atmosphere.

It had taken ten thousand years for the inhabitants of Europe to replace the post-Pleistocene splendor of their ecology with the squalor of industry, domestication, and overpopulation. Their American offspring were much more diligent: we accomplished the same task in a mere three centuries.

Precisely this historical compression may help explain why radical environmentalism has put down such strong roots in America. The loss of the natural world was felt more acutely on this continent; it was thematized early on and became part of our intellectual and political heritage. This in no way suggests that the American radical environmental movement speaks with more authority than radical groups in Australia, Africa, Indonesia, or Europe, which have contributed their own significant and thoughtful expressions of outrage at civilization's assault on nature. But it is true that on this continent radical environmentalism finally found its own tumultuous voice.

To grasp the historical significance of the radical environmental movement, we need to consider the path not taken, the path of environmental sanity and accommodation. Between the mad inspiration of our ancestors to defoliate the green world and the present reality of biological meltdown, there were other visions of human community, other voices in defense of the wild, of which in a real sense the present radical environmental movement is but a reprise. There were a number of historical opportunities that are usually passed over in the paean to progress characterizing most historiography — paths our culture could have taken and at times almost did, if only we had listened, not to some fanatical voices on the cultural fringe, but to those who embodied the core values of human community: the Jeffersons, the Thoreaus, the Muirs.

In *The Radical Politics of Thomas Jefferson*, Richard Matthews introduces us to a Jefferson quite unlike the bland patriot after whom we name high schools. The Jefferson of history, Matthews argues, rejected the market economy of ever-expanding industry this nation has come to represent and held up the ideal of a steady-state agrarian society in which "moderation in material desires is . . . essential."[3] His fascination with and admiration for American Indian culture led him to the conclusion that communal anarchism was preferable to the oppressive institutions of civilization. Indeed, as Charles Miller adds in *Jefferson and Nature*, Jefferson believed that ultimately the Europeans and Indians of the continent were destined to become "one people," bonded by marriage and by a new culture that would combine the freedom of the Indians' tribal society with the tradition of Western pastoralism.[4] According to Matthews, Jefferson's pastoral vision of the nation was meant to strike a balance between "the extremes of primitivism and what may be called 'over-civilization,' " — a balance that contained the promise of "a healthy, beautiful environment in which men can grow and develop. . . . By bringing this aesthetic dimension back into the American ethos, a sense of order, harmony, and limits would result."[5] The best political form to express this agrarian ideal, Jeffersonian democracy as *Jefferson* conceived it (not his successors) was radical, grassroots democracy, based on the ward level and ever prepared to overturn any accumulation of power by those in leadership roles.

Jefferson was hardly a radical environmentalist, and he often did not live up to his ideal in his own public or private life. Nevertheless, had this country followed the path he suggested, of minimal industry and an emphasis on the small-scale rural freehold, of creating a harmonious community rather than a powerful empire, we might have been spared the environmental trauma now under way. The great hardwood forests of the East and South would perhaps still be intact, the bays free of pollution and filled with life, the ancient cultures of the Indians still thriving and providing a reference for Western culture to dwell peaceably in nature. There would have been no Love Canal, no PCBs in Lake Michigan, no Three Mile Island. But industry and Alexander Hamilton — including the Hamilton in Jefferson himself — won out over Jefferson, sending America on its way to Order, Empire, and the *Exxon Valdez*.

After Jefferson's death another advocate for environmental modesty emerged. Sounding the theme of biocentrism, Henry David Thoreau began his natural history field studies, because, as he explained, "I wanted to know my neighbors, to get a little nearer to them." In attempting to do so, he was one of the first Americans to come to grips with the environmentally destructive character of our culture, and just as it had been for his successors a century and a half later, the death of the ancient forests was the catalyst. Aware that the woods were being pushed back rapidly from his hometown of Concord, Massachusetts, Thoreau condemned contemporary timber practices, calling them "a greediness that defeats its own purposes." The epithet might just as well have been used by Thoreau to describe the entire industrial economy that was springing up around him. In contrast, Thoreau saw humanity as part of the larger biotic community, which prompted him to call the plants and animals and even the natural objects that existed near Concord his "co-inhabitants" and "fellow-creatures." Thoreau anticipated the pernicious effects of anthropocentrism, warning, "There is no place for man-worship."[6]

But again, man-worship won out. As a kind of objective correlative of the path our culture took, Thoreau's beloved Walden Pond was destined to lie within a mile of a four-lane highway. By the time of Thoreau's death the East Coast was well on its way to becoming a powerhouse of heavy industry and a biological desert.

There was, however, still hope. The West of the late 1800s was in some places still the domain of nature, with vast and majestic conifer forests, three-hundred-foot-tall redwoods, raging rivers, and some of the most diverse animal and plant communities on Earth. The western wilderness found its voice in John Muir. Like Thoreau, Muir also saw humans as part of a larger nonhuman community, over which they had usurped the role of "Lord Man": "Nature's object in making animals and plants might possibly be first of all the happiness of each one of them, not the creation of all for the happiness of one. Why ought man to value himself as more than an infinitely small composing unit of the one great unit of creation?"[7] The anthropocentrism Muir so abhorred took on tangible form when plans were made to place a dam inside the boundaries of Yosemite National Park to provide cheap water for San Francisco. For Muir the dam represented more than just a foolish project; it was a fork in the road, a moment for deciding how we were to treat the natural world — as a resource or as a thing with value in its own right. The decision was made. The dam was built, and since then every major waterway in the West has been dammed, the old-growth forests have dwindled to almost nothing, the oceans have become dumping grounds and oil fields. Muir saw it happening.

There were others. Aldo Leopold, Sigurd Olson, Rachel Carson, Edward Abbey — all expressed the theme that by learning to accommodate the natural world, we and our children obtain benefits that are ten times superior to any short-term gains from industry and anthropocentric arrogance. But before the ecological and political disappointments of the past could crystallize into a radical movement proclaiming this message, America had to experience one more forsaken opportunity. The moderate environmental movement of the 1970s rose to the occasion, abandoning the message of environmental modesty for stratagems, influence, and prestige. It is within this context, a history of lost possibility — both political and ecological — that the radical environmental movement comes into focus.

Radical environmentalism presents itself as one more chance, perhaps the last chance, to turn from the path of environmental imperialism and reconsider our place in the biosphere. Every other time such a reevaluation has beckoned, civilization has triumphed. And yet it has not. By continually undermining the integrity of the environment it has set in motion forces of social unrest and resistance it never could have imagined. "The whole grandiose structure," writes Abbey, "is self-destructive: by enshrining the profit motive (power) as our guiding ideal, we encourage the intensive and accelerating use and abuse of land, air, water — the natural world — on which the structure depends for its continued existence."[8] A greediness that defeats its own purposes, he might have said.

It may already be too late, as William Catton argues. In the coming world of population overshoot, warns Catton, "affluence, equity, democracy, human tolerance, peaceful coexistence between nations, races, sects, sexes, parties, all are in jeopardy."[9] Catton still retains a dim hope that ecological collapse may be avoided, but a dim hope it remains. Even as that sentence was written, another species unique to the universe flickered out, another thread in the complex weave of human and nonhuman life was unraveled . . .

We are living in a time of rage — humanitarian rage against impoverishment, famine, wars; political rage against right-wing death squads, oppressive communist bureaucracies, military occupations; economic rage against the marginalization of the underclass and the monolithic power of multinational corporations. And there is a growing green rage against the destruction of the Earth and its breathtaking profusion of life. Dave Foreman has called for a new warrior society to defend what remains of the Earth's beauty. For all its controversies and shortcomings, perhaps radical environmentalism is the spearhead of that warrior society, and perhaps it will be able to put the rage of the times, that warrior spirit, to use in the best context — the defense of the integrity of life on this planet.

John Muir once wrote that in a war between humans and bears he would be sorely tempted to side with the bears. For Foreman, Mike Roselle, Paul Watson, John Seed, Bill Devall, the growing ranks of radical environmentalists around the world, and perhaps for all of us, the time to make the choice between the natural and cultural world has come.

NOTES
―――――

CHAPTER 1. THE ECOLOGY OF CONFRONTATION

1. See Michael P. Cohen, *The History of the Sierra Club*, pp. 172–180.

2. *Lake Powell: Jewel of the Colorado*. It is generally conceded that Floyd Dominy wrote the entire book.

3. *Lake Powell*, p. 13. Dominy is also quoted as saying, "On balance, I can't lament what's been covered up" (John McPhee, *Encounters with the Archdruid*, p. 200).

4. Edward Abbey, *Beyond the Wall*, p. 100. Abbey also suggested that after the dam was blown up, the "splendid new rapids thus created we will name Floyd E. Dominy Falls" (*Desert Solitaire*, p. 165).

5. Whether the plastic should be unfurled or unrolled was the subject of an almost scholastic debate among the dam crackers the night before at the Lone Rock Campground, about five miles from the dam. Several of them were afraid that if the entire plastic roll was thrown over the side, its weight would jerk the crack from its moorings. Thus the pro-unrollers proposed that the end of the plastic be slowly unrolled, like a giant roll of toilet paper, over the side (noting the appropriateness of the simile). The pro-unfurlers argued that there would be no jerk, since the inertia of the roll would decrease as it unfurled. The sounder physics of the pro-unfurlers won the day, as did the fact that it would have taken too much time to unroll the crack anyway.

6. Fortuitously, the incident was videotaped by three students from the University of San Francisco — Randall Hayes, Christopher McLeod, and Glen Switkes — who had come to interview Abbey. Wolke and Roselle saw the students' audiovideo equipment in their van the day before and began questioning them, thinking they were with the police. The Earth First!ers changed their mind only when Switkes pulled out a jug of homemade beer and offered them some. McLeod went on to make several acclaimed environmental documentaries, Hayes became director of the Rainforest Action Network, and Switkes became an activist in the Amazon Project.

7. Speech by Abbey, March 21, 1981, recorded on the video documentary *The Cracking of the Glen Canyon Damn* [sic].

8. Technically it was the group's second public act, since in April 1980, Foreman, Kezar, and a few other Earth First!ers had gone into New Mexico's Gila Wilderness to put up a plaque commemorating the last raid of Victorio, an Apache, which had wiped out a mining camp in the area. The plaque is discussed in Chapter 4.

9. "A Petition to the United States Congress," printed in *Earth First! Newsletter*, December 21, 1981, p. 3. The text read: "The Construction of Glen Canyon Dam and the filling of Lake Powell on the Utah/Arizona border was probably the single most destructive project to the environment ever undertaken in the United States. It destroyed an incomparable area of red rock canyon wilderness. We, the undersigned citizens of the United States of America, hereby petition our elected representatives in Congress assemble to pass legislation directing the breaching of Glen Canyon Dam and the draining of Lake Powell to allow the Colorado and San Juan Rivers to cleanse their canyons and begin to recreate their wilderness." The petition was signed by several thousand people.

10. Interview with Mike Roselle, San Francisco, July 7, 1989.

11. Interview with Sue Joerger, Medford, Oreg., October 10, 1987.

12. "Bulldozers into Boat Anchors," *Earth First!*, August 1, 1985, p. 25.

13. Telephone interview with Ben Hull, September 11, 1989.

14. Telephone interview with Gary Herbert, attorney with the Mountain States Legal Foundation, August 28, 1989; Jennifer Foote, "Trying to Take Back the Planet," *Newsweek*, February 5, 1990, p. 24.

15. Telephone interview with Jim McCauley, August 8, 1989.

16. Quoted in Fred Setterberg, "The Wild Bunch: Earth First! Shakes Up the Environmental Movement," *Utne Reader*, May–June 1987, p. 71.

17. It was first mentioned as an ecological tool by a folksy Leroy Watson in the *Earth First! Newsletter*, December 21, 1981, p. 6, in a column that would later be entitled "Dear Ned Ludd," created to dispense advice on monkeywrenching.

18. Telephone interview with William Derr, September 10, 1989.

19. "Tree Sabotage Claims Its First Victim," *San Francisco Chronicle*, May 15, 1987.

20. "Earth First! Blamed for Worker's Injuries," *Eureka Times-Standard*, May 14, 1987.

21. In reality, mills encounter metal in logs all the time — camp nails, bits of barbed wire — and timber companies have used metal detectors in their mills for years. The saw at the Cloverdale mill, for instance, hits metal about once every two weeks without the benefit of radical environmentalist intervention. The issue that never arose in the incident but should have was the inadequate safety practices of

Louisiana-Pacific, which allow a worker protected only by a face shield to be in such close proximity to the head rig.

22. Since only a single spike was used and no warning was given, it is very unlikely that radical environmentalists were involved. The connection with a right-wing extremist is discussed in Peter Steinhart, "Respecting the Law," p. 12.

23. "Environmental Radicals Target of Probe into Lumber Mill Accident," *Los Angeles Times*, May 14, 1987.

24. Telephone interview with Judi Bari, October 10, 1989.

25. 18 USCA Sec. 1864.

26. Quoted in "Officials Assail Use of Nails to Block Logging," *New York Times*, June 22, 1988.

27. Telephone interview with McCauley.

28. The owner of the mill, Gregory Forest Products, did not believe this event could be the work of radical environmentalists, even those with the most impeccable sense of timing. But Greg Miller, of the Southern Oregon Timber Industries Association, sent a number of letters to the local press suggesting it was.

29. Telephone interview with Hull.

30. The Washington recision was at the Icicle Creek sale in the Wenatchee National Forest; the Virginia recision was in the Big Schloss roadless area of the George Washington National Forest. In both incidents the timber company demanded a reappraisal and reauction of the timber sale, which meant the Forest Service had to remove the spikes. However, since the service could not guarantee that all the spikes were removed, it could not find any new purchasers.

31. The petition to Fish and Wildlife that finally forced the service to hold hearings was filed by a small Maine-based environmental group called Green World. The large national organizations such as Audubon and the Sierra Club refused to do so for fear of alienating the congressional delegations from timber states — in particular, Hatfield.

32. Earth First! v. Block, 569 F. Supp. 415 (U.S.D.C. Oreg. 1983). It was the first lawsuit brought by the fledgling group.

33. Interview with Ron Huber, Grand Canyon, Ariz., July 8, 1987.

34. Quoted in *Earth First!*, September 22, 1988, p. 1.

35. *Earth First!*, November 1, 1986, p. 1.

36. *Grants Pass Daily Courier*, July 17, 1989.

37. In the Siskiyou National Forest, in southern Oregon, and in Humboldt County, California. See *Grants Pass Daily Courier*, July 13, 1989; *San Francisco Chronicle*, August 17, 1989.

38. *Grants Pass Daily Courier*, June 22, 1987.

39. Interview with Dave Foreman, Grand Canyon, Ariz., July 8, 1987.

40. Paul Watson and Warren Rogers, *Sea Shepherd*, pp. 171 ff.

41. Watson, "Occurrence in the Ferocious Isles: Sea Shepherd Takes on Whale Butchers," *Earth First!*, September 23, 1986, p. 1.

42. Watson, "Raid on Reykjavik," *Earth First!*, December 21, 1986, p. 1; Robert W. Stewart, "Militants Damage Iceland Whale Processing Plant," *Los Angeles Times*, November 10, 1986.

43. Extensive coverage of ecotage worldwide for the past decade can be found in *Earth First!*.

44. During an environmental exchange program, members of the Earth Island Institute, Mike Roselle among them, talked with militant environmentalists in Leningrad, who suggested they were engaged in ecotage. Roselle was even able to smuggle in for them a copy of Foreman's book *Ecodefense: A Field Guide to Monkeywrenching*, a how-to manual on ecological sabotage.

45. Interview with Darryl Cherney, Jemez Mountains, N. Mex., June 23, 1989.

46. As quoted in Joe Kane, "Mother Nature's Army: Guerrilla Warfare Comes to the American Forest," *Esquire*, February 1987, p. 102. Hair also denounced Earth First! as terrorists in Fred Setterberg, "The Wild Bunch: Earth First! Shakes Up the Environmental Movement," *Utne Reader*, May–June 1987, p. 71.

47. Letter to the president of Iceland from Greenpeace International, London, November 11, 1986, printed in *Morganbladith* (Reykjavík), November 12, 1986.

48. Interview with Barbara Dugleby, Grand Canyon, Ariz., July 7, 1987.

49. Interview with Robert Hattoy, Los Angeles, September 9, 1987.

50. Howie Wolke, "The Grizzly Den," *Earth First!*, May 1, 1983, p. 2.

51. Interview with Nancy Morton, Grand Canyon, Ariz., July 8, 1987. Morton not only met Earth First!, but also married it, in the form of Dave Foreman.

52. Speech by Foreman, Seventh Annual Round River Rendezvous, Grand Canyon, Ariz., July 10, 1987.

53. As indicated by their presence in significant numbers at the 1989 Earth First! Round River Rendezvous and by the publication of a journal, *Live Wild or Die!*, as an alternative to the national *Earth First!* journal, with its more "amicable" — if that's the right word — relations with the mainstream environmental movement.

54. Alston Chase, *Playing God in Yellowstone*, p. 347.

55. Chase, "Missionaries of Environmentalism," *Orange County Register*, August 6, 1989.

56. Murray Bookchin, "Social Ecology Versus 'Deep Ecology.'"

57. Speech by Foreman.

58. For a succinct discussion of ideas central to radical environmental-

ism, see Foreman, "Whither Earth First!?," *Earth First!*, November 1, 1987, pp. 20–21.

59. See Roderick Nash, *The Rights of Nature*.

CHAPTER 2. THE CULTURE OF EXTINCTION

1. Aldo Leopold, *A Sand County Almanac*, p. 130.

2. Ibid., pp. 224–225.

3. Interview with Rick Bailey, Grand Canyon, Ariz., July 7, 1987.

4. "The Current State of Biological Diversity," in Edward O. Wilson, ed., *Biodiversity*, p. 13.

5. Norman Myers, *The Sinking Ark*, p. 31.

6. Robert MacArthur and Edward O. Wilson, *The Theory of Island Biogeography;* D. S. Siberloff, "Mass Extinctions and the Destruction of Moist Tropical Forests," in M. E. Soulé and Bruce A. Wilcox, eds., *Conservation Biology*.

7. Myers, "A Look at the Present Extinction Spasm and What It Means for the Evolution of Species," in E. J. Hoage, ed., *Animal Extinctions: What Everyone Should Know* (Washington, D.C.: Smithsonian Institution Press, 1985), p. 55.

8. William D. Newmark, "A Land-Bridge Island Perspective"; James Gleick, "Species Vanishing from Many Parks," *New York Times*, February 3, 1987.

9. Quoted in Gaylord Nelson, " 'Teach-In' to Save the Earth," *Reader's Digest*, April 1970, p. 111.

10. See Table 6-2 in Ariel E. Lugo, "Estimating Reductions in the Diversity of Tropical Forest Species," in Edward O. Wilson, ed., *Biodiversity*, p. 64.

11. Conversation with Jasper Carlton, Berkeley, Calif., February 9, 1989.

12. A. H. Knoll, "Patterns of Extinction in the Fossil Record," in M. H. Nitecki, ed., *Animal Extinctions*, pp. 21–68.

13. Paul Ehrlich, "Extinctions and Ecosystem Functions: Implications for Humankind," in M. H. Nitecki, ed., *Animal Extinctions*, p. 164.

14. D. Jablonski, "Causes and Consequences of Mass Extinctions: A Comparative Approach," pp. 183–230.

15. Ghillean T. Prance, ed., *Biological Diversification in the Tropics* (New York: Columbia University Press, 1982).

16. Myers, "A Look at the Present Extinction Spasm," p. 54.

17. Murray Bookchin, "Social Ecology Versus 'Deep Ecology,' " p. 20. An exaggerated sense of humanity's grandeur, often reflected in their titles, characterizes the writings of all these men. Chase insists we have to "play God" in Yellowstone; Anderson wants to "govern evolution"; Schmookler would have humankind arise "out of weakness" and become the consciousness of the Earth. It is as if these writers, forced

to concede that humanity is part of nature, try to rescue their humanism by chalking up the blunders of human history to some grandiose mission not otherwise apparent to this author.

18. Alston Chase, *Playing God in Yellowstone*, p. 374.

19. Walter Truett Anderson, *To Govern Evolution*, p. 346.

20. Ron Arnold, *Ecology Wars*, p. 118.

21. Ibid., pp. 115–116.

22. See Gordon V. Childe, *Man Makes Himself;* Alfred W. Crosby, *Ecological Imperialism*, pp. 17–21.

23. George Perkins Marsh, *Man and Nature*.

24. Vernon Carter and Tom Dale, *Topsoil and Civilization*, pp. 6–7.

25. Robert Paehlke, *Environmentalism and the Future of Progressive Politics*, p. 2.

26. "Summit Stresses Ecological Threat," *Los Angeles Times*, July 17, 1989.

27. German Green Party, *The Federal Programme of the German Green Party*, p. 31.

28. Michael Redclift, "Turning Nightmares into Dreams," p. 180.

29. See Max Nicholson, *The New Environmental Age* (Cambridge: Cambridge University Press, 1987); Donald Worster, *Nature's Economy*, pp. 339–348; Thomas Berry, "The Ecological Age," in Peter Borrelli, ed., *Crossroads*.

30. World Wildlife Fund — U.S., "Linking Conservation and Development."

31. Thomas J. Kimball, "Status of the Environment and Our Efforts to Improve It," *Proceedings of the 1972 International Conference on Nuclear Solutions to World Energy Problems*, p. 6.

32. William R. Catton, Jr., *Overshoot*, p. 173.

33. Petr Beckmann, *Eco-Hysterics and the Technophobes*, p. 6. Of course, Beckmann is something of an easy target, but even more reasoned paeans to technology, such as Peter Vajk's *Doomsday Has Been Cancelled*, are filled with embarrassing assurances that the environment is in no danger.

34. *An Environmental Agenda for the Future* (Washington, D.C.: Island Press, 1985).

35. Langdon Winner, *The Whale and the Reactor*, p. 83.

36. Michael Soulé, "Conservation Biology: Its Scope and Its Challenge," in M. E. Soulé and Bruce A. Wilcox, eds., *Conservation Biology*, p. 166.

37. Martin Heidegger, *The End of Philosophy*, p. 109.

38. Arnold Toynbee, *London Observer*, April 14, 1974.

39. William Ophuls, *Ecology and the Politics of Scarcity*, p. 151.

40. Robert Heilbroner, *An Inquiry into the Human Prospect*, p. 26.

41. Thus big-game hunts in Alaska, for example, may cost up to ten thousand dollars, limiting them to corporate clients and the wealthy. They are less an instance of recreation than of status.

42. Mark A. Stein, "First Open-Air Bacteria Test Goes Smoothly," *Los Angeles Times*, April 25, 1987.

43. For an excellent discussion of extending legal rights to nature, see Christopher D. Stone, *Should Trees Have Standing?*

44. Lloyd Timberlake and Jon Tinker, *Environment and Conflict*.

45. See Cynthia Pollock, "Decommissioning Nuclear Power Plants," pp. 119–138.

46. Colin M. Turnbull, "Cultural Loss Can Foreshadow Human Extinctions: The Influence of Modern Civilization," in M. H. Nitecki, ed., *Animal Extinctions*, pp. 175–192; and Turnbull, *The Mountain People*.

47. Ehrlich, "The Loss of Diversity," in Edward O. Wilson, ed., *Biodiversity*, p. 22.

48. Roland Barthes, *Mythologies*, p. 155.

49. Michel Foucault, *The Birth of the Clinic*.

50. Speech by Dave Foreman, Grand Canyon, Ariz., July 7, 1987.

51. Winner, *The Whale and the Reactor*, p. 129.

52. Vajk, *Doomsday Has Been Cancelled*.

53. Gregg Easterbrook, *Newsweek*, July 24, 1989, p. 35.

CHAPTER 3. THE RISE AND FALL OF REFORM
ENVIRONMENTALISM

1. Barry Commoner spoke at Harvard, M.I.T., and Rhode Island College; Gaylord Nelson outdid everyone by speaking at nine colleges, from Harvard to Berkeley.

2. Senators Nelson, Ted Kennedy, and Edmund Muskie gave addresses at major universities. With an extraordinary sense of bad timing, Secretary of the Interior Walter Hickel spoke at the University of Alaska to proclaim that the Alaskan oil pipeline would be built.

3. "The Dawning of Earth Day," *Time*, April 27, 1970, p. 46.

4. John G. Mitchell and Constance L. Stallings, eds., *Ecotactics*, p. 12.

5. Speech by Nelson, April 22, 1970, quoted in *Time*, May 4, 1970, p. 16.

6. The Wilderness Society refused to join Merritt and Ruckel in the suit, mindful as always of its financial resources and impressed with the bad advice of a Washington, D.C., attorney who anachronistically thought the U.S. government could not be sued.

7. Gary Soucie to David Brower, April 19, 1967, quoted in Susan R. Schrepfer, *The Fight to Save the Redwoods*, p. 164.

8. By 1983 the heads of the Sierra Club, the Natural Resources Defense Council, the Audubon Society, the Environmental Defense Fund, and the Wilderness Society were all attorneys.

9. Ten years later the two hundred thousandth member joined, who was — some might say significantly — a volunteer in an environmental museum. See *Sierra*, July-August 1981, p. 66; and Sierra Club membership reports, Sierra Club San Francisco office.

10. Thomas Dunlap, *Saving America's Wildlife*, p. 102.

11. Minutes, Board of Directors, May 2–3, 1970; editorial, *Sierra Club Bulletin*, June 1970, p. 2.

12. Minutes, Board of Directors, February 14–15, 1970, exhibit A. This fear of infiltration by undesirable elements is a recurrent theme throughout the history of the mainstream environmental movement. Thus, twelve years later, in an editorial in *Sierra* (May-June 1982, p. 10), Brock Evans, the director of the Sierra Club's Washington office, still felt it necessary to defend the club against charges of anti-Americanism and communist influence. And in a 1987 book, *The New Environmental Age*, environmental writer Max Nicholson worries out loud that there are those "who may plot to take over some influential and possibly well-funded organization, which can then serve as a platform for their ulterior aims."

13. Michael McCloskey, "Sierra Club Executive Director, the Evolving Sierra Club and the Environmental Movement, 1961–1981," interview conducted by Susan R. Schrepfer, Regional Oral History Office, Bancroft Library, Berkeley, Calif., 1983, p. 122.

14. *Audubon*, January 1977, inside cover.

15. Paul Rauber, "With Friends Like These . . . ," *Mother Jones*, November 1986, p. 36.

16. Dave Foreman, "Earth First!," p. 39.

17. "The Rise of Anti-Ecology," *Time*, August 31, 1970, p. 42.

18. Robert Chrisman, "Ecology, a Racist Shuck," *Scanlan's*, August 1979, p. 46.

19. "This Ecology Craze," *New Republic*, March 7, 1970, p. 9.

20. Barry Commoner, "Beyond the Teach-In," *Saturday Review*, April 4, 1970, p. 63.

21. Gaylord Nelson, " 'Teach-In' to Save the Earth," *Reader's Digest*, April 1970, p. 112.

22. James Ridgeway, *The Politics of Ecology;* Barry Weisberg, *Beyond Repair.*

23. Edward Clebsch, "The Campus Teach-In on the Environmental Crisis — 1970," *Living Wilderness*, Spring 1970, p. 12.

24. Douglas Scott, "Student Activism on Environmental Crisis," p. 9.

25. Quoted in Peter Borrelli, "Environmentalism at a Crossroads," p. 24.

26. "Earth Day," *Newsweek*, April 13, 1970, p. 26.

27. Brock Evans, *Sierra*, January-February 1980, p. 9.

28. "A Talk with Mike McCloskey, Executive Director of the Sierra Club," *Sierra*, March-April 1982, p. 36.

29. "The Rise of Anti-Ecology," *Time*, August 31, 1970, p. 42.

30. "This Ecology Craze," *New Republic*, March 7, 1970, p. 8.

31. Quoted in John McPhee, *Encounters with the Archdruid*, p. 212.

32. Ibid., p. 215.

33. Michael P. Cohen, *The History of the Sierra Club*, p. 396.

34. H. Jeffrey Leonard et al., *Business and Environment*.

35. William K. Reilly, "After the Environmental Rally," *The Conservation Foundation: A Report for the Year 1977* (Washington, D.C.: 1977).

36. Dennis M. Roth, *The Wilderness Movement and the National Forests*, p. 64.

37. H. J. McCloskey, in *Ecological Ethics and Politics*, cavils pointlessly that the reasons Leopold gives for preserving the natural world are sometimes pragmatic and sometimes Deep Ecology.

38. Robert Marshall, "The Problem of the Wilderness," *Scientific Monthly*, 30 (1930), p. 144.

39. Robert Hunter, *Warriors of the Rainbow*, p. 301.

40. Quoted in Robert A. Jones, "Environmental Movement — Wholesale Changes at Top," *Los Angeles Times*, December 27, 1984.

41. Jones, "Environmental Movement."

42. Interview with Robert Hattoy, Los Angeles, September 1, 1987.

43. Peter Borrelli, "Environmentalism at a Crossroads," pp. 26, 27.

44. Quoted in Seth Zuckerman, "Environmentalism Turns Sixteen," *Nation*, October 18, 1986, p. 368.

45. Zuckerman, "Environmentalism Turns Sixteen," p. 369.

46. Rupert Cutler quoted in Roth, *The Wilderness Movement and the National Forests*, p. 53.

47. Interview with Foreman, Grand Canyon, Ariz., July 7, 1987.

48. "Statement of Eliot Porter at Board Meeting," September 15, 1968; quoted in Cohen, *The History of the Sierra Club*, p. 416.

49. *Audubon*, June 1977, p. 84.

50. Ibid., p. 83.

51. Larry Moss, "Beyond Conflict — The Art of Environmental Mediation," *Sierra*, March-April 1981, p. 40.

52. See "Environmental Mediation and Conflict Management," *Environmental Professional*, 2 (1980), entire issue.

53. "Readers' Turn," *Audubon*, July 1978, pp. 116–117.

54. Arne Naess, "The Shallow and the Deep, Long-Range Ecology Movement. A Summary," pp. 95–100.

55. Deep Ecology is discussed at length in Chapter 7.

56. Douglas Scott quoted in Roth, *The Wilderness Movement and the National Forests*, p. 54.

57. Ibid., p. 61.

58. Johnson later became a supporter of Earth First!, giving a speech on April 21, 1984, at an Earth First! gathering celebrating John Muir's birthday, in which he told the crowd: "Don't compromise."

59. Johnson won the suit, California v. Bergland, 483 F. Supp. 465 (U.S.D.C. Calif. 1980).

60. Foreman, "Earth First!," p. 39.

CHAPTER 4. EARTH FIRST!

1. Edward Abbey, *Beyond the Wall*, p. 137.

2. Howie Wolke, "The Grizzly Den," *Earth First! Newsletter*, March 20, 1982, p. 4.

3. Interview with Mike Roselle, San Francisco, July 7, 1989.

4. Roselle, "Roadkill," *Earth First!*, March 20, 1985, p. 21.

5. Dave Foreman, quoted in the video documentary *The Cracking of the Glen Canyon Damn*.

6. Wolke, "The Grizzly Den," *Earth First!*, May 1, 1983, p. 3.

7. Samuel S. Epstein et al., *Hazardous Waste in America*, p. 6.

8. Quoted in Richard A. Watson, "A Critique of Anti-Anthropocentric Biocentrism," *Environmental Ethics*, Fall 1983, p. 247.

9. Speech by Foreman, Santa Fe, N. Mex., June 25, 1989.

10. Speech by Foreman, Grand Canyon, Ariz., July 7, 1987.

11. Interview with Roselle, Grand Canyon, Ariz., July 5, 1987.

12. *Dry Country News*, quoted in *Earth First! Newsletter*, March 20, 1982, p. 3.

13. *Earth First! Newsletter*, June 1980, p. 1.

14. *Earth First!*, June 21, 1983, p. 9.

15. Ibid.

16. *Earth First! Newsletter*, December 21, 1981, p. 3.

17. "Environmental Activists Shifting from Preservation to Restoration," *Los Angeles Times*, January 17, 1988.

18. William Tucker, "Is Nature Too Good for Us?," *Harper's*, March 1982, p. 29.

19. "Out, damned spot!" says Lady Macbeth, act 5, scene 1. I haven't been able to track down which Earth First!er came up with this mysterious allusion, or how he or she expected the likes of James Watt to understand it.

20. "Earth First!," *Earth First! Newsletter*, March 20, 1982, p. 10.

21. Based on his contacts with a number of environmental groups, Roselle estimates there are some one hundred thousand Earth First!ers "at heart" in the mainstream environmental movement: "Mike Ro-

selle, Co-Founder of Earth First!, on Direct Action," *Ecology Center Newsletter* (Berkeley, Calif.), July 1989, p. 3.

22. A 1978 survey of five major environmental groups conducted by Resources for the Future suggested that about 19 percent of their members held views "that might be associated with the deep ecology movement."

23. Interview with Nancy Morton, Grand Canyon, Ariz., July 8, 1987.

24. "Cracking the Elwha Damn," *Earth First!*, September 23, 1987, p. 4.

25. Ron Arnold, *At the Eye of the Storm*, p. 196. Arnold's work is a tour de force of sycophancy, unintentional humor, and factual inaccuracy (he says only forty Earth First!ers were present, and he omits, for obvious reasons, the handshaking incident). It is must reading for those who want to understand the prodevelopment mentality of the Watt Department of the Interior. Funded by the right-wing Free Congress Research and Education Foundation, the book was not a bestseller, so the resource corporation Georgia-Pacific took it upon itself to donate copies to hundreds of libraries across the nation as a public service.

26. Quoted in *New York Times*, June 8, 1983.

27. *Environmental Action*, June 1984, p. 4.

28. Richard Costley, letter to J. W. Deinema, March 19, 1971, Forest Service Historical Series. Quoted in Dennis M. Roth, *The Wilderness Movement and the National Forests*, p. 7.

29. Foreman, "Standing Firm," *Earth First! Newsletter*, December 21, 1981, p. 3.

30. Ibid.

31. *Denver Post*, July 5, 1982.

32. Interview with Roselle, San Francisco, July 7, 1989.

33. Michael Kerrick, "Ecotage from Our Perspective."

34. Quoted in Kirkpatrick Sale, "The Forest for the Trees," p. 33.

35. Interview with Roselle.

CHAPTER 5. ESCALATIONS

1. *The Epic of Gilgamesh*, trans. N. K. Sandars (New York: Penguin Books, 1972), p. 72.

2. George Perkins Marsh, *Man and Nature*.

3. Quoted in the *Kalmiopsis Action Alert*, August 7, 1989, p. 1.

4. See T.S. Map F.Y. 82-85, U.S. Forest Service files.

5. Defining old growth has not been easy. In 1986 the Forest Service set up a task force to do so but eventually left it to the supervisors of each national forest to come up with their own meaning. Not surprisingly, they have overwhelmingly used definitions that favor the timber industry. See Jerry F. Franklin et al., *Ecological Characteristics*

of Old-Growth Douglas-Fir Forests (U.S. Department of Agriculture, Pacific Northwest Forest and Range Experiment Station, February 1981). But whatever reasonable definition one attaches to old growth, the important point is that there will not be any of it left if present harvest rates continue.

6. Earth First! v. Block, 569 F. Supp. 415 (U.S.D.C. Oreg. 1983).

7. Details of the Kalmiopsis campaign can be found in the following issues of *Earth First!:* May 1, 1983; June 21, 1983; August 1, 1983.

8. Interview with Mike Roselle, San Francisco, July 7, 1989.

9. "Reminiscences of Mendocino," *Hutchings California Magazine,* October 1858, quoted in Ray Raphael, *Tree Talk,* p. 4.

10. Interview with Bob Watson, Grants Pass, Oreg., September 12, 1987.

11. Ellen Schultz, "A Raider's Ruckus in the Redwoods," *Fortune,* April 24, 1989, pp. 172–180.

12. "Redwood Battle," *Oakland Tribune,* August 20, 1989.

13. Ibid.

14. See Timothy Egan, "Where Have All The Forests Gone?," *New York Times,* February 15, 1989.

15. For example, in 1864, President Lincoln gave Northern Pacific Railroad 38.5 million acres of public land in exchange for laying track from Lake Superior to the Puget Sound. Northern Pacific eventually became Burlington Resources.

16. Under the Organic Act the Forest Service was authorized to allow the cutting only of mature trees, not the entire stand involved in clear-cutting.

17. For an excellent description of the fight against clear-cutting, see Edward C. Fritz, *Sterile Forest.*

18. See Orville Camp, *The Forest Farmer's Handbook.* See also Camp, "Natural Selection Forest Farming," *Trumpeter,* Summer 1989, pp. 103–108; and Raphael, *Tree Talk.*

19. *Seattle Post-Intelligencer,* July 5, 1988.

20. See Robert MacArthur and E. O. Wilson, *The Theory of Island Biogeography;* and Larry D. Harris, *The Fragmented Forest.*

21. Quoted in Nancy Wood, *Clearcut: The Deforestation of America* (San Francisco: The Sierra Club, 1971), p. 17.

22. As quoted in Mike Gienella, "Timber Chief Recalls Roots," *Press Democrat* (Ukiah, Calif.), February 5, 1989.

23. Interview with Sue Joerger, Grants Pass, Oreg., September 11, 1987.

24. Arnold, *Ecology Wars,* p. 144.

25. Speech by Arnold, "Loggerheads Over Land Use: Organizing Against Environmentalists," to the Ontario Forest Industries Association, February 1988, reprinted in *Logging and Sawmilling Journal,* April 1988, and *New Catalyst,* Winter 1988/89, p. 10.

26. Ibid.

27. For logger protests, see *Grants Pass Daily Courier*, August 3, 1987; *Medford Mail Tribune Extra*, August 6–12, 1987.

28. *Earth First!*, December 21, 1989, p. 12.

29. "Panel Votes for Dr. Seuss Book," *San Francisco Chronicle*, October 6, 1989; John M. Glionna, " 'Lorax' Survives Ax, Still on Reading List," *Los Angeles Times*, October 6, 1989.

30. *Eco-News*, January 1, 1983; NEC report, December 12, 1983.

31. Gifford Pinchot, *The Fight For Conservation* (Seattle: University of Washington Press, 1967), pp. 15–16.

32. Pinchot, *Breaking New Ground*, pp. 31–32.

33. David A. Clary, *Timber and the Forest Service*, p. 28.

34. Quoted in *Wilderness*, Summer 1983. Forplan is actually a program, not a computer, which the Forest Service uses to plot maximum timber harvests within the scope of certain restraints, such as soil erosion, sedimentation of rivers, destruction of wildlife. It is often described by environmentalists as Orwellian.

35. Quoted in *Oregonian*, August 6, 1989.

36. Quoted in "Biologist Warns of Clearcutting," *Grants Pass Daily Courier*, August 26, 1987.

37. Quoted in "Forest Supervisor Kisses Louisiana-Pacific's Feet," *Earth First!*, December 21, 1984, p. 1.

38. "Economics Policy Statement," *Forest Planning*, December 1983.

39. See *Subsidizing the Timber Industry: The Economics of National Forest Mismanagement* (Eugene, Oreg.: Cascade Holistic Economic Consultants, 1980).

40. *Sandpiper* (monthly newsletter of the Redwood Regional Audubon Society), April 1989, reprinted in *Inner Voice* (publication of the Association of Forest Service Employees for Environmental Ethics), Summer 1989, p. 7.

41. The full text of the letter is printed in *Inner Voice*, Summer 1989, p. 4.

42. The text, which Pinchot wrote over the signature of Secretary of Agriculture James Wilson, can be found in Pinchot's *Breaking New Ground*, pp. 261–262.

43. Letter from Jeff DeBonis to Dale Robertson, *Inner Voice*, Summer 1989, p. 4.

44. Roselle admitted to the spiking only after the statute of limitations had expired.

45. Interview with Ron Huber, Grand Canyon, Ariz., July 9, 1987.

46. Quoted in "Redwood Battle," *Oakland Tribune*, August 20, 1989.

47. Speech by Greg King, Berkeley, Calif., March 18, 1989.

48. Mike Jakubal, "Stumps Suck! on the Okanogan," *Anarchy, a Journal of Desire Armed*, Fall/Winter 1988–89, p. 1.

49. The name "Stumps Suck!" came from a banner that Rick Bailey, an Oregon Earth First!er, brought to a protest. Its directness caught Jakubal's fancy.

50. David Pease, "Save a Tree, Maim a Human," *Forest Industries*, May 1986.

51. Quoted in Raphael, *Tree Talk*, pp. 220–221.

52. Camp, *The Forest Farmer's Handbook*, p. 53.

CHAPTER 6. THE GREEN WORLD

1. Robert Hunter, *Warriors of the Rainbow*, p. 369.

2. Paul Watson, "Occurrence in the Ferocious Isles," *Earth First!*, September 23, 1986, p. 1.

3. Quoted in Dick Russell, "The Monkeywrenchers," in *Crossroads: Environmental Priorities for the Future*, ed. Peter Borrelli (Washington, D.C.: Island Press, 1988), p. 37. See also Watson and Warren Rogers, *Sea Shepherd*, p. 70.

4. "Earth First! Founder Busted in Possible Set-up," *Animal Agenda*, September 1989, p. 20.

5. Watson, "Occurrence in the Ferocious Isles," p. 1.

6. Speech by Watson, Big Basin, Calif., California Earth First! Rendezvous, October 1986.

7. "Sea Shepherd Returns to Iceland," *Sea Shepherd Log*, March 1988, p. 1.

8. Watson, "Raid on Reykjavik," *Earth First!*, December 21, 1986, p. 1.

9. Russell, "The Monkeywrenchers," p. 40.

10. Telephone interview with Scott Trimingham, January 18, 1990.

11. Watson, "Occurrence in the Ferocious Isles," p. 1.

12. *Sun* (British Columbia), November 10, 1986.

13. Interview with Rod Coronado, Salmon Creek, Idaho, July 3, 1987.

14. Interview with John Seed, Jemez Mountains, N. Mex., June 23, 1989.

15. Quoted in Bill Devall, "The Edge: The Ecology Movement in Australia," *Ecophilosophy Newsletter*, Spring 1984, p. 11.

16. Interview with Seed.

17. Quoted in Devall, "The Edge," p. 11.

18. Seed, "An Immodest Proposal," *Earth First!*, May 1, 1986, p. 20.

19. Seed, "Beyond Anthropocentrism," p. 35.

20. The same Randall Hayes who helped make *The Cracking of the Glen Canyon Damn*.

21. Interview with Seed.

22. Seed, "Beyond Anthropocentrism," p. 37.

23. Graham Innes, "Buried Protest: Words from the Daintree," *Earth First!*, December 21, 1984, p. 15.

24. Quoted in Seed, "Letter from the Solomon Islands," *Earth First!*, December 21, 1984, p. 14.

25. Interview with Mike Roselle, San Francisco, July 7, 1989.

26. Mary Davis, "Environmental Sabotage in Western Europe," *Earth First!*, June 21, 1988, p. 22.

27. Quoted in Davis.

28. Gertrude Shilling, Green member of the Hesse legislature, was quoted in the *Frankfurter Allgemeine Zeitung*, July 23, 1982, as saying, "It is the goal of the Greens to do away with Parliament and to practice direct democracy."

29. See John McCormick, *Reclaiming Paradise*, pp. 40–42.

30. Michael Redclift, "Turning Nightmares into Dreams," p. 182.

31. Interview with Claus Sievert, Berkeley, Calif., October 8, 1989.

32. *Tageszeitung*, January 15, 1980.

33. Winfried Schlaffke, ed., *Vorsicht: Gruene Faelle! Die Partei der falschen Hoffnungen* (Koeln: Tiberius Verlag, 1987), p. 25.

34. *Tageszeitung*, March 24, 1980.

35. See Elim Papadakis, *The Green Movement in West Germany*, p. 179.

36. Howie Wolke, editorial, *Earth First!*, March 20, 1982, p. 5.

37. Petra Kelly, *Fighting for Hope*, p. 18.

38. Rudolf Bahro, *Socialism and Survival*, p. 2.

39. As quoted in Papadakis, *The Green Movement*, p. 180.

40. GAL Hamburg, *Programme*, p. 8; quoted in Papadakis, *The Green Movement*, p. 179.

41. German Green Party, *The Federal Programme of the German Green Party*, p. 7.

42. Herbert Kitschelt, *The Logics of Party Formation*, p. 91.

43. Interview with Dave Foreman, Grand Canyon, Ariz., July 8, 1987.

CHAPTER 7. DEEP ECOLOGY

1. Arne Naess, "Deep Ecology and Ultimate Premises," p. 128.

2. Bill Devall, *Simple in Means, Rich in Ends*, pp. 6–8.

3. John Seed, "Beyond Anthropocentrism," p. 38.

4. Interview with Devall, Grand Canyon, Ariz., July 10, 1987.

5. Naess, "Deep Ecology and Ultimate Premises," p. 128.

6. Devall and George Sessions, *Deep Ecology*, pp. 18–19.

7. David Ehrenfeld, *The Arrogance of Humanism*.

8. See John Passmore, *Man's Responsibility for Nature*, p. 116; H. J. McCloskey, *Ecological Ethics and Politics*, pp. 48–55.

9. Aldo Leopold, *A Sand County Almanac*, p. 204.

10. Sessions, "Deep Ecology and the New Age," p. 27.

11. Henryk Skolimowski, *Eco-Philosophy*, p. 68.

12. Dave Foreman, "Cat Tracks," *Earth First!*, June 21, 1986, p. 21.

13. See David Parice Greanville, "Environmentalists and Animal Rightists — The New Odd Couple?" *Animal Agenda*, October 1989, pp. 22–24.

14. See Gene Spitler, "Justifying a Respect for Nature," pp. 255–260.

15. John Livingstone, *The Fallacy of Wildlife Conservation*, p. 54.

16. See Christopher Manes, "Philosophy and the Environmental Task," pp. 75–82.

17. Paul Shepard, "Ecology and Man — A Viewpoint," p. 2.

18. Naess, "Self-Realization: An Ecological Approach to Being in the World," in *Thinking Like a Mountain*, p. 20.

19. Interview with Devall.

20. David Abram, "Merleau-Ponty," p. 101.

21. Ibid., p. 109.

22. Letter to author, October 17, 1988.

23. Langdon Winner, *The Whale and the Reactor*, p. 133.

24. Peter Borrelli, "The Ecophilosophers," p. 74.

25. Ibid., p. 72.

CHAPTER 8. THE CRITICS

1. *Interaction*, Fall 1983, p. 5.

2. As quoted in *High Country News*, October 23, 1989.

3. Roland Barthes, *Mythologies*, p. 148.

4. Donella H. Meadows et al., *The Limits to Growth*.

5. H.S.D. Cole et al., eds., *Models of Doom;* Cy A. Adler, *Ecological Fantasies;* and Petr Beckmann, *Eco-Hysterics and the Technophobes*.

6. As quoted in Ron Arnold, *At the Eye of the Storm*, p. 254.

7. Lewis Mumford, "Authoritarian and Democratic Technics."

8. Gregory H. Davis, *Technology — Humanism or Nihilism: A Critical Analysis of the Philosophical Basis and Practice of Modern Technology* (Washington, D.C.: University Press of America, 1981), p. 3.

9. Richard Neuhaus, *In Defense of People: Ecology and the Seduction of Radicalism* (New York: Macmillan, 1971), p. 157.

10. Interview with Sue Joerger, Grants Pass, Oreg., September 11, 1987.

11. Interview with Dave Foreman, Grand Canyon, Ariz., July 8, 1987.

12. Murray Bookchin, "Social Ecology Versus 'Deep Ecology.'"

13. As quoted in Peter Borrelli, "The Ecophilosophers," p. 81.

14. Brian Tokar, "Social Ecology, Deep Ecology, and the Future of Green Political Thought," p. 132.

15. George Bradford, "How Deep Is Deep Ecology?"

16. Alston Chase, *Playing God in Yellowstone.*

17. Arne Naess, "Deep Ecology and Ultimate Premises," p. 128.

18. Chim Blea, "Why the Venom," *Earth First!*, November 1, 1987, p. 19.

19. Henryk Skolimowski, "To Continue the Dialogue with Deep Ecology," *Trumpeter*, Fall 1987, p. 31.

20. George Lukacs, *History and Class Consciousness*, p. 234.

21. Bradford, "How Deep Is Deep Ecology?" p. 8.

22. Warwick Fox, "Further Notes in Response to Skolimowski," *Trumpeter*, Fall 1987, p. 34.

23. Bookchin, "Social Ecology Versus 'Deep Ecology,' " p. 21.

24. Quoted in George Sessions, "Deep Ecology and the New Age," p. 29.

25. James Lovelock, *Gaia*, p. 127.

26. Walter Truett Anderson, *To Govern Evolution*, p. 338.

27. Peter Vajk, *Doomsday Has Been Cancelled*, p. 61.

28. Arnold, *Ecology Wars*, pp. 116–117.

29. Ibid., p. 255.

30. Roderick Nash, *Wilderness and the American Mind;* and Lynn White, Jr., "The Historical Roots of Our Ecologic Crisis."

31. Immanuel Kant, "Duties to Animals and Spirits," pp. 239–240.

32. Bookchin, "Social Ecology Versus 'Deep Ecology,' " p. 20.

33. Christina Hoff, "Kant's Invidious Humanism," p. 67.

CHAPTER 9. CIVIL DISOBEDIENCE

1. Roderick Nash, *The Rights of Nature.*

2. Nash, "Rounding Out the American Revolution," p. 178.

3. George Wuerthner, "Tree-Spiking and Moral Maturity," p. 20.

4. Mike Roselle, "Deep Ecology and the New Civil Rights Movement," p. 23.

5. "Wild Rockies EF! Demand Equal Rights for All Species," *Earth First!*, March 21, 1989, p. 5.

6. Henry David Thoreau, *Walden, or Life in the Woods*, p. 243.

7. Tim Palmer, *Stanislaus*, p. 178.

8. Transcript sent to author.

9. "When the Earth Comes First, the Law Comes Later," *Register-Guard* (Eugene, Oreg.), August 16, 1987.

10. Dave Foreman, editorial, *Earth First!*, June 21, 1985, p. 2.

11. Quoted in *Medford Mail Tribune Extra*, August 13–19, 1987.

12. Bill Devall, *Simple in Means, Rich in Ends*, p. 126.

13. Brian Heath, "What Do You Expect to Accomplish — Anyway?," *Earth First!*, November 1, 1986, p. 5.

14. See Judge Field's dissent in *The Slaughter House Cases* 83 U.S. 36 (1872).

15. Interview with Foreman, Grand Canyon, Ariz., July 8, 1987; and interview with Roselle, Grand Canyon, Ariz., July 9, 1987.

16. Nash, *The Rights of Nature*, p. 12.

17. Interview with Jeff Hoffman, Grand Canyon, Ariz., July 8, 1987.

18. Interview with Devall, Grand Canyon, Ariz., July 10, 1987.

19. Roselle, "Deep Ecology and the New Civil Rights Movement," p. 23.

20. Devall and George Sessions, *Deep Ecology*, p. 18.

21. "The people must cease to hold slaves, and to war on Mexico, though it cost them their existence as a people," Thoreau, *Walden, or Life in the Woods*, p. 239.

22. Keith Ervin, *Fragile Majesty*, p. 232.

23. Quoted in "Non-Violent Direct Action Training: Our Tactic vs. Their Interiority of Pacifism," *Earth First!*, August 1, 1989, p. 29.

CHAPTER 10. ECOTAGE

1. Interview with Dave Foreman, Grand Canyon, Ariz., July 8, 1987.

2. "Who Is the Real Rapist?," *Southern Utah News*, July 15, 1987.

3. Peter Steinhart, "Respecting the Law," p. 13.

4. Foreman, ed., *Ecodefense*, p. 16.

5. George Wuerthner, "Tree-Spiking and Moral Maturity," p. 20.

6. Interview with Bill Devall, Grand Canyon, Ariz., July 10, 1987.

7. Interview with Foreman.

8. Harold Gilliam, "Violence Begets Violence," *San Francisco Chronicle*, November 1, 1987.

9. *Forest Industries*, June 1987, p. 2.

10. As quoted in Steinhart, "Respecting the Law," p. 12.

11. Interview with Mike Roselle, Grand Canyon, Ariz., July 9, 1987.

12. Interview with Roselle, San Francisco, July 7, 1989.

13. Steinhart, "Respecting the Law," p. 13.

14. Interview with Devall.

15. The issue is directly addressed by the Supreme Court in Andrus v. Allard, 444 U.S. 51 (1979).

16. Interview with Sue Joerger, Grants Pass, Oreg., September 11, 1987.

17. As quoted in Margaret L. Knox, "Horns of a Dilemma," *Sierra*, November/December 1989, p. 61.

18. Interview with Claus Sievert, Berkeley, Calif., October 15, 1989.

19. Foreman, ed., *Ecodefense*, p. 17.

20. Ed Marston, "Ecotage Isn't a Solution, It's Part of the Problem," *High Country News*, June 19, 1989.

21. See *Hold That Line: Powerline Protest Newsletter of Central Minnesota* (Lowry, Minn.); "Bolt Weevils," *Earth First!*, May 1, 1984, pp. 10–11.

22. As quoted in *Mother Earth News*, January/February 1985, p. 22.

23. Ibid.

24. Marston, "Ecotage Isn't a Solution," p. 15.

25. Foreman, ed., *Ecodefense*, p. 14.

26. See Chapter 1.

27. Wuerthner, "Tree-Spiking and Moral Maturity," p. 20.

28. Devall, *Simple in Means, Rich in Ends*, p. 144.

29. Howie Wolke, "Thoughtful Radicalism," *Earth First!*, December 21, 1989, p. 29.

30. T. O. Hellenbach, "The Future of Monkeywrenching," in Foreman, ed., *Ecodefense*, p. 22.

31. Devall, *Simple in Means, Rich in Ends*, p. 145.

32. Hellenbach, "The Future of Monkeywrenching," p. 22.

33. Foreman, ed., *Ecodefense*, p. 16.

34. Interview with Roselle, Grand Canyon, Ariz., July 9, 1987.

35. Speech by Foreman, Grand Canyon, Ariz., July 10, 1987.

36. Robert Paehlke, *Environmentalism and the Future of Progressive Politics*, pp. 7–8.

37. Interview with Peg Millett, Grand Canyon, Ariz., July 10, 1987.

38. Interview with Howie Wolke, Grand Canyon, Ariz., July 10, 1987.

CHAPTER 11. THE TRIALS OF RADICAL ENVIRONMENTALISM

1. Paul Feldman and Richard E. Meyer, "Four Held in Plot to Cut Lines Near Nuclear Plants," *Los Angeles Times*, June 1, 1989.

2. Interview with Mike Roselle, San Francisco, July 7, 1989.

3. Quoted in *Earth First!*, June 21, 1989, p. 6.

4. Feldman and Meyer, "Four Held in Plot to Cut Lines."

5. Sandy Tolan, "Inside Earth First!," *Arizona Republic*, August 6, 1989; "Arizona Arrestees Released from Jail," *Earth First!*, August 1, 1989, p. 1. The identities of the infiltrators were confirmed by one of the defense attorneys through a review of the FBI tapes.

6. Interview with Jesse Hardin, Canyon, Calif., August 22, 1989.

7. Quoted in "Inside Earth First!," *Arizona Republic*, August 6, 1989.

8. Quoted in *Earth First!* (special section), June 16, 1989, p. 2.

9. "Earth First! Founder Busted in Possible Set-up," *Animal Agenda*, September 1989, p. 20; Nick Ravo, "U.S. Surgical Admits Spying on Animal-Rights Groups," *New York Times*, January 26, 1989.

10. "The Entrapment of Fran Trutt," *Ecomedia #46*, February 21–March 7, 1989.

11. "Earth First! Founder Busted in Possible Set-up," p. 21.

12. "Inside Earth First!."

13. Interview in *Current* (quarterly newsletter of Big River Earth First!), Summer 1989.

14. *L'Express*, August 16–22, 1985.

15. Alex Shoumatoff, "Murder in the Rainforest," *Vanity Fair*, September 1989.

16. Quoted in Eve Pell, "The High Cost of Speaking Out," *California*, November 1988, p. 145.

17. Pell, "The High Cost of Speaking Out," p. 145.

18. Penelope Canan and George W. Pring, "Strategic Lawsuits Against Public Participation," *Social Problems*, 35 (December 1988).

19. Quoted in "Defamation Suits 'Chill' Activists," *National Law Journal*, July 25, 1988.

20. Interview with Roselle, Grand Canyon, Ariz., July 9, 1987.

21. Pacific Lumber v. Sally Bell, "Complaint for Damages," Case Number 80156, Superior Court of California, County of Humboldt, pp. 3–4.

22. Quoted in "PL Files Lawsuit Against Protesters," *Humboldt Beacon*, July 25, 1987.

CHAPTER 12. THE NATURAL RESOURCES STATE

1. Interview with Tim Jackson, Berkeley, Calif., July 10, 1989.

2. Telephone interview with Karen Wood, August 25, 1989.

3. Michael Kerrick, "Ecotage from Our Perspective."

4. 36 CFR Sec. 261.58.

5. Interview with Jackson.

6. Order, Occupancy and Use, Siuslaw National Forest, Attachment A.

7. Telephone interview with Tim Moran (arrested for violating a closure order), November 5, 1989.

8. Ibid.

9. "Timber Industry, Foes Fear Violence Potential," *Grants Pass Daily Courier*, July 17, 1989.

10. United States v. Gemmill, 535 F.2d 1145, 1152 (9th Cir. 1976).

11. Kerrick, "Ecotage from Our Perspective," p. 11.

12. Telephone interview with Wood.

13. "Timber Industry, Foes Fear Violence Potential."

14. "Timber Industry, Foes Fear Violence Potential"; "Escalation! The Kalmiopsis 24," *Earth First!*, August 1, 1989, p. 6; interview with Tim Jackson.

15. Interview with Hal Carlstad, Berkeley, Calif., August 20, 1989.

16. Speech by Jim Weed, printed in *Loggers World*, November 1988.

17. Quoted in Ron Arnold, *At the Eye of the Storm*, p. 241.
18. Quoted in *Business Week*, January 24, 1983, p. 85.
19. Quoted in Nolan Hester, "Forest Service Chief Aims to Double Logging," *Albuquerque Journal*, March 12, 1982.
20. Quoted in Arnold, *At the Eye of the Storm*, p. 122.
21. Denzel Ferguson and Nancy Ferguson, *Sacred Cows at the Public Trough*, p. 195.
22. Quoted in Mark A. Stein and Louis Sahagun, "BLM Woes Spill onto Public Lands," *Los Angeles Times*, May 12, 1989.
23. Edward Relph, *Rational Landscapes and Humanistic Geography*, pp. 14–15.
24. Wayland Drew, "Killing Wilderness," p. 15.

CHAPTER 13. CIVILIZATION AND OTHER ERRATA

1. Donald Worster, *Nature's Economy*, p. 58.
2. Interview with Dave Foreman, Grand Canyon, Ariz., July 8, 1987.
3. Ron Arnold, *At the Eye of the Storm*, p. 41.
4. Interview with Foreman.
5. Bill Devall and George Sessions, *Deep Ecology*, p. 48.
6. Morris Berman, *The Reenchantment of the World*, p. 50.
7. Michel Foucault, *The Order of Things*, p. 310.
8. Theodore Roszak, *Where the Wasteland Ends*, p. xxx.
9. Interview with Mike Roselle, Grand Canyon, Ariz., July 9, 1987.
10. Speech by Foreman, Santa Fe, N. Mex., June 25, 1989.
11. Murray Bookchin, *The Ecology of Freedom*, p. 43.
12. Devall, *Simple in Means, Rich in Ends*, p. 125.
13. Interview with Foreman.
14. William R. Catton, Jr., *Overshoot*, p. 170.
15. Ibid., p. 12.
16. See Miss Ann Thropy (pseud.), "Population and AIDS," p. 32; Daniel Conner, "Is AIDS the Answer to an Environmentalist's Prayer?," pp. 14–16.
17. See "Alien Nation," printed in *Earth First!*, November 1, 1987, p. 17.
18. See George Bradford, "How Deep Is Deep Ecology?"

CHAPTER 14. BEYOND THE GREEN WALL

1. Yevgeny Zamyatin, *We*, p. 89.
2. Ernest Callenbach, *Ecotopia*.
3. Theodore Roszak, *Where the Wasteland Ends*, pp. 413–445.
4. Interview with Mike Roselle, Grand Canyon, Ariz., July 9, 1987.
5. Interview with John Davis, Grand Canyon, Ariz., July 8, 1987.

6. Arthur O. Lovejoy and George Boas, *Primitivism and Related Ideas in Antiquity.*

7. Donald Worster, *Nature's Economy,* p. 378.

8. Conversation with Alston Chase, Jemez Mountains, N. Mex., June 22, 1989.

9. Walter Truett Anderson, *To Govern Evolution,* pp. 322–330.

10. Stanley Diamond, *In Search of the Primitive,* p. 172.

11. Bill Devall and George Sessions, *Deep Ecology,* p. 96.

12. Speech by Dave Foreman, Seventh Annual Round River Rendezvous, Grand Canyon, Ariz., July 10, 1987.

13. Edward Abbey, "A Response to Schmookler on Anarchy," p. 22.

EPILOGUE

1. Quoted in Peter Matthiessen, *Wildlife in America,* p. 150.

2. Paul R. Cutright, *Theodore Roosevelt, the Naturalist,* p. 41.

3. Richard K. Matthews, *The Radical Politics of Thomas Jefferson,* p. 123.

4. Charles A. Miller, *Jefferson and Nature,* p. 65.

5. Matthews, *The Radical Politics of Thomas Jefferson,* p. 125.

6. Quoted in Donald Worster, *Nature's Economy,* p. 60.

7. Quoted in Bill Devall and George Sessions, *Deep Ecology,* p. 104.

8. Edward Abbey, "A Response to Schmookler on Anarchy," p. 22.

9. William R. Catton, Jr., *Overshoot,* p. 262.

SELECTED BIBLIOGRAPHY

Abbey, Edward. *Beyond the Wall: Essays from the Outside*. New York: Holt, Rinehart and Winston, 1971.

———. *Desert Solitaire*. Salt Lake City, Utah: Peregrine Smith, 1981.

———. "A Response to Schmookler on Anarchy." *Earth First!*, August 1, 1986: p. 22.

Abram, David. "Merleau-Ponty and the Voice of the Earth." *Environmental Ethics* 10 (Summer 1988): pp. 101–120.

Adler, Cy A. *Ecological Fantasies*. New York: Glen Eagle Press, 1973.

Anderson, Walter Truett. *To Govern Evolution: Further Adventures of the Political Animal*. San Diego: Harcourt Brace Jovanovich, 1987.

Arnold, Ron. *At the Eye of the Storm: James Watt and the Environmentalists*. Chicago: Regnery Gateway, 1982.

———. *Ecology Wars: Environmentalism As If People Mattered*. Bellevue, Wash.: Free Enterprise Press, 1987.

———. "Loggerheads Over Land Use: Organizing Against Environmentalists." *New Catalyst* (Winter 1988/89): p. 10.

Bahro, Rudolf. *Socialism and Survival*. London: Heretic Books, 1982.

Barthes, Roland. *Mythologies*. Translated by Annette Lavers. New York: Hill and Wang, 1972.

Beckmann, Petr. *Eco-Hysterics and the Technophobes*. Boulder, Colo.: Golem Press, 1973.

Berger, John. *Restoring the Earth: How Americans Are Working to Renew Our Damaged Earth*. New York: Alfred A. Knopf, 1985.

Berman, Morris. *The Reenchantment of the World*. Ithaca, N.Y.: Cornell University Press, 1981.

Bookchin, Murray. *The Ecology of Freedom: The Emergence and Dissolution of Hierarchy*. Palo Alto, Calif.: Cheshire, 1982.

———. "Social Ecology Versus 'Deep Ecology': A Challenge for the Ecology Movement," *Green Perspectives, Newsletter of the Green Program Project* 4 and 5 (Summer 1987).

Borrelli, Peter. "Environmentalism at a Crossroads." In *Crossroads: Governmental Priorities for the Future*, edited by Peter Borrelli. Washington, D.C.: Island Press, 1988, pp. 3–25.

———. "The Ecophilosophers." In *Crossroads: Environmental Priorities for the Future*, edited by Peter Borrelli. Washington, D.C.: Island Press, 1988.

Bradford, George. "How Deep Is Deep Ecology?: A Challenge to Radical Environmentalism." *Fifth Estate* 22 (Fall 1987).

Cahn, Robert, ed. *An Environmental Agenda for the Future*. Washington, D.C.: Island Press, 1985.

Caldwell, Lynton Keith. *International Environmental Policy: Emergence and Dimensions*. Durham, N.C.: Duke University Press, 1984.

Callenbach, Ernest. *Ectopia*. Berkeley, Calif.: Banyan Tree Books, 1975.

Camp, Orville. *The Forest Farmer's Handbook: A Guide to Natural Selection Forest Management*. Ashland, Oreg.: Sky River Press, 1981.

Carter, Vernon, and Tom Dale. *Topsoil and Civilization*. Norman: University of Oklahoma Press, 1955.

Catton, William R., Jr., *Overshoot: The Ecological Basis of Revolutionary Change*. Champaign: University of Illinois Press, 1980.

Chase, Alston. *Playing God in Yellowstone: The Destruction of America's First National Park*. Boston: Atlantic Monthly Press, 1986.

Childe, Gordon V. *Man Makes Himself*. London: Watts, 1956.

Clary, David A. *Timber and the Forest Service*. Lawrence: University of Kansas Press, 1986.

Cohen, Michael P. *The History of the Sierra Club: 1892–1970*. San Francisco: Sierra Club Books, 1988.

Cole, H.S.D. et al., eds., *Models of Doom: A Critique of "The Limits to Growth."* London: Chatto and Windus, for Sussex Press, 1973.

Conner, Daniel. "Is AIDS the Answer to an Environmentalist's Prayer?" *Earth First!*, December 22, 1987: pp. 14–16.

Crosby, Alfred W. *Ecological Imperialism: The Biological Expansion of Europe 900–1900*. Cambridge: Cambridge University Press, 1986.

Cutright, Paul R. *Theodore Roosevelt, the Naturalist*. New York: Harpers, 1956.

Devall, Bill. *Simple in Means, Rich in Ends: Practicing Deep Ecology*. Salt Lake City, Utah: Peregrine Smith, 1988.

——— and George Sessions. *Deep Ecology: Living As If Nature Mattered*. Salt Lake City, Utah: Peregrine Smith, 1985.

Diamond, Stanley. *In Search of the Primitive: A Critique of Civilization*. New Brunswick, N.J.: Transaction, 1974.

Drew, Wayland. "Killing Wilderness." *Ontario Naturalist*, September 1972.

Dunlap, Thomas. *Saving America's Wildlife*. Princeton, N.J.: Princeton University Press, 1988.

Ehrenfeld, David. *The Arrogance of Humanism*. New York: Oxford University Press, 1978.

Epstein, Samuel S., Lester O. Brown, and Carl Pope. *Hazardous Waste in America*. San Francisco: Sierra Club Books, 1982.

Ervin, Keith. *Fragile Majesty: The Battle for North America's Last Great Forest*. Seattle: The Mountaineers, 1989.

Ferguson, Denzel, and Nancy Ferguson. *Sacred Cows at the Public Trough.* Bend, Oreg.: Maverick Publications, 1983.

Foreman, David. "Earth First!" *Progressive* (October 1981): pp. 39–42.

————, ed. *Ecodefense: A Field Guide to Monkeywrenching.* Tucson, Ariz.: Ned Ludd Books, 1985.

Foucault, Michel. *The Birth of the Clinic: An Archaeology of Medical Perception.* Translated by Alan Sheridan. New York: Pantheon, 1973.

————. *The Order of Things: An Archaeology of the Human Sciences.* New York: Vintage Books, 1973.

Fox, Warwick. "Further Notes in Response to Skolimowski." *Trumpeter* 4 (Fall 1987): pp. 32–34.

Fritz, Edward C. *Sterile Forest: The Case Against Clearcutting.* Austin, Tex.: Eakin Press, 1983.

German Green Party. *The Federal Programme of the German Green Party.* Translated by Hans Fernbach. London: Heretic Books, 1983.

Harris, Larry D. *The Fragmented Forest: Island Biogeography Theory and the Preservation of Biotic Diversity.* Chicago: University of Chicago Press, 1984.

Hays, Samuel P. *Beauty, Health, and Permanence: Environmental Politics in the United States, 1955–1985.* Cambridge: Cambridge University Press, 1987.

Heidegger, Martin. *The End of Philosophy.* Translated by Joan Stambaugh. London: Souvenir Press, 1975.

Heilbroner, Robert. *An Inquiry into the Human Prospect, Updated and Reconsidered for the 1980s.* New York: W. W. Norton, 1980.

Hoff, Christina. "Kant's Invidious Humanism." *Environmental Ethics* 5 (Spring 1983): pp. 63–70.

Hunter, Robert. *Warriors of the Rainbow: A Chronicle of the Greenpeace Movement.* New York: Holt, Rinehart and Winston, 1979.

Jablonski, D. "Causes and Consequences of Mass Extinctions: A Comparative Approach." In *Dynamics of Extinction,* edited by D. K. Elliott. New York: Wiley Interscience, 1986.

Kant, Immanuel. "Duties to Animals and Spirits." In *Lectures and Ethics,* translated by Louis Infield. New York: Harper and Row, 1963.

Kelly, Petra. *Fighting for Hope.* Translated by Marianne Howarth. Boston: South End Press, 1983.

Kerrick, Michael. "Ecotage from Our Perspective: An Explanation of the Willamette National Forest's Policy on Environmental Sabotage Known as 'Ecotage.' " Read into *Congressional Record,* Hearing Before the Subcommittee on Tax, Access to Equity Capital and Business Opportunities of the Committee on Small Business, U.S. House of Representatives, 99th Congress, October 14, 1985. Washington, D.C.: GPO, 1986.

Kitschelt, Herbert. *The Logics of Party Formations: Ecological Politics in Belgium and West Germany.* Ithaca, N.Y.: Cornell University Press, 1989.

Knoll, A. H. "Patterns of Extinction in the Fossil Record." In *Animal Extinctions*, edited by M. H. Nitecki. Chicago: University of Chicago Press, 1984.

Lake Powell: Jewel of the Colorado. Washington, D.C.: GPO, 1965.

Leonard, H. Jeffrey, J. Clarence Davies III, and Gordon Binder. *Business and Environment: Toward Common Ground*. Washington, D.C.: Conservation Society, 1977.

Leopold, Aldo. *A Sand County Almanac and Sketches Here and There*. New York: Oxford University Press, 1949.

Livingstone, John. *The Fallacy of Wildlife Conservation*. Toronto: University of Toronto Press, 1981.

Lovejoy, Arthur O., and George Boas. *Primitivism and Related Ideas in Antiquity*. Baltimore: Johns Hopkins University Press, 1935. Reprint. New York: Octagon Books, 1965.

Lovelock, James. *Gaia: A New Look at Life on Earth*. New York: Oxford University Press, 1979.

Lukacs, George. *History and Class Consciousness*. Translated by Rodney Livingstone. Cambridge: M.I.T. Press, 1968.

MacArthur, Robert, and Edward O. Wilson. *The Theory of Island Biogeography*. Princeton, N.J.: Princeton University Press, 1967.

McCloskey, H. J. *Ecological Ethics and Politics*. Totowa, N.J.: Rowman and Littlefield, 1983.

McCormick, John. *Reclaiming Paradise: The Global Environmental Movement*. Bloomington: Indiana University Press, 1989.

McPhee, John. *Encounters with the Archdruid*. New York: Farrar, Straus and Giroux, 1971.

Manes, Christopher. "Philosophy and the Environmental Task." *Environmental Ethics* 4 (1982): pp. 255–260.

Marsh, George Perkins. *Man and Nature*. Edited by David Lowenthal. Cambridge: Harvard University Press, 1965.

Matthews, Richard K. *The Radical Politics of Thomas Jefferson: A Revisionist View*. Lawrence: University of Kansas Press, 1984.

Matthiessen, Peter. *Wildlife in America*. New York: Viking, 1987.

Meadows, Donella H., Dennis L. Meadows, Jorgen Randers, and William W. Behrens. *The Limits to Growth*. New York: Universe Books, 1972.

Meeker, Joseph W. *Minding the Earth: Thinly Disguised Essays on Human Ecology*. Alameda, Calif.: Latham Foundation, 1988.

Miller, Charles A. *Jefferson and Nature*. Baltimore: Johns Hopkins University Press, 1988.

Miss Ann Thropy (pseud.). "Population and AIDS." *Earth First!*, May 1, 1987: p. 32.

Mitchell, John G., and Constance L. Stallings, eds. *Ecotactics: The Sierra Club Handbook for Environmental Activists*. New York: Pocket Books, 1970.

Mumford, Lewis. "Authoritarian and Democratic Technics." *Technology and Culture* 5 (1964): pp. 1–8.

Myers, Norman. *The Sinking Ark: A New Look at the Problem of Disappearing Species*. New York: Pergamon, 1979.

Naess, Arne. "Deep Ecology and Ultimate Premises." *Ecologist* 18 (1988): pp. 128–131.

———. "The Shallow and the Deep, Long-Range Ecology Movement. A Summary." *Inquiry* 16 (1973): pp. 95–100.

Nash, Roderick. *The Rights of Nature: A History of Environmental Ethics.* Madison: University of Wisconsin Press, 1989.

———. "Rounding Out the American Revolution: Ethical Extension and the New Environmentalism." In *Deep Ecology*, edited by Michael Tobias. San Diego: Avant Books, 1985.

———. *Wilderness and the American Mind.* New Haven, Conn.: Yale University Press, 1967.

Newmark, William D. "A Land-Bridge Island Perspective on Mammalian Extinctions in Western North American Parks." *Nature*, January 29, 1987.

Nitecki, M. H., ed. *Animal Extinctions.* Chicago: University of Chicago Press, 1984.

Ophuls, William. *Ecology and the Politics of Scarcity.* San Francisco: W. H. Freeman, 1977.

O'Toole, Randal. *Reforming the Forest Service.* Washington, D.C.: Island Press, 1988.

Paehlke, Robert. *Environmentalism and the Future of Progressive Politics.* New Haven, Conn.: Yale University Press, 1989.

Palmer, Tim. *Stanislaus: The Struggle for a River.* Berkeley: University of California Press, 1982.

Papadakis, Elim. *The Green Movement in West Germany.* New York: St. Martin's Press, 1984.

Passmore, John. *Man's Responsibility for Nature.* New York: Scribner's, 1974.

Pinchot, Gifford. *Breaking New Ground.* New York: Harcourt Brace, 1947.

Pollock, Cynthia. "Decommissioning Nuclear Power Plants." In *State of the World 1986*, edited by Linda Strake. New York: W. W. Norton, 1986.

Porritt, Jonathan. *Seeing Green: The Politics of Ecology Explained.* New York: Basil Blackwell, 1984.

Raphael, Ray. *Tree Talk: The People and Politics of Timber.* Covelo, Calif.: Island Press, 1981.

Redclift, Michael. "Turning Nightmares into Dreams: The Green Movement in Eastern Europe." *Ecologist* 19 (September/October 1989): pp. 177–183.

Relph, Edward. *Rational Landscapes and Humanistic Geography.* New York: Barnes and Noble Imports, 1981.

Ridgeway, James. *The Politics of Ecology.* New York: E. P. Dutton, 1970.

Roselle, Michael. "Deep Ecology and the New Civil Rights Movement." *Earth First!*, May 1, 1988: p. 23.

Roszak, Theodore. *Where the Wasteland Ends: Politics and Transcendence in Postindustrial Society.* Garden City, N.Y.: Doubleday, 1972.

Roth, Dennis M. *The Wilderness Movement and the National Forests: 1964–1980*. Washington, D.C.: U.S. Department of Agriculture, 1984.

Sale, Kirkpatrick. "The Forest for the Trees: Can Today's Environmentalists Tell the Difference?" *Mother Jones*, November 1986: pp. 33–37.

Schmookler, Andrew Bard. *Out of Weakness: Healing the Wounds That Drive Us to War*. New York: Bantam, 1988.

Schrepfer, Susan R. *The Fight to Save the Redwoods: A History of Environmental Reform, 1917–1978*. Madison: University of Wisconsin Press, 1983.

Scott, Douglas. "Student Activism on Environmental Crisis." *Living Wilderness* 34 (Spring 1970): p. 24.

Seed, John. "Beyond Anthropocentrism." In *Thinking Like a Mountain, Toward a Council of All Beings*, edited by John Seed, Joanna Macy, Pat Fleming, and Arne Naess. Philadelphia: New Society Publishers, 1988.

Sessions, George. "Deep Ecology and the New Age." *Earth First!*, September 23, 1987: p. 27.

Shepard, Paul. "Ecology and Man — A Viewpoint." In *The Subversive Science*, edited by Paul Shepard and Daniel McKinley. Boston: Houghton Mifflin, 1969.

Skolimowski, Henryk. *Eco-Philosophy*. Boston: Marion Boyers, 1981.

Soulé, M. E., and Bruce A. Wilcox, eds. *Conservation Biology: An Evolutionary-Ecological Perspective*. Sunderland, Mass.: Sinauer Associates, 1980.

Spitler, Gene. "Justifying a Respect for Nature." *Environmental Ethics* 4 (Fall 1982): pp. 255–260.

Steinhart, Peter. "Respecting the Law." *Audubon* 89 (November 1987): pp. 10–13.

Stone, Christopher D. *Should Trees Have Standing?: Toward Legal Rights for Natural Objects*. Los Altos, Calif.: William Kaufmann, 1974.

Thoreau, Henry David. *Walden, or Life in the Woods, and On the Duty of Civil Disobedience*. New York: Collier Books, 1972.

Timberlake, Lloyd, and Jon Tinker. *Environment and Conflict*. Boulder, Colo.: Earthscan Press, 1985.

Tokar, Brian. "Social Ecology, Deep Ecology, and the Future of Green Political Thought." *Ecologist* 18 (1988): pp. 132–141.

Tucker, William. "Is Nature Too Good for Us?" *Harper's*, March 1982: pp. 27–35.

Turnbull, Colin M. *The Mountain People*. New York: Simon and Schuster, 1972.

Vajk, Peter. *Doomsday Has Been Cancelled*. Culver City, Calif.: Peace Press, 1978.

Watson, Paul, and Warren Rogers. *Sea Shepherd: My Fight for Whales and Seals*. New York: W. W. Norton, 1982.

Weisberg, Barry. *Beyond Repair: The Ecology of Capitalism*. Boston: Beacon Press, 1971.

White, Lynn, Jr. "The Historical Roots of Our Ecologic Crisis." *Science* 155 (1967): pp. 1203–1207.

Wilson, Edward O. "The Current State of Biological Diversity." In *Biodiversity*, edited by Edward O. Wilson. Washington, D.C.: National Academy Press, 1988.

Winner, Langdon. *The Whale and the Reactor: A Search for Limits in an Age of High Technology*. Chicago: University of Chicago Press, 1986.

World Wildlife Fund — U.S. "Linking Conservation and Development: The Program in Wildlands and Human Needs of the World Wildlife Fund." Washington, D.C., 1986.

Worster, Donald. *Nature's Economy: The Roots of Ecology*. San Francisco: Sierra Club Books, 1977.

Wuerthner, George. "Tree-Spiking and Moral Maturity." *Earth First!*, August 1, 1985: p. 20.

Zamiatin, Eugene (Yevgeny Zamyatin). *We*. Translated by Gregory Zilboorg. New York: E. P. Dutton, 1952.

INDEX

Abalone Alliance, 205
Abbey, Edward, 3, 5, 6, 21, 68, 111, 114, 151, 241, 247; ecotage philosophy, 4, 8, 69, 81, 175
Abram, David, 148–149
acid rain, 30, 31, 125, 133
Adat concept, 172–173, 185, 239
Adler, Cy, 152
Advanced Genetic Sciences, 37
Africa, 43, 109n, 111, 112, 201, 233, 244
Agriculture Department, U.S., 47, 79
AIDS, 233
Alaska, 62, 205; oil spill, 43; old-growth forests, 91
Alaska Lands Bill, 62, 63
Alaska Pulp Company, 97
Alexander, George, 12
Alta Dam, Norway, 17
Amazon basin, Brazil, 30, 122, 202
American Indian Movement, 109
Amicus Journal, 150
Amory, Cleveland, 109
Anderson, Walter Truett, 27, 159, 238
Animal Agenda, 198
animal control, 92, 218
Animal Farm (Orwell), 65
Animal Rights Alliance, 198
animal rights movement, 17, 108, 110–111, 116, 198–199; biocentrism and, 145; Deep Ecology and, 146; German, 134; philosophy, 146–147
anthropocentrism, 141–145, 157, 232, 247

antiecology (antienvironmentalism, antinature), 43; activism, 94; animal rights movement and, 146; culture and, 139; industry and, 92–93; violence and, 215; writers, 75, 151–154, 160
Arizona, 193–194, 196, 199
Army Corps of Engineers, U.S., 203–204
Arnado, Bill, 15
Arnold, Ron, 27, 78, 93–94, 160–161, 205, 225–226
Arrogance of Humanism, The (Ehrenfeld), 143
Association of Oregon Loggers, 9
At the Eye of the Storm (Arnold), 225–226
Audubon (National Audubon Society publication), 50
Audubon Society, 45, 47, 49, 50, 57, 217
Australia, 17, 100, 117–121, 123, 124; Forestry Commission, 117; radical environmental movement, 129, 170, 244
Austria, 128

Bahro, Rudolf, 133–134
Bailey, Rick, 24
Baker, Marc, 194
Baker bird sanctuary, MI, 59
Bald Mountain, OR, 85, 86, 88, 89, 120n, 199. *See also* Kalmiopsis roadless area, OR
Baldrige, Malcolm, 114
Bardot, Brigitte, 108

Barthes, Roland, 41, 152
Basque separatist movement, 126
bears: black, 78; grizzly, 27, 34, 75, 78, 97, 172, 180, 241, 243
Becking, Rudolf, 104
Beckmann, Petr, 152
Belgium, 127
Berger, John, 75
Bergland, Bob, 61
Berman, Morris, 227
Berry, Philip, 49–50
Beyond Repair: The Ecology of Capitalism (Weisberg), 52
Big Scrub, New South Wales, 117, 118, 119, 120
biocentrism, 185; civil rights movement, 166–168, 170; criticism of, 156–157; Deep Ecologists and, 72, 144, 145; Earth First! and, 70–71, 72, 73, 74, 76–77, 82, 110–111, 119, 132, 166–167; ethics and, 73, 147–148; land ethics and, 144–145. *See also* Deep Ecology movement
Biodiversity Task Force, 19, 25–26
biological meltdown, 26, 28, 29, 42, 43, 52, 95, 183, 188, 233
bison/buffalo, 161, 241, 243–244
Black Scholar (journal), 51
Boesky, Ivan, 91
bolt weevils (farmer protesters), 184–185, 188, 190
Bonnie Abbzug Feminist Garden Party, 99–100
Bonzai, Conrad, 159
Bookchin, Murray, 20–21, 27, 51, 103; Deep Ecology and, 154–156, 159; Green party and, 135, 164; social ecology philosophy, 156, 158–159, 160, 161, 162, 163, 228–229, 230
Borneo, 122. *See also* Penan people of Borneo
Borrelli, Peter, 150
Bradford, George, 155, 156–157, 158
Brazil, 32, 34, 107, 122, 200, 202–203
Bridger-Teton National Forest, WY, 10, 96
British Columbia, 112, 115

British Columbia Hydro Substation, 16–17
Brower, David, 45, 49, 59, 121; founds Earth Island Institute, 55; founds Friends of the Earth, 55, 67, 127; mainstream environmentalism and, 108; ousted from Sierra Club board, 53–54
Brown, Lester, 71
Brown, Lisa, 215
Bulgaria, 128
Bureau of Land Management, U.S., 15, 179, 190, 218, 219
Bureau of Reclamation, U.S., 3, 4–5
Burger King, 119, 197
Burlington Resources, 91
Bush, George, 59
Business and Environment: Toward Common Ground (Conservation Foundation), 55

Caldwell, Lynton, 141
California, 11, 12, 14, 18, 54, 92, 116, 130, 168; Deep Ecology movement in, 154–155; nuclear facilities, 194, 205; old-growth initiative, 102; protected land, 74, 179; Resources Agency, 64; timber industry, 94, 206–207; Water Resources Control Board, 180; wilderness destruction, 89–90
California Desert Protection Act, 19
California v. *Block*, 88, 179
Callenbach, Ernest, 236
Camp, Orville, 92, 105
Canada, 16, 94, 107, 108, 116
Canan, Penelope, 204
Cape York Peninsula, Australia, 120
Capra, Fritjof, 227
Carlton, Jasper, 19, 25
Carson, Rachel, 49, 247
Carter, Jimmy, 58, 61, 63
Carter, Vernon, 29, 30, 228
cattle and livestock, 68, 161, 219, 244
Catton, William, 32, 233, 234, 248

Center for the Defense of Free
    Enterprise, 93
Center of Environmental Conflict
    Resolution, 60
Central America, 28, 199, 204
Central Arizona Project, 194, 197
Chase, Alston, 156; humanist
    philosophy, 27, 159, 160, 161,
    162; radical environmental
    movement and, 20, 21, 155, 238
Cherney, Darryl, 17, 102, 207
Chernobyl accident, 31
Chrisman, Robert, 51
Christiansen, Jim, 101
civil disobedience, 13–14, 19, 99,
    167, 184, 199, 207–209; in
    Australia, 121; ecological/
    environmental, 168, 171–172,
    173, 174; in Iceland, 116; and
    pacifism, 169; and radical
    environmentalism, 169–170,
    206; social change and, 207–209
"Civil Disobedience" (Thoreau),
    167
civilization complex, 35, 40, 41,
    42, 141, 231, 232, 235, 238
civil rights movement, 173, 207;
    biocentric, 166–168, 170, 172–
    174
Clark, Katherine, 196
Clary, David, 95
clear-cutting, 12, 14, 89, 90, 91–
    92, 100, 104, 179
Clebsch, Edward, 52
Cohen, Mark, 231
Cole, H.S.D., 152
Colorado, 48, 95, 194, 205
Colorado Civil Liberties Union,
    205
Colorado River, 4, 6, 7. *See also*
    Glen Canyon Dam, AZ, protest
Colville National Forest, WA, 180
Commoner, Barry, 25, 46, 51, 228
Conference on the Human
    Environment, 32
Conner, Daniel, 197
Conservation Foundation, 55, 58
Conservation Foundation
    (Australia), 118
Cooney, NM, 72–73
Coronado, Rod, 114–115
Costley, Richard, 80

Councils of All Beings, 120
court decisions and environmental
    litigation, 48, 179–181, 204–208,
    213–214
Cranston, Alan, 19
Cromwell, John, 79–80, 95, 96, 97,
    217
Cutler, Rupert, 58, 61–62
Czechoslovakia, 31

Daintree rain forest, Australia, 120
Dale, Tom, 29, 30, 228
Darwin, Charles/Darwinism, 35,
    140, 142
Davis, Gregory, 153
Davis, John, 237
Davis, Mark, 194, 195, 196, 197
Davis, Mary, 126
DDT, 49
Debonis, Jeff, 98–99
"Deep Ecology and the New Age"
    (Sessions), 145
"Deep Ecology and the New Civil
    Rights Movement" (Roselle),
    166, 172
Deep Ecology movement, 56, 60–
    61, 72, 110, 125, 128, 185, 232;
    anthropocentrism and, 144, 157;
    in Australia, 119, 120, 122;
    biocentrism and, 144, 145; in
    California, 154–155; criticism
    of, 151, 154–158, 159, 161;
    Ecological Self concept and,
    176–177; ecotage and, 176;
    Green party and, 136; New Age
    philosophy and, 146, 155;
    philosophy of, 139–142, 147–
    150, 153, 158, 164, 172, 225, 238.
    See also Earth First!
Defenders of Wildlife, 47, 49
Democratic Ecology party (West
    Germany), 132
Denmark, 16
Derr, William, 11
Descartes, René, 227
Devall, Bill, 119, 140, 141, 144,
    149, 173, 248; Deep Ecology
    and, 226, 240; direct action
    philosophy and ecotage
    activities, 170, 176, 180, 186–
    188, 231–232; Ecological Self
    concept and, 148, 176

Diablo Canyon nuclear facility, CA, 54, 194, 205
Diamond, Stanley, 238–239
Dinosaur National Monument, 4
Direct Action, 16–17
direct action philosophy, 231–232. *See also* civil disobedience; ecotage
Discipline and Punish (Foucault), 230
Dodge, R. I., 243
Dokken, Roger, 197
Dominy, Floyd, 5
Doomsday Has Been Cancelled (Vajk), 152
Doran, Jerry, 112
Drew, Wayland, 220
Dubois, Mark, 168, 169
Dubos, Rene, 46
Duffus, James, III, 219
Dugleby, Barbara, 18, 166
Dunstad, Peter, 184

Earth Day (1970), 25, 45–47, 49, 50–51, 52, 53
Earth First!, 17, 18–19, 127, 233; animal rights and, 198; in Australia, 119–120; biocentrism (ecosystem) philosophy, 70–71, 72, 73, 74, 76–77, 82, 110–111, 119, 132, 166–167; Biodiversity Task Force, 19, 25–26; Deep Ecology and, 155; ecotage activities, 19, 177, 183, 184 (*see also* Glen Canyon Dam, AZ, protest; Oregon, protest activities in; Willamette National Forest, OR, protest); environmental policy influenced by, 8; FBI investigation of, 6, 193–194, 196–199; founding and early activities, 4, 69–73, 117, 132; Glen Canyon Dam, AZ, protest, 5–7, 16, 77–78; goals, 72; Green party and, 136; lawsuits against, 9, 195, 206–207; lawsuits by, 19, 180, 189; media attention, 113; membership, 76; Oregon protest, 86–87, 99–102, 168, 212–213, 215; radical faction

and politics, 100, 102–103, 110, 136, 150, 187–188, 205; restoration ecology policy, 75; Shakespeare and, 76; timber industry and, 8–9, 11, 14, 16; violence vs., 200, 213, 215; Wilderness Preserve System, 74; Willamette National Forest, OR, protest, 99–102. *See also* Deep Ecology movement
Earth First! (journal), 74, 110, 111, 155, 166, 174, 184, 195, 237
Earth First! Newsletter, 74
Earth First! v. *Block*, 180
Earth Force, 108–109
Earth Island Institute, 55
ecocide, 29, 189, 241
Ecodefense (Foreman), 82–83, 114, 121, 126, 185, 186, 187, 189
Ecoglasnost, 128
Eco-Hysterics and the Technophobes (Beckmann), 152
Ecological Fantasies (Adler), 152
Ecological Self concept, 148, 153, 176–177
Ecology and the Politics of Scarcity (Ophuls), 36
Ecology of Freedom, The (Bookchin), 229
Ecology Wars (Arnold), 93, 160
Ecotactics (Sierra Club), 46
ecotage, 8–9, 12–13, 19, 69, 170, 174, 176, 185–187, 190, 199, 208, 209; in Australia, 121; in Borneo, 122; Deep Ecology and, 176–177; ethics and, 175–176, 178–179, 182–184; in Europe, 17, 126, 127; growth of, 185, 189; and law, 179, 180–181, 216; manual about, 82–83; in Pacific Northwest, 102, 183; social change and, 189–190; theory of, 16, 186–188; whaling protest, 114–115
Ecotage from Our Perspective (government document), 211
Ecotopia (Callenbach), 236
ecowars, 34
Egler, Frank, 71
Ehrenfeld, David, 143–144
Ehrlich, Paul, 40, 46, 54, 232–233
elephant poaching, 109n

Ellul, Jacques, 227, 231
Elwha Dam, WA, 77
Endangered Species Act, 47
Endangered Species Conservation
    Act, 47
Energy Department, U.S., 62
Energy Fuels Nuclear, 14, 214–
    215
England, 16, 109, 110, 127
Enlightenment, 142, 143;
    ecological destruction and, 162–
    163, 164, 234; technology and,
    227
Environmental Action for
    Survival, 52
*Environmental Agenda for the
    Future, An* (Group of Ten), 33
Environmental Defense Fund, 50
environmental elite, 36–37
Environmental Ethics (journal),
    181
environmental impact statements,
    63, 82, 88, 179, 180
environmental imperialism, 154,
    229, 235, 247
*Environmentalism and the Future
    of Progressive Politics* (Paehlke),
    189–190
Environmental Law Society, 46
Environmental Protection Agency,
    U.S., 47, 58
Ervin, Keith, 174
Estonia, 31
Europe, 30–31, 189; antinuclear
    protests, 125–127, 128–129,
    200–201; ecotage activities, 17,
    126, 127; forestry methods, 90;
    radical environmental
    movement and demonstrations,
    210, 244
Evan Mecham Eco-Terrorist
    International Conspiracy
    (EMETIC), 194
Evans, Brock, 53
Everhart, Kevin, 86–87
evolution, 26, 27, 161, 163;
    biotechnology and, 37; control
    of 160, 161, 239; end of, 35, 41;
    humanist environmentalists
    and, 158, 161, 162; man and, 42,
    142, 156, 164; New Age and,
    145, 159

extinction patterns, 26–27
Exxon, 43, 190

Faeroe Islands, 16, 114
Fain, Mike, 104n, 196, 197, 198,
    199
*Fallacy of Wildlife Conservation,
    The* (Livingstone), 147
famine, 233–234, 248
FBI, 104n, 110, 184, 207; Earth
    First! investigation, 6, 193–196;
    ecotage investigation, 194–196;
    Foreman investigation, 193–194,
    195–198, 207
Ferguson, Denzel, 219
Ferguson, Nancy, 219
Fifth Estate (journal), 103, 155
Finaldi, Lisa, 58
Finland, 128
Fish and Wildlife Service, U.S., 13,
    15, 94
Foreman, Dave, 5, 6, 9, 20, 21, 59,
    185, 200; arrest on felony
    charges, 193–198; as cofounder
    of Earth First!, 4, 66–67, 68, 70;
    on conservation movement and
    groups, 50, 225; ecological
    philosophy, 72, 75; ecotage
    manual, 82; FBI investigation
    of, 193–194, 195, 196–198, 207;
    on goals of Earth First!, 72;
    protest activities, 76, 81, 88,
    104n; publishes *Ecodefense*, 82–
    83; publishes newsletter, 74;
    radical methods and philosophy,
    19, 42, 66, 84, 108, 110, 119, 146,
    154, 169, 171, 175, 176, 184, 186,
    189, 193, 226, 228, 232, 240, 248
Forest Industries (magazine), 104,
    177
Forest Service, U.S., 9, 10, 12, 13,
    15, 16, 54, 56, 95, 174, 190, 209;
    closure of public lands, 14–15,
    88, 174, 212, 213–214, 218;
    dissent within, 98–99; herbicide
    use, 179; land policy, 61–63,
    98–99; lawsuits against, 15, 48,
    88, 180; lobbying efforts and,
    92; policy affected by ecotage,
    186; pot commandos, 15, 209–
    211, 212, 214; purity doctrine,
    79–80; response to ecotage

Forest Service (*continued*)
  activites, 211–213; revenues of,
  97–98; timber industry and, 85,
  89, 95, 96–97, 105; timber
  policy, 91, 176; timber-supply
  projections, 95–96
Fossey, Dian, 201
Foucault, Michel, 42, 143, 227,
  229–230, 231
Four Notch Area, TX, 15
Fox (saboteur), 185, 188
Fox, Warwick, 144, 147, 156, 157
Fragile Majesty (Ervin), 174
France, 125, 126, 127, 200–201
Frazier, Ron, 196
Friedman, Milton, 53
Friends of Animals, 198
Friends of the Earth, 55, 67, 83,
  127; in France, 127; in Malaysia,
  123
Frostban, 37
Fuerst, Michael, 210, 225
Fund for Animals, 109, 110

George Washington National For-
  est, VA, 12
Germany, 123, 125; antinuclear
  demonstrations, 129–130, 170;
  Green party, 17, 31, 107, 128–
  129, 130–133, 134, 183
Getty Oil Company, 10, 79, 80, 81,
  82, 83
Gila Wilderness, NM, 72–73
Gilliam, Harold, 177
Glen Canyon Dam, AZ, protest, 3,
  4–5, 6, 7, 10, 16, 77
Grand Canyon, 14, 175, 214
Gray Wolf Clear Water (Paul Watson), 109–110, 111, 117
Greater Yellowstone ecosystem,
  78–79
Green Alternative (Tokar), 155
Green Conference, 20
greenhouse effect, 175
Green List for the Protection of
  the Environment, 130
Green movement/party, 123–124,
  125; American, 135, 154, 164;
  antinuclear protests, 17, 127,
  201; Eastern bloc, 128; philosophy and policies, 30–31, 127,
  134–135; political power of,

127–128; in West Germany, 17,
  31, 107, 128–129, 130–133, 134,
  183
Greenpeace, 16, 18, 57, 115, 125;
  antinuclear protests, 200–201;
  seal-hunting protest, 107, 108
Gros Ventre Range, WY, 78–80,
  81, 82, 86, 217
Group of Ten, 33
Gruhl, Herbert, 131–132

Hair, Jay, 17, 57
Hardesty Mountain, OR, 11
Hardin, Jesse (Long Wolf), 107,
  196
Hargrove, Eugene, 181
Hascom, Ed, 215
Hatfield, Mark, 12, 13, 85
Hattoy, Robert, 18, 57–58
Hayes, Dennis, 53
Hayes, Randall, 119, 121
Health, Education and Welfare
  Department, U.S., 47
Heidegger, Martin, 36, 143, 226,
  231
Heilbroner, Robert, 36
Hellenbach, T. O., 187–188
herbicides, 92, 179
Hetch Hetchy Valley, CA, 77
Hirsh, Leon, 198
History of Sexuality, The (Fou-
  cault), 229
History of the Idea of Progress, The
  (Nisbet), 230
Hodel, Donald, 43, 77, 209
Hoff, Christina, 163
Hoffman, Abbie, 50, 67
Hoffman, Jeffrey, 165, 172
Holistic Range Management, 161
"How Deep Is Deep Ecology?"
  (Bradford), 156–157
Howe, Sydney, 55
Howitt, David, 114–115
Huber, Ron, 100, 101–102, 169
Hull, Ben, 9
humanism, 143, 153, 157, 163,
  227, 230
humanist environmentalism, 27,
  156, 161–162, 163–164
Hungary, 31
Hunter, Robert, 57

Hvalvinurfelag ("Friends of the Whale"), 116

Iceland, 16, 17, 18, 113–116, 117, 147
Idaho, 12, 74, 218
Ik people of Uganda, 39
In Defense of People (Neuhaus), 154
Independent Oglala Sioux Nation, 109
Innes, Graham, 120
In Search of the Primitive (Diamond), 238–239
Institute for Environment and Development, 38
Institute for Social Ecology, 154, 156
Interior Department, U.S., 47, 79, 209
International Environmental Policy (Caldwell), 141
International Whaling Commission (IWC), 16, 113, 114
island ecology model, 25
Italy, 128
ivory trade, 107–108, 109n

Jackson, Reid, 96
Jackson, Spurs, 5
Jackson, Tim, 207, 209, 212
Jackson Hole Alliance for Responsible Planning, 80–81
Jakubal, Mike, 100–101, 103, 106
Japan, 111, 112; timber imports, 91, 94, 97; whale-product imports, 113, 114
Jefferson, Thomas, 144, 166, 171, 172, 181, 232, 245–246
Jefferson and Nature (Miller), 245
Joerger, Sue, 7, 154, 182
Johnson, Al "Jet," 108–109
Johnson, Betty, 205
Johnson, Huey, 64, 88
Jungk, Robert, 130, 220

Kalmiopsis roadless area, OR, 13–14, 15, 84–88, 89, 92, 99, 100, 120n, 168, 169, 213; lawsuit and decision, 180, 206; security measures in, 214–215. *See also* Bald Mountain, OR

Kant, Immanuel, 162–163
Karlinski, Joel, 199
Karlton, Lawrence K., 63
Kayapo Indians, 200, 231
Kelly, Petra, 133
Kerr-McGee Corporation, 195
Kerrick, Michael, 82–83, 211, 212, 214
Kezar, Ron, 4, 76, 119; as cofounder of Earth First!, 4, 68, 70
King, Greg, 102
King, Martin Luther, Jr., 165, 166–167, 174
Kitschelt, Herbert, 135
Knutson-Vandenberg Act, 97
Koehler, Bart: as cofounder of Earth First!, 4, 68, 69, 70; protest activities, 76, 82, 119
Koroga tribe of Solomon Islands, 121
Kung, Pierre, 125

Lalonde, Brice, 127
Lancaster Timber Company, 215
Lang, Scott, 46
Latvia, 31
lawsuits and court decisions, 48, 179–181, 204–208, 213–214
Leonard, Richard, 54
Leopold, Aldo, 23–24, 31, 42, 54, 56, 61, 81, 247; land ethic, 72, 144–145
"Letter on Humanism" (Heidegger), 143
Lever Brothers, 121–122
Limits to Growth (Meadows and Meadows), 152
Lithuania, 31, 128
Little Granite Creek, WY, protest, 79, 81, 82, 83, 171, 217
Livermore, Ike, 55
Live Wild or Die!, 103
Livingstone, John, 147
Living Wilderness (Wilderness Society), 52
Locke, John, 166, 181
Loftson, Jon, 113, 116
Louisiana-Pacific Corporation, 8, 10, 11–12, 79, 93, 94, 96, 177, 188, 190; antitrust violations, 79, 97; government contract, 97; lawsuits against, 180

Love Canal, 73, 246
Lovejoy, Arthur, 237–238
Lovelock, James, 24, 30, 159
Ludd, Ned, 82
Lukacs, George, 156, 158

Macy, Joanna, 120
Malaysia, 32, 122–123, 200, 231, 239
Malthus, Thomas, 233–234
Malville nuclear facility, France, 201
Man and Nature (Marsh), 29, 85
Marcuse, Herbert, 190, 226, 227, 231
Marsden, Steve, 87
Marsh, George Perkins, 29, 85, 228
Marshall, Robert, 56, 85, 86, 95
Marston, Ed, 184, 186, 188–189
Marxism, 129, 133–134, 140, 151, 154, 155
Matthews, Richard, 245
Maxxam Corporation, 14, 102, 206
McCauley, Jim, 9
McCloskey, Michael, 46, 49, 53, 57
McClure, James, 12
McNamee, Stephen, 195–196
Meadows, Dennis, 152
Meadows, Donella, 152
Mecham, Evan, 194
media coverage: of environmentalist actions, 13, 101, 113; of protest activities, 108, 115, 173–174, 187–188; of radical methods, 175–176
Meeker, Joseph, 144
Meese, Edwin, 6, 197
Mendes, Chico, 200, 202–203
Merleau-Ponty, Maurice, 148–149
Merlo, Harry, 79, 93, 177, 180
Merritt, Clif, 48
Mexico, 4, 68, 94
Michigan, 58, 59
Middle Santiam Cathedral Forest, OR, 99, 100, 173, 174, 210. *See also* Willamette National Forest, OR
Millennium Grove, OR, 100–102, 120n. *See also* Willamette National Forest, OR
Miller, Charles, 245
Miller, Greg, 15

Millett, Peg, 190, 194, 196, 199
Minding the Earth (Meeker), 144
mining industry, 9, 14; and national security issues, 216–217; uranium, 126, 214
Minnesota farmer protest, 184–185, 188
Mobil Oil, 59
Models of Doom (Cole), 152
Mohamed, Mahathir Bin, 122
Monkey Wrench Gang, The (Abbey), 4, 8, 69, 100
monkeywrenching. *See* ecotage
Monongahela case, 91
Monongahela National Forest, WV, 179
Montana, 12, 166–167, 243–244
Moore, Les, 86, 87, 88
Mooreman, James, 58
Moss, Larry, 59–60
Mountain States Legal Foundation, 9, 10, 151
Mount Hood, OR, 13
Muir, John, 54, 61, 72, 245, 246, 248; conservation movement and, 56; founds Sierra Club, 57; political activism, 77, 247
Multiple Use–Sustained Yield Act, 91, 96, 179, 180
Mumford, Lewis, 153, 227, 231
murder of environmentalists, 201–203
Myers, Norman, 27
Myth of the Machine (Mumford), 227

Nader, Ralph, 46
Naess, Arne, 60–61, 119, 127; Deep Ecology and, 125, 128, 139, 140–141, 155; Ecological Self concept, 148, 176
Naish, Don, 59
Nash, Roderick, 161, 165, 173; radical philosophy, 166, 171–172, 176
National Association of Environmental Professionals, 60
National Coal Association, 217
National Environmental Policy Act (NEPA), 47, 91, 179
National Forest Drug Enforcement Act, 15, 209

National Forest Management Act, 92, 180

National Forest Timber Conservation and Management Act, 48

National Park Service, 15, 54

national security vs. environmental issues, 216–218, 220–221

National Wildlife Federation, 17, 47, 57, 58

Natural Resources Defense Council, 48

natural rights theory, 171–172

Nature's Economy (Worster), 225

Nazism, 163, 176

Nearing, Mary Beth, 210

Nelson, Gaylord, 46–47, 51, 52

Neolithic revolution, 29, 35

Netherlands, 128

Neuhaus, Richard, 154

Nevada, 74, 218

New Age movement, 119, 145–146, 154–155, 156, 159, 160

New Mexico, 66, 67, 72–73

New South Wales, Australia, 117, 118

New Zealand, 201

Nigeria, 32

Nisbet, Robert, 230–231

Nixon, Richard M., 47, 49, 51, 53

Nomadic Action Group (NAG), 119

Norlen, Doug, 87

Norway, 17, 112, 125, 126

nuclear facilities, 17, 220; accidents at, 30; contamination from, 38; ecotage and, 126; protest actions, Europe, 17, 125–127, 128–129, 170, 200–201; protest actions, U.S., 193–194, 195, 205

Nuclear State, The (Jungk), 130, 219–220

oil industry, 78–79

Okanogan National Forest, WA, 103

old-growth forests, 86, 87, 88, 89, 92, 94, 100, 101, 102, 103, 109, 247; closures, 212; and ecotage, 186, 206; and environmental ethics, 176, 177, 178; and profit, 86, 98, 102; radical environmentalism and, 14–15, 85, 171, 173, 174, 200, 203, 206, 210, 214

Olsen, David, 101

Olson, Sigurd, 247

Olympic Mountains, WA, 77

One Dimensional Man (Marcuse), 190, 226

Ophuls, William, 36

Oregon, 9, 12, 13–14, 82, 206; Bureau of Land Management, 96; designated wilderness land, 62–63, 74, 93; Natural Resources Council, 14, 88; protest activities in, 84–88, 89, 92, 94. *See also* Kalmiopsis roadless area, OR; Willamette National Forest, OR

Organic Act, 91, 179

Origin of Species (Darwin), 142

O'Shaughnessy (Hetch Hetchy) Dam, CA, 77

O'Toole, Randal, 97

Out of Weakness (Schmookler), 159–160

Overshoot (Catton), 233

owl, spotted, 13, 14, 19, 84, 89, 94, 98

ozone layer depletion, 30, 43, 71, 175

Pacific Legal Foundation, 205

Pacific Lumber Company, 90–91, 206–207

Pacific Northwest, 8, 9, 94, 100; ecotage in, 102, 183, 215; forests, 180, 183; wilderness destruction, 89–90. *See also specific locations*

Paehlke, Robert, 30, 189

Paleopathology at the Origin of Agriculture (Cohen), 231

Palo Verde nuclear facility, AZ, 194, 196, 199

Parable of the Tribes (Schmookler), 231

Peaceful Direct Action Code, 168–169

Pease, David, 104, 177

Penan people of Borneo, 122–123, 200, 231, 238, 239

Pendley, William, 151

People for the Ethical Treatment of Animals, 116
Perceptions International, 198–199
Pereira, Fernando, 201
Perini Land and Development Company, 203–204
Peru, 32, 122
pesticides, 34, 49, 71, 92, 218
Pinchot, Gifford, 56, 95, 98, 145, 214
Piromasco Indians of Peru, 122
Pit River Indian tribe, 213
Playing God in Yellowstone (Chase), 20, 155
Plumas National Forest, CA, 12
Plum Creek Timber Company, 91
Plumley Construction Company, 86, 88
Plundering of the Planet, The (Gruhl), 131
Poland, 31
Politics of Ecology (Ridgeway), 52
pollution, 27, 30; control, 35, 71; infant mortality and, 31
Population Bomb (Ehrlich), 54, 232–233
Porter, Eliot, 59
Portugal, 16, 111–112, 126–127
pot commandos, 15, 209–211, 212, 214
Potomac conservationists, 58, 63, 64
Presidential Council on Environmental Quality, 47
Prevent Ecological Sabotage Today, 12
Primitivism and Related Ideas (Lovejoy), 237
Prince, Randy, 169
Pring, George, 204, 205
Public Lands Council, 218–219
Pyramid Creek, OR, 210

radiation, 37, 38, 71
Radical Politics of Thomas Jefferson, The (Matthews), 245
radical protest methods. *See* civil disobedience; ecotage
Rainbow Warrior (ship), 201
Rainforest Action Network, 121, 123

Rainforest Information Centre, 121
rain forests: Amazonian, 30, 202; Australian, 117–120, 121; U.S., 28, 40, 92, 97
RARE II, 62–64, 65, 66, 67, 68, 88
Rational Landscapes and Humanistic Geography (Relph), 220
Reagan, Ronald, 6, 43, 49, 54, 60, 77; antienvironmental policies, 66, 79, 197, 209, 216, 225; defense policy, 114; land management policy, 219
Redclift, Michael, 31, 128
Redden, James, 88
redwood trees, 90, 92, 94, 102, 140, 206–207, 241
reform environmentalism, 44, 49, 86, 188–190; credibility and, 52–54; conservative politics of, 52, 54, 55; Deep Ecology and, 60–61, 139, 144; failure of, 64–65, 188–189, 213, 247; professionalism and, 57–61; radical environmentalism and, 17–19, 83, 89
Reforming the Forest Service (O'Toole), 97
Reilly, William, 55, 58
Relph, Edward, 220, 221
Resolve, 60
restoration ecology, 75
Restoring the Earth (Berger), 75
Revolutionary Ecoterrorist Pie Brigade, 103
Reykjavík, Iceland, 16, 113–115, 117
Ridgeway, James, 52
road blockading, 13–14, 86–87, 100, 102, 118, 168, 206; in Malaysia, 122, 123. *See also* Bald Mountain, OR; Kalmiopsis roadless area, OR
Roadless Area Review and Evaluation (RARE II), 62–64, 65, 66, 67, 68, 88
Robertson, F. Dale, 98
Robin Wood, 125
Rocky Flats nuclear facility, CO, 194, 195
Rocky Mountain National Park, CO, 25

Romania, 128
Roselle, Mike, 7, 20, 45, 72, 121, 195; as cofounder of Earth First!, 4, 67–68, 69–70; Earth First! protests and activities, 86–87, 88, 99, 119; ecological philosophy, 82, 83, 123, 144, 170, 171, 172–173, 177–178, 182, 189, 206, 227–228, 237, 248; new civil rights movement and, 166
Roszak, Theodore, 227, 231, 236
Round River Rendezvous, 81
Rousseau, Jean-Jacques, 42, 166
Royal Society for Prevention of Cruelty to Animals (U.K.), 109
r-selected creatures, 26–27
Rubin, Jerry, 67
Ruckel, Tony, 48
Ruhrgebiet, 123
Rwanda, 201

Sacred Cows at the Public Trough (Ferguson and Ferguson), 219
Sagebrush Revolution, 218–219
Sand County Almanac (Leopold), 144
Sanders, Ken, 74
Sapone, Mary Lou, 198
Savory, Allan, 151, 161
Scandinavia, 117, 126
Schmookler, Andrew Bard, 27, 159–160, 162, 231
Scott, Douglas, 52–53, 55–56, 63
Sears, Paul, 225
Sea Shepherd (ship), 16, 109, 110, 111, 112
Sea Shepherd II (ship), 112, 114
Sea Shepherd Conservation Society, 16, 17, 18, 109, 110, 112, 117, 127, 136; Iceland protest, 113, 114–116; protest guidelines, 111, 117; TV commercial by, 116
Seed, John, 243; back-to-the-land philosophy, 117, 119–120, 121, 123, 248; Deep Ecology and, 122, 140, 155; Earth First! and, 119; protest activities, 117–118
Sessions, George, 173; biocentrism and, 144; Deep Ecology and, 141, 145, 156, 226, 240

"Shallow and the Deep, Long-Range Ecology Movement, The" (Naess), 60, 140
Shasta National Forest, CA, 213
Shee Atika timber company, 205
Shell Oil Company, 122
Shepard, Paul, 148
Sierra (ship), 111–112
Sierra Club, 4, 18, 19, 44, 45, 52, 53, 57, 64, 77, 118; budget, 58; Concerned Members for Conservation faction, 54; conservative policy, 52, 53, 54–55, 70, 225; Deep Ecology and, 150; Earth Day and, 46; lawsuits against, 205; lawsuits by, 63, 86, 203; Legal Defense Fund, 20, 48, 58; legislation and, 47; membership, 48–50, 217; political influence, 58, 59; pollution policy, 71; salaries and staff, 57, 58
Silent Spring (Carson), 49
Silkwood, Karen, 195
Simon, Julian, 151, 152, 153
Sioux Indians, 109–110
Siskiyou National Forest, OR, 14, 85, 210
Siuslaw National Forest, OR, 179, 212
Skarphedinsson, Magnus, 116
Skolimowski, Henryk, 145, 156, 157, 158
Society of Conservation Biologists, 34
Solar Energy Research Institute, 53
Solomon Islands, 121
Soulé, Michael, 34–35, 42
Southeast Alaska Conservation Council, 68
Southern Oregon Timber Industries Association, 7, 15, 93, 154, 182
Soviet Union, 17, 31, 128, 216–217
Spain, 126
Spence, Gerry, 195, 196
spotted owl, 13, 14, 19, 84, 89, 94, 98
Springman, Baldur, 132
Stanislaus River, CA, 168
Steinhart, Peter, 176, 179, 180
Stillwater Mountains, NV, 218

Strategic Lawsuits Against Public Participation (SLAPPs), 204–205
Students for a Democratic Society, 51
Stumps Suck!, 103
surveillance, electronic, 213, 214
Sweden, 124, 128
Switzerland, 104, 105, 106, 128
Sylvester, Rick, 203, 204

Taiyo Fishing Corporation, 112
Tama, Pedro, 87
Tasmania, 120n, 170
Tausinga, Job, 121
Technological Society, The (Ellul), 227
Technology—Humanism or Nihilism (Davis), 153
technology vs. environment, 32–34, 43, 52–54, 183, 188, 226–227, 232, 236, 237, 241
Teilhard de Chardin, Pierre, 159
"terrorism," ecological. See ecotage
Teton County Chamber of Commerce, 80
Texas, 15, 91, 179
Thailand, 17
Third World, 32–33, 34, 124
Thompson, Tom, 212
Thoreau, Henry David, 42, 144, 165, 167, 169, 173, 232, 245, 246
Three Mile Island, 73, 246
Timber and the Forest Service (Clary), 95
timber industry, 8–15, 17, 19, 34, 47–48, 92–93; deforestation and, 90–92, 104–106; Forest Service and, 85, 89, 95, 96–97, 105; greed and, 93; and Kalmiopsis roadless area, OR, 84–88; public relations campaign, 94; and radical protests, 210–212, 214; security measures, 214–215; short-term profits and, 91; value system of, 182; violence and, 213
To Govern Evolution (Anderson), 27
Tokar, Brian, 155
Tongass National Forest, AK, 97, 98

Topsoil and Civilization (Carter and Dale), 29, 228
Torrence, James F., 96
toxic waste, 34
Toynbee, Arnold, 36
tree pinning, 12–13
tree sitting, 14, 15, 100–102, 120, 168–169, 206–207, 210
tree spiking, 10–12, 13, 82, 99, 102, 169, 175, 176, 177, 178–179, 183, 186, 188, 210
tribal peoples, life-style of, 122–123, 172–173, 239–240
Trimingham, Scott, 113
Trinity National Forest, CA, 213
Trutt, Fran, 198
Tucker, William, 75–76, 154
Turning Point, The (Capra), 227

Uganda, 39
Ultimate Resource (Simon), 152
Union of Indigenous Nations, 122
United Nations, 32; Conference on the Human Environment, 185; Environmental Program Global 500 award, 202
United States: energy consumption, 32; Green party in, 135, 154, 164; natural law concept, 171–172; nuclear reactors, 38; radical environmental movement, 129, 135, 244
uranium mining, 126, 214
U.S. Steel, 185, 188
U.S. Surgical Corporation, 198
Utah, 74

Vajk, Peter, 152, 160
Vancouver, Canada, 108, 109, 115
Vancouver Island, 16
Versteylen, Luc, 127
Victorio incident, 73, 77
Virginia, 12, 13, 91
vivisection, 110, 198

Wade, Valeri, 166
Walden Pond, 246
Wallace, George, 51
Warren, Diana, 87
Washington, D.C., 45, 166
Washington (state), 12, 13, 91;

ecotage activities in, 102, 103–104

Washington Contract Loggers' Association, 215

Watson, Bob, 90

Watson, Paul, 16, 107–109, 110, 111–112, 114, 115, 116–117, 125, 248

Watt, James, 9, 43, 49, 76, 78, 152, 197, 226; energy policy, 216–217; Good Neighbor policy, 219; and livestock land, 219; wilderness classification and, 80, 81

Webb, Geoff, 83

Weed, Jim, 215, 216

Weisberg, Barry, 52

Western Forestry and Conservation Association, 103

Weyerhaeuser, 8

Whale and the Reactor, The (Winner), 33–34

whales/whaling, 16, 18, 110, 111–112, 113–116, 117, 241

Whales Limited, 113

Wheeler, Doug, 50

Where the Wasteland Ends (Roszak), 236

White, Lynn, 161

White River National Forest, CO, 48

Wilderness Act, 48, 80, 85, 92, 179

Wilderness Society, 23, 44, 45, 52, 66, 68; budget, 58; lawsuits and, 64; membership, 49; political influence and lobbying activities, 59, 65; salaries, 57

Willamette Industries, 14, 100

Willamette National Forest, OR, 14, 82, 98, 211; protest, 99–102

Willis, David, 88

Willson, Brian, 204–205

Wilson, E. O., 24–25

Winner, Langdon, 33–34, 42–43, 149

Wolke, Howie, 5, 10, 20; as cofounder of Earth First!, 4, 18, 66, 67, 68, 69, 70, 132; protest activities, 78, 190; radical philosophy, 187

wolves, 23–24, 34, 110, 112, 218

Woof, Peter, 112

World Future Research Conference, 128, 140

Worldwatch Institute, 71

World Wildlife Fund, 58

Worster, Donald, 225, 238

Wounded Knee, SD, 109, 111

Wuerthner, George, 166, 176, 186–187

Wyoming, 78, 243; designated wilderness, 83; mining industry, 62. *See also* Gros Ventre Range, WY; Louisiana-Pacific Corporation

Yellowstone National Park, WY, 10, 27, 172

Yosemite National Park, CA, 25, 77, 247

Zimbabwe, 183